PARSONS AND PEDAGOGUES

PARSONS
AND PEDAGOGUES:

THE S.P.G. ADVENTURE
IN AMERICAN EDUCATION.

JOHN CALAM

COLUMBIA UNIVERSITY PRESS
NEW YORK AND LONDON
1971

Copyright © 1971 Columbia University Press
Library of Congress Catalog Card Number: 77-139603
SBN: 0-231-03371-0
Manufactured in the United States of America

FOR RENÉE

PREFACE

THIS IS A BOOK about American education. It deals with the work of the Society for the Propagation of the Gospel in Foreign Parts, missionary arm of the Anglican Church. For the Society's emissaries, as well as for those who struggled to define their work, the enterprise constituted a true adventure. It led participants into unknown territory. It subjected Society preachers and teachers in the American colonial field to unanticipated dangers. Moreover, it involved both personal and institutional financial risk.

Had this book been written a few years earlier, its cast might have been less numerous and its scope narrower. Until quite recently such a historical undertaking predictably would have equated education with schooling. Over the last decade or so, however, historians of American education have found themselves under mounting provocation to break away from institutional histories. Precisely when this trend began is not clear. More certain is the fact that provocateurs like Richard Hofstadter, Bernard Bailyn, and Lawrence A. Cremin have goaded several generations of seminars to develop hitherto neglected educational themes, regardless of their divergence from tales of the schoolroom. At certain junctures these revisionists have gathered together to chart new approaches. Such was the case in 1954 when the Committee on the Role of Education in American History met in New York and subsequently released a report calling for a "full understanding of education as a moving force in American history." At other times these same scholars elaborated their views in slim volumes whose heuristic properties have since proved unusually influential. One such analysis, Bernard Bailyn's *Education in the Forming of American Society* (1960), produced the now-famous dictum that education is not just pedagogy but "the entire process by which a culture transmits itself across the generations." A second, Lawrence A. Cremin's *The Wonderful World of Ellwood Patterson Cubberley* (1965), challenged historians to come up with fuller, more imaginative analyses of the relationship between American education and American civilization. In this respect Professor Cremin has been quick to pick up his own gauntlet; his definitive history of American education is well on the way to publication.

It should be clear from the start, then, that this widely accommodating notion of the diverse activities one may examine under the rubric of education serves this book as an important premise. Granted, S.P.G. resources extensively supported classroom instruction in a wide variety of colonial schools. Nor has there been a shortage of historical accounts to this effect. A fine early example is William Webb Kemp's *The Support of Schools in Colonial New York by the S.P.G.* (1913) which, although anachronistically seeking public school beginnings in America's colonial past, nonetheless stands as a model of meticulous scholarship.

But even the most casual sifting of the S.P.G. archives readily indicates that from the Society's point of view there existed more important educational quests in North America than mere rudimentary classroom teaching. The Society charter itself leaves much unanswered about this. Establishment and maintenance of an Anglican clergy abroad serves as its principal clause of purpose. Conversely, the S.P.G. anniversary sermons, abstracts of Society business, special sermons and essays printed in the mission field, libraries shipped for colonial edification, and the thousands of Society letters crisscrossing the Atlantic between 1702 and 1783 reveal an S.P.G. posture toward America of particular interest to educational historians, regardless of the fact that S.P.G. men struck this attitude elsewhere than the schoolhouse.

Examining the nature of this assumed relationship between Britain and America and studying the way it was articulated thus become central concerns in the chapters to follow. According to the criteria adopted by Bailyn, Cremin, and their revisionist colleagues, moreover, the task is legitimately one for the educationist. Yet, here is no brand new enterprise. Although he would scarcely have considered himself as an educational historian, David Humphreys produced in 1730 *An Historical Account of the Incorporated Society for the Propagation of the Gospel in Foreign Parts* which told how, through Church authority, the S.P.G. brought tone to an otherwise barbarous America by process of direct cultural transfer. More recently, at half-century intervals, self-congratulatory works sharing this culturally unflattering view of colonial America continued to appear. Ernest Hawkins' *Historical Notices* (1845) celebrated the colonizing as well as the civilizing effects of the Society's American experience. C. F. Pascoe's encyclopedic *Two Hundred Years of the S.P.G.* (1901) chronicled the S.P.G.'s ameliorating effect on colonial Americans in danger of shedding all vestiges of common decency. H. P. Thompson's *Into All Lands* (1951) related an S.P.G. campaign against crass American ignorance.

Since these pioneer works were written by Society officers, of course, it is understandable that they paid but minimal attention to internal criticism of their data—the wealth of documents making up the S.P.G. archives. To the contrary, the fundamental strength of these broad treatments springs from their comprehensive sampling. But their very fidelity to the words of long-departed correspondents adds up to a greatly distorted image of North American culture. And it is this very distortion which, I believe, dictates still another reaction with education widely construed as historical catalyst.

Parsons and Pedagogues seeks, then, to lend fresh perspective to a subject which has prompted at least two and a quarter centuries of periodic investigation. Its unifying theme is education, by which I mean not just the daily routines of schoolmasters, but likewise the application of preachers, catechists, administrators, bibliophiles, and authors to the task of extending Church and empire unanimity in America. Its mood remains realistic. In fact, document upon document testifies to institutional as well as personal misunderstanding and disappointment marking the Society educational adventure abroad. In contrast with official histories sharing a questionable optimism about Society success throughout the period 1701-1783, this book enquires further into those aspects of colonial existence that blocked S.P.G. educational attempts. As a result, it draws to the conclusion that, after eighty years of systematic educational exertion in America's thirteen colonies, S.P.G. effectiveness in stemming the republican tide proved negligible in comparison with initial Society expectations.

In offering this analysis, I wish to thank Professor Lawrence A. Cremin, who encouraged me from the beginning, reading countless outlines and drafts along the way. I must express appreciation, also, to members of Professor Cremin's history seminar who, from 1965 to the present, listened to accounts of what I had found and asked a great many challenging questions. My indebtedness extends to Professor Jonathan C. Messerli, Professor Robert T. Handy, Professor Robert D. Cross, and Mr. Martin S. Dworkin for their many helpful criticisms, as well as to Professor Philip H. Phenix and Professor Richard F. W. Whittemore for their searching queries. Microfilms of pertinent S.P.G. documents were made available through the generosity of the Institute of Philosophy and Politics of Education, Teachers College, Columbia University. In the matter of arranging for use of this and other invaluable material, special recognition is due S.P.G. archivist Isobel Pridmore, Judy F. Suratt, and the staffs of Teachers College Library, Butler Library, and the main and missionary libraries of Union Theological Seminary.

I am especially pleased to acknowledge with gratitude permission graciously proffered by the United Society for the Propagation of the Gospel, London, England, to quote extensively from S.P.G. manuscripts.

John Calam

New York
November, 1970

CONTENTS

PARSONS AND PEDAGOGUES

I

EDUCATING THE S.P.G.

SINCE HIS EMERGENCE from a vague past, historic man has recorded both his accomplishments and his shortcomings. The intellectual triumphs of Newtonian England, for instance, stand amply documented. So do the moral inadequacies of the time. Indeed, between the 1688 Revolution Settlement and the early years of the eighteenth century, wicked men and women seemed to observant contemporaries to flourish in Britain as never before. Excessive drinking appeared widespread among all classes. Obscene books found eager buyers. Prostitutes and gamblers plagued magistrate and minister alike. Private masquerades and public theatres earned episcopal condemnation as ultimate degredations.

But this post-revolution concern over moral laxity was something other than a minority puritan lament for departed innocence. Immorality, in fact, caused wide concern throughout England, and the numerous societies founded for relieving debtors, aiding the poor, or improving manners fought it relentlessly. Some estimate that from 1692 to 1702 moral improvement associations pressed charges against 20,000 people accused of profanity and 3,000 "lewd and disorderly persons" in London and Westminster alone.[1] Thomas Bray, one of the builders of the Society for the Propagation of the Gospel in Foreign Parts, himself took the common view that since England's power and reputation were menaced by internal moral deterioration, responsible citizens should play public informer in an effort to eradicate evil.[2]

Tale-bearing and subsequent prosecution for moral misconduct was, however, an unreliable means of resisting corruption. Many well-meaning Englishmen hesitated to risk public scandal. Moreover, since reform societies often welcomed interdenominational membership, High Churchmen generally declined to cooperate. Even so, alternative remedies for moral retrogression presented themselves. With prevention rather than retribution as their guiding principle, certain religious societies aimed through education at preserving national integrity in law, politics, and religion. Dating back to England's conversion to protestantism, these religious societies had a long history and a corresponding interest in Britain's overseas possessions. As early as 1534, Archbishop Cranmer furnished two chaplains to serve Calais. In 1578, when Frobisher embarked on his search for the Northwest Passage, Queen Elizabeth's council dispatched "Maister Wolfall" as first reformed Church of England parson to see American service. Similar arrangements attended Sir Humphrey Gilbert's expedition to Newfoundland (1583) and Sir Walter Raleigh's voyage to Virginia (1584).[3]

1. See J. H. Overton, *Life in the English Church, 1660–1714*, p. 214, cited in H. P. Thompson, *Thomas Bray* (London: S.P.C.K., 1954), p. 7. The figures are striking when compared with a London metropolitan population of 674,350, based on parish records, suggested by M. Dorothy George, *London Life in the 18th Century* (New York: Capricorn Books, 1965), p. 329.

2. See Thomas Bray, *For God or for Satan*, pp. 23–24, cited in Dudley W. R. Bahlman, *The Moral Revolution of 1688* (New Haven: Yale University Press, 1957), Chapter 1.

3. C. F. Pascoe, *Two Hundred Years of the S.P.G.: An Historical Account of the Society for the Propagation of the Gospel in Foreign Parts, 1701–1900* (London: S.P.G., 1901), pp. 1–2.

In general, thought, such minimal provisions for ensuring Christian living according to newly constituted Anglicanism failed from the outset to impress English colonial settlers or native populations. And, although they enjoyed royal endorsement, later arrangements to bring American colonial provinces under the bishop of London's ecclesiastical jurisdiction inspired little home enthusiasm for moral reform abroad through Church teaching. Conversely, several privately motivated enterprises obtained royal charters and met with more success. Two deserve mention as S.P.G. precursors. One, the Society for the Propagation of the Gospel in New England, institutionalized in 1649 the work started by John Eliot three years previously. Composed of Anglicans as well as dissenters, it carried on its work up to the American War of Independence. The other, established in 1699, was the Society for Promoting Christian Knowledge, which among other projects energetically supplied parochial libraries to North American plantations. So burdened became the S.P.C.K. with home affairs, however, that its overseas responsibilities lagged. As a result, S.P.C.K. founding father Thomas Bray proposed a further religious society with the unique function of attending to American provincial instruction.

Few phases of that seventeenth- and eighteenth-century yearning for human perfection better exemplify the genius of British social, political, and religious institutions for concerted effort than do the discussions that culminated in the formation of the Society for the Propagation of the Gospel in Foreign Parts. Missionary arm of the established Church, the Society, Venerable Society, or S.P.G. as it is variously designated can trace its origins to the determination of Thomas Bray. Following his 1696 appointment as bishop of London's commissary[4] to Maryland, but prior to his departure for that colony, Bray had con-

4. These officials acted as bishop's representative. They made visitations, held conventions, and recommended applicants for holy orders, but they lacked the authority either to ordain or confirm.

trived to send parsons abroad and had shipped books for their use in extending Anglicanism. Native generosity plus modest status in the Church hierarchy left Bray poor. Nevertheless, by selling and borrowing he raised enough money to sail to Maryland, where he drafted a provincial bill for Church establishment. Eager to get royal assent for this legislative proposal, he returned to England in 1700. Both Archbishop Tenison of Canterbury and Bishop Compton of London granted a sympathetic hearing, clearing the way for discussing fully in convocation the far wider issue of spreading Church doctrine throughout the colonies and among His Majesty's ships at sea. In addition, then, to his political responsibility to procure ratification of Maryland's establishment bill, Bray found himself the nominee of an Anglican convocation committee. His specific task was petitioning William III for a royal charter in aid of yet another religious society.

Although a relatively minor Church official, Bray brought special qualifications to his job of persuading the king. As parson, he recognized the connection between good books and good sermons. As bibliophile and philanthropist well beyond his means, he knew how to distinguish useful books from less serviceable ones. As S.P.C.K. charter member, he appreciated the importance of political lobbying in order to secure the resources vital to extending Christian morality. His American experience, moreover, led him to conclude that without the combined efforts of Church officers and private citizens American Anglicanism stood in jeopardy. Episcopal trust in this entire matter proved to be well placed. Bray lodged his petition. The king sought constitutional opinion. Thenceforth, the Society for the Propagation of the Gospel in Foreign Parts assumed corporate responsibility for an assault on immorality and encroachments on established English protestantism. In so doing, it exercised a hitherto unknown function. For, as the charter declared, here was royal endorsement of an Anglican scheme of reform outside the realm, in those "Plantacons, Colonies, and Factories beyond the Seas."[5] And S.P.G. charity would reach white settler, Negro, and Indian alike. Above all, a learned ministry was to instruct a people assumed to be ill versed in Christian living. Thus began a most ambitious educational enterprise.

During the first dozen years or so of incorporation the Society worked out routines for dealing with its overseas educational adventure. By far the most successful early realization of the 1701 charter lay in the initiative of S.P.G. officers and the solid institutional structure these men created as a result. Appearing in days when clubs and societies of every kind permeated English life, the Society for the Propagation of the Gospel in Foreign Parts stood second to none in organizational thoroughness. Presidents, vice-presidents, secretaries, and treasurers emerged from membership as elected executives. When need arose, committee chairmen, auditors, messengers, scribes, and caretakers served as appointees of a general body meeting every week or two in the Lambeth Palace library or at the vestries of London's more important churches. Secretaries saw to the transcription of minutes, proceedings, and correspondence into folio journals. These told of subcommittees struck to consider bylaws and standing orders, overseas news, translations, finances, maps and charts, real estate, and colonial acts of assembly.

As early records testify, the Society's confidence in its ability to educate sprang not only from sound corporate superstructure but also from the range and influence of its membership. As ex officio president, the archbishop of Canterbury headed a list of episcopal charter and nominated members embracing the prestige bishoprics of Britain. Several of the former occupied the ecclesiastical bench in the House of Lords, and the bishop of London, always prominent in S.P.G. affairs, numbered among the Lords Commissioners of Trade and Plantations. Foreign

5. The Charter of 1701, reprinted in Pascoe, *Two Hundred Years*, p. 932. More detailed accounts of the founding of the S.P.G. may be read in this comprehensive work, pp. 1–9, as well as in William Webb Kemp, *The Support of Schools in Colonial New York by the S.P.G.* (New York: Teachers College, Columbia University, 1913), Chapters 1 and 2.

orthodox protestantism established rapport with the Society, which in turn strengthened its own university connections, first by virtue of the bishop of London's status as chancellor of Virginia's William and Mary College, and second through S.P.G. membership extended to professors at Oxford and Cambridge, Utrecht, Heidelberg, Anhalts, Leipswick, Basel, Bern, and Lausanne.[6] Moreover, in recognition of past services and present need for practical advice, membership was sparingly bestowed upon such men as Commissary Thomas Bray and George Keith, first Society missionary in America.

To these clerical components were added military, commercial, and political lay members. In regularity of attendance and participation, captains, colonels, and lieutenants general rivaled doctors of divinity. Lawyers willingly proffered opinions whenever litigation threatened. London, Amsterdam, Barbadoes, and New York merchants, including Elihu Yale donated time, money, and investment recommendations. Meanwhile, the combined experience of legislators and colonial administrators helped the S.P.G. find support for its American mission, particularly through addresses to royalty or by means of private parliamentary bills.[7] In financial matters, too, the S.P.G. quickly

---

6. Church charter members included the archbishops of Canterbury and York, and the bishops of London, Gloucester, Chichester, Chester, Bath and Wells, and Bangor. See "Charter of the Society, June 16, 1701," in Pascoe, *Two Hundred Years*, p. 932. Soon to be added were the bishops of Durham, Winchester, Carlisle, Exeter, Salisbury, Lichfield and Coventry, Norwich, Peterborough, Bristol, Lincoln, and Oxford. See *S.P.G. Journals*, Vol. I, entry for November 21, 1701, p. 20, #6. Over the first decade or so of S.P.G. history, foreign membership included ministers of the French and Dutch churches in London, chaplains at the Prussian Court, clergymen of the French churches in Amsterdam and Rotterdam, the provost and the superintendent general of all the churches in Brunswick and Luneberg, the president and deans of the Grisons Synod, a Swedish bishop, and officials in Zurich, Bern, Neufchatel, Geneva, and Halle. See *S.P.G. Journals*, Vol. I, pp. 340, 375, 381, 472, 483; Vol. II, pp. 18, 53, 73, 91, 265; Vol. III, pp. 117, 254, 327. For details of extended university connections, see *S.P.G. Journals*, Vol. I, pp. 247, 308, 418, 444; Vol. II, p. 364; Vol. III, pp. 57, 254, 327, 346.

7. Although an Anglican, Elihu Yale yielded to the overtures of Cotton Mather and Jeremiah Dummer and subsidized the Congregational New Haven college that adopted his name. See. E. S. Gaustad, *A Religious History of America* (New York: Harper and Row, 1966), pp. 59–60. A short time pre-

placed itself on a firm, if limited, footing. It printed forms of subscription and deputation. It deposited specie or bonds with London goldsmiths or the newly-formed Bank of England. It invested in East India and Exchequer bonds and other securities, at the same time conferring with agents regarding land speculation in Barbadoes, New Jersey, Pennsylvania, and on Long Island.

That such meticulous planning involving a wide range of influential British and colonial society established a steady foundation for future building may readily be verified by noting that the S.P.G. celebrated in 1970 two hundred sixty-nine years of continuous missionary activity,[8] despite the blow it sustained in North America as a consequence of American independence.

Fundamental to its eighteenth-century American operation

---

viously, Yale had offered the Society interest-free loans for general purposes, and gifts for a combination London meeting place, chapel, library, and charity school, as well as for support of bishops in America. See *S.P.G. Journals,* Vol. III, entries for December 20, 1717, p. 328, #6, and April 18, 1718, p. 363, #5. In view of the younger Mather's earlier complaints about S.P.G. inroads upon Long Island dissent, Yale's philanthropy serves as a reminder that time and circumstances can readily blur the lines of rigid sectarianism. *Ibid.,* Vol. II, entry for June 15, 1711, p. 57, #12.

In addition to such strategically placed members as Messrs. Langhorne and Heysham, members of parliament, and Mr. John Basket, queen's printer, the Society numbered among its ranks people like Sir Robert Atkyns, once chief baron of the exchequer and speaker of the House of Lords, Sir Nathaniel Lloyd, a fellow of All Soul's, Oxford, who became deputy admiral advocate, king's advocate, and master of Trinity Hall, Oxford, and John Carteret, First Earl Granville, successively gentleman of the bedchamber to George I, bailiff of Jersey, lord-lieutenant of Devon, ambassador to Sweden, and lord-lieutenant of Ireland. See Sir Leslie Stephens and Sir Sidney Lee (eds.), *The Dictionary of National Biography* (Oxford: Oxford University Press, 1959–1960), Vol. XI, p. 1309; Vol. III, pp. 1119–24. Those familiar with America included Mr. John Bridges, surveyor general of all the king's woods on the continent of America, Colonel Robert Quarry, Mr. Nicholas Trott, attorney general of South Carolina, merchants like Lewis Morris and Caleb Heathcote, and such notable colonial chief and lieutenants governor as Sir Francis Nicholson, Joseph Dudley, Sir Nathaniel Johnson, Edward Hyde, Robert Hunter, Alexander Spotswood, Edward Tynte, Captain Gooking, Robert Lowther, John Perne, Charles Craven, Sir Nicholas Laws, and Richard Philipps.

For details of royal and parliamentary appeals, see *S.P.G. Journals,* Vol. I, entry for March 20, 1701/2, p. 47, #4; Vol. III, entry for August 19, 1715, p. 73.

8. In 1965, through a merger with the Universities' Mission to Central Africa (U.M.C.A.), the S.P.G. became the United Society for the Propagation of the Gospel (U.S.P.G.). Belle Pridmore, U.S.P.G. archivist, letter to the author, London, March 26, 1968.

was the Society's charter granted by William III on June 16, 1701, which read in part:

Whereas Wee are credibly informed that in many of our Plantacons, Colonies, and Factories beyond the Seas, belonging to Our Kingdome of England, the Provision for Ministers is very mean. And many others of Our said Plantacons, Colonies, and Factories are wholy destitute, and unprovided of a Mainteynance for Ministers, and the Publick Worshipp of God; and for Lack of Support and Mainteynance for such, many of our Loveing Subjects doe want the Administration of God's Word and Sacraments, and seem to be abandoned to Atheism and Infidelity and alsoe for Want of Learned and Orthodox Ministers to instruct Our said Loveing Subjects in the Principles of true Religion, divers Romish Preists and Jesuits are the more incouraged to pervert and draw over Our Loving Subjects to Popish Superstition and Idolatry

And whereas Wee think it Our Duty as much as in Us lyes, to promote the Glory of God, by the Instruccon of Our People in the Christian Religion And that it will be highly conducive for accomplishing those Ends, that a sufficient Mainteynance be provided for an Orthodox Clergy to live amongst them, and that such other Provision be made, as may be necessary for the Propagation of the Gospell in those Parts:

And whereas Wee have been well assured, That if Wee would be gratiously pleased to erect and settle a Corporacon for the receiving, manageing, and disposeing of the Charity of Our Loveing Subjects, divers Persons would be induced to extend their Charity to the Uses and Purposes aforesaid

Know yee therefore, that We have [incorporated] . . . THE SOCIETY FOR THE PROPAGATION OF THE GOSPELL IN FORREIGNE PARTS: . . .[9]

Although it came in for divergent interpretation during the first decades of its existence, and was augmented by a supplemental charter in 1882,[10] the original charter pointed the way to future S.P.G. accomplishment. Activities at first developed

9. Pascoe, *Two Hundred Years,* pp. 932–33.
10. Dated April 6, 1882, the supplemental charter made provisions for a very much extended field of endeavor. It included waiving the oath of office, removing from standing committees the power of granting leases, and clarifying mortgage, property improvement, and other property holding clauses. See Pascoe, *Two Hundred Years,* pp. 936–38.

in the thirteen American colonies. Transmitting the Anglican message through missionary work, schools, and the distribution of books and pamphlets, the Society helped support 329 missionaries, 82 schoolmasters, and 18 catechists before its last United States missionary departed in 1783. And although this event marked the end of an era in S.P.G. history, it increased rather than diminished Society resolution to propagate the gospel throughout the world. In Newfoundland, Bermuda, Canada, the West Indies, Central and South America, Africa, Madagascar, Australasia, India, Burma, Ceylon, Borneo, China, Korea, and Japan, as well as in numerous European countries, S.P.G. emissaries or local Society representatives continued to teach Anglican Christianity up to the time that funds dwindled or national policy in the mission field dictated otherwise.

When reading the full record of the Society's undertakings in many lands, one detects a remarkable approximation of institutional aims and goals. Indeed, this record verifies the development overseas of a variously modified Anglicanism that does credit to charter expectations. It is risky to conclude, on the other hand, that the S.P.G. always possessed anything approaching a clear sense of orientation respecting the fulfillment of its ambitions. Taken as a whole, the 1701 charter provided a straightforward statement of purpose. But royal approval of this document merely set the stage for action in the Society's first theatre, the New World. How to proceed was another matter; and in its attempts to educate itself to the realities of the task ahead, the Society considered advice in every quarter. From Thomas Bray, from officials concerned with trade or Indian affairs, from Churchmen anxious to shift certain English social problems abroad, from colonial residents and government appointees, as well as from S.P.G. envoys touring North America, recommendations poured in.

What life was really like in America and how best to improve it through Anglican instruction remained central queries during the Society's maiden years. As the S.P.G. journals and home letters generally revealed, a vaguely romantic, geographically imprecise notion of America pervaded early discussions concerning Society responsibilities. In this regard, Thomas Bray's counsel appeared something of an exception. As the bishop of London's Commissary for Maryland, Bray had promoted various kinds of libraries—traveling libraries to accompany indigent parsons on their journeys to distant colonies, rural libraries for country curates, parochial libraries for the personal use of parish priests, laymen libraries for parishioners, lending libraries located in market towns, even libraries for rough seaports as alternatives to taverns. An unassuming man, Bray nevertheless brought forward many such practicable suggestions. When the S.P.G. named George Keith for a colonial tour of inspection, Bray not only provided an itinerary, with Boston, New York, Philadelphia, Annapolis, and Williamsburg as important centers, but also packaged and shipped to these places a great many books and pamphlets for Keith's use there. Concerned over Church discipline in Maryland, he urged the purchase for some £1,500 of a plantation to serve as the official seat of Anglican supervision in the colony. In addition to these more sweeping concerns, he supplied a lot of detailed information necessary to a charter society gathering up the loose ends of private philanthropy,[11] thereby simplifying the start of careful bookkeeping that enabled the S.P.G. to correlate policy with legers from then on.

Less altruistic vested interests like the Lords Commissioners of Trade and Plantations signified special interest in the politi-

11. *Sion College MSS*, p. 323, cited by H. P. Thompson, *Into All Lands* (London: S.P.C.K., 1951), p. 74; "Dr. Bray's Memorial shewing the Necessity of one to Superintend the Church and Clergy in Maryland . . . ," V. J., June 26, 1702, *S.P.G. Journals*, Appendix, A, No. XVI; Dr. Bray to the Secretary, Sheldon near Birmingham, March 24, 1704, *S.P.G. Letter Books*, Series A, Vol. I, No. CLXIV; Dr. Bray to the Secretary, Sheldon, June 24, 1704, *ibid.*, Series A, Vol. I, No. CLXVI; Dr. Bray to the Secretary, Sheldon, March 24, 1702, *S.P.G. Journals*, Appendix A, No. XVI; Dr. Bray to the Secretary, *English Church History: S.P.C.K. Minutes and Correspondence 1698–1704*, cited by Thompson, *Into All Lands*, p. 75.

cal, military, and economic significance of Indians occupying strategic frontier positions. Six months before the Society's incorporation, the commissioners (whose membership included the bishop of London) had written to the archbishop of Canterbury expressing concern over the Five Nations Indians on the New York borderland. What troubled them was later reflected in the S.P.G. charter. French Jesuits, they asserted, were conversant with this primitive people in a technical sense; that is, priests understood and spoke the Indian languages and thereby gained Catholic converts as well as allies for France. Responding, the Society enquired further about funds. In reply, the lords reminded the S.P.G. of the queen's bounty—a £20 subsidy for outward-bound missionaries first secured by London's Bishop Compton under Charles II. They further proposed an eventual benefice in England as the most likely encouragement to a minister contemplating several years teaching along the Indian trails. They suggested as well that the Society for Evangelizing Indians in New England might be willing to help out.[12]

The S.P.G. apparently acted on this advice. In due course, Sir William Ashurst wrote the Society for the Propagation of the Gospel in Foreign Parts on behalf of the New England Society. He promised no financial support, but discussed at length the many-sidedness of Indian missionary ventures and the principal obstacles to success. These, he said, comprised Jesuit trickery, limited assets, English encroachment on Indian

12. "A Letter from the Lords Commissioners of Trade and Plantations to the Archbishop of Canterbury concerning the Conversion of the Indians," Vide Journal, White Hall, October 25, 1700, *S.P.G. Journals,* Appendix A, No. V; Mr. Popple Jnr. to the Secretary, White Hall, February 3, 1703/4, *S.P.G. Letter Books,* Series A, Vol. I, No. CXXVI. Curiously enough, the Society for Evangelizing Indians in New England was the 1649 design of John Eliot, a puritan missionary to the Indians whose theocratic work *Christian Commonwealth* in 1661 was banned by the Massachusetts General Court as "justly offensive . . . to kingly Gouvernment in England," see *Massachusetts Historical Society Publications,* Vol. IX, Third Series, p. 128, cited by Vernon Parrington, *Main Currents in American Thought,* Vol. I: *1620–1800: The Colonial Mind* (New York: Harcourt, Brace and World, Inc., 1927, 1954), p. 81.

lands, and nomadism. Ashurst stressed the relationship between proselytizing and Indian trade; in addition, he emphasized that receiving presents greatly improved an Indian's disposition to instruction and allegiance. He also underscored the successes of Dutch ministers adept at tribal tongues, a belief in language skills later echoed by Robert Livingston, secretary for Indian affairs in New York, and by Godfrey Dellius, a Netherlands pastor who constantly offered advice based on his former work among the Iroquois.[13]

Other home correspondents lectured the new Society in a rather more general fashion about the many good works it was capable of accomplishing. Sometime navy chaplain the Reverend Patrick Gordon suggested voluntary support from British freeholders, merchants, and clergy, and prescribed mandatory English as a simplistic solution to the Indian language barrier. Citizens Thomas Hughes and Albert Dunlop showed how the S.P.G. might better regulate navy manners by arranging preferment ashore for chaplains of five years maritime service. Few gratuitous proposals better infer missionary recruiting problems than did several from Thomas, bishop of Sodor and Man. Insularity, claimed the prelate, supplied the best environment for missionary training. On the Isle of Man, youths lived under strict discipline and frugality. They were used to the sea, and could be trained at existing schools in expectation of colonial missions. As captive scholars, moreover, they could be denied departure from the island and all hopes of advancement at home

13. Sir William Ashurst to the Secretary, London, June 30, 1703, *S.P.G. Letter Books,* Series A, Vol. I, No. XCII; "The Memorial of Robert Livingston," Vide Journal, September 17, 1703, *S.P.G. Journals,* Appendix A, No. XXIX. A persistent correspondent, Dellius lectured the Society on the iniquities of rum, trade licenses, the advantages of Christian Indian guides during time of war, colonial expansion, the duties of governors, and the problems of rendering devotional treatises into the Indian idiom. In return for this advice, Dellius expected the rectorship of London's St. James' Dutch Church, but never achieved his ambition. See Mr. Dellius to the Secretary between May 29, 1702, and December 25, 1708, *S.P.G. Letter Books,* Series A, Vol. I, Nos. VII, LXX, LXXII, LXXXIX, CVII, CXIII, CXXXII, CXLIX, CL; Vol. II, Nos. VII, LIII; Vol. III, Nos. XLI, CXLVIII, CXLIX, CLXXXVIII.

in order to ensure obedience to S.P.G. commands regarding their going abroad.[14]

If home schemes like these hinted at easy solutions to often-times obscurely stated problems, the voice of colonial Anglicanism at the time sounded more precise. To wealthy Anglican governors and settlers along America's Atlantic seaboard, for example, the Church lay in dire need of defense against nonconformist challenge, and chances of Anglican survival depended on the Society's ability to send over properly trained, well-paid missionaries.

Typical of these S.P.G. members at large was New England Governor Joseph Dudley. Born at Roxbury, educated at Harvard, during his life convinced of the advantages of close colonial obedience to England, Dudley volunteered a good deal of local information about how the Society might begin its work. As a highly placed official with excellent intercolonial connections, Governor Dudley scanned wider horizons too. In his *Account of the State of Religion in the English Plantations in North America,*[15] he presented a province-by-province estimate of population, potential for Church success, and denominational patterns, and he took as a matter of course the vital coexistence of churches and ministers on the one hand and schools and schoolmasters on the other. Society parsons and pedagogues, he

14. "Proposals for Propagating the Gospel in all Pagan Countreys," Vide Journal, January 16, 1701, *S.P.G. Journals,* Appendix A, No. VIII; "Scheme for Regulation of Manners in the Navy," Journal, May 19, 1704, *ibid.,* Appendix A, No. XL; "The Bishop of Man's Proposal for Propogating [*sic*] the Gospel etc.," *S.P.G. Letters,* Series C, Vol. XIV, No. I, dated May 12, 1707; Addition, dated February 26, 1710, *ibid.,* Series C, Vol. XIV, No. III.

15. For an interpretation of Dudley as constitutional legalist in colonial affairs, see Everett Kimball, *The Public Life of Joseph Dudley* (New York: Longmans, Green and Company, 1911). See also Governor of New England to the Secretary, n.p., November 8, 1702, *S.P.G. Letter Books,* Series A, Vol. I, No. XLIII; The Governor of New England and other The Members of the Church at Boston to his Grace the Lord Archbishop of Canterbury, Boston, December 23, 1703, *ibid.,* Series A, Vol. I, No. CLIX; Governor Dudley to the Secretary, Boston, October 10, 1706, *ibid.,* Series A, Vol. III, No. IV; *S.P.G. Journals,* Appendix A, No. III.

implied, ideally should be middle-aged, moral, learned men of sufficient means to avoid contempt, particularly in New England where children seemed well taught by socially recognized schoolmasters.

New York's Governor Cornbury shared several of Dudley's views. Society schoolteachers, he argued, ought to be mature scholars in holy orders. They needed to cooperate with Anglican ministers to ensure that colonial boys and girls received a proper upbringing. Cornbury likewise reviewed provincial needs as a whole. He indicated that settlers in isolated East Long Island stood in unusual need of S.P.G. assistance since they had hitherto postponed efforts in that direction because they incorrectly supposed that securing Anglican ministers would be contingent on an act of assembly. Dutch ministers, he observed, would do well at Albany, at Kingston in Ulster County, and in King's County, Long Island. As these Low Country men died, they might profitably be replaced by S.P.G. nominees whose churches and schools would gradually help transform all New York into a thoroughly English colony. Indians required special consideration. Those sent to teach them should learn the native dialects, he said, for it was out of the question to expect a minister of the Church of England to convert an Indian through a Dutch interpreter.[16]

Cornbury's most impassioned observation, though, involved an early Society missionary to Albany who fitted few of his lordship's specifications. Thorougood Moore suffered house arrest in the fort at New York for refusal to consider the governor his superior in S.P.G. affairs. Moore's eventual escape to England with a counter-petition against his jailer prompted Cornbury to strenuous objection. If, he reasoned, S.P.G. servants

16. Lord Cornbury to Colonel Quarry, New York, July 15, 1705, *S.P.G. Letter Books,* Series A, Vol. II, No. XCI. A later letter admitted that the assembly "were not in a Temper" to pass such legislation. See Lord Cornbury to the Secretary, New York, November 22, 1705, *ibid.,* Series A, Vol. II, No. CXXXII; Lord Cornbury to the Secretary, New York, November 29, 1707, *ibid.,* Series A, Vol. III, No. CLV.

were to act independently of colonial government control and move about at will, was it not logical to assume that governors ought to be so advised to prevent them intermeddling with things beyond their mandates?[17] Here, to be sure, was a valid question. If the Society were to subscribe to a theory of missionary imperialism, the resulting problem of overlapping church and state responsibilities arising from the lack of a colonial bishop loomed very large indeed.

In addition to governors, prominent colonial residents holding Society membership habitually addressed the S.P.G., advising how best to effectuate the charter. One of these was Colonel Lewis Morris. Like Cornbury, he disliked Quakers and Congregationalists on point of principle. He dismissed New England independency as a sort of theological pollutant, and refused to consider East Jersey dissenters as Christians. He warned both governors that sending young missionaries to America on minimal allowances would be false economy detrimental to Church interests. As in Dudley's case, he wrote a detailed memorandum on the state of religion in which he described many other things as well. He differentiated between usually tightly knit English towns in the old land and East Jersey settlements strewn over areas as great as 225 square miles. He gave one of the earliest indications of colonial population mobility, showing that many Jersey residents had arrived not directly from Europe but from New England, New York, and Rhode Island, bringing with them every sort of religious persuasion. The youth of the entire province he indicated as an ignorant, debauched, riotous, drunken lot. An Anglocentric thinker, Morris showed the path to improvement. It lay, he believed, in parliament's assurance that all governors, council members, and magistrates should be firm Churchmen. Churchmen in general would have special privileges. And ministers who volunteered to preach gratis in

17. *Ibid.*

America would be guaranteed benefices upon their return to England.[18]

There was one colonial Society member, however, who in frequency, volume, and variety of advice to the Society outdistanced Dudley, Cornbury, and Morris put together. That man was Colonel Caleb Heathcote, a Westchester landowner held by some as the most useful colonial layman in the history of the American Anglican Church. If multiplicity of position be the measure of influence, Heathcote was a powerful person. At one time or another he served as military officer, judge, surveyor general of customs, and mayor of Westchester and New York. As merchant, land speculator, publicist, and Churchman he enjoyed the widest range of social contacts.[19] Such knowledgeable S.P.G. members were certainly hard to come by.

Among the hundreds of laymen's opinions recorded by the Society, few condemnations of colonial morality plumb such depths of iniquity as those of Caleb Heathcote, master of Scarsdale Manor. In an often-quoted assessment of New York and vicinity, Heathcote told of a heathenish country with a passion for ungodly Sundays which, as militia commander, he claimed to have improved by offering the reserve force under his orders the choice between Bible-reading and compulsory drill. He objected to New England congregationalism which, in spite of colleges at Boston and Saybrook, and a large contingent of

18. Like Dudley, Morris was colonial born. He was successively judge of the court of common rights in East Jersey, president of the council, member of Cornbury's council, speaker of the general assembly, chief justice of New York, and governor of New Jersey. See William A. Whitehead (ed.), *The Papers of Lewis Morris, Governor of New Jersey, from 1738–1746* (New York: George Putnam, 1852), pp. 1–30. See also Colonel Lewis Morris to Mr. Archdeacon Beveridge, East Jersey, September 3, 1702, *S.P.G. Letter Books*, Series A, Vol. I, No. XLV; "The Memorial of Col: Morris Concerning the State of Religion in the Jerseys," Vide Journall [*sic*], September 19, 1702, *S.P.G. Journals*, Appendix A, No. II.

19. Dixon Ryan Fox, *Caleb Heathcote* (New York: Charles Scribner's Sons, 1926), p. 273. Heathcote's community reach in matters of taxation can readily be seen by his quadruplicate office in Westchester. As a member of the council, he consented to the levy of taxes. As presiding judge of the Westchester court of sessions, he supervised the assessment of taxes. As farmer of the excise he collected the money himself. And as a contractor he spent the money so secured for outfitting troops or furnishing supplies. *Ibid.*, p. 53.

ministers, left hundreds unbaptised and denied others liberty of conscience.[20] Just the same, the mayor of Westchester believed the recently established S.P.G. could refine the tone of colonial living if only it would follow his proposals.

Heathcote's notion of Society organization predicated a steadfast belief in the easy transmission to America of hierarchical social control. Thus, according to Heathcote, effective colonial settlement of Society-sponsored schools and churches was to hinge upon the authority of a resident superior, preferably a bishop, responsible for calling quarterly meetings, ordaining Anglican priests, and seeing that S.P.G. preachers and teachers regularly furnished him and the Society with particulars of their work. About this theoretical framework, Heathcote constructed his ideal of total Society performance. Questions of finance as well as of conscience would require the legislative cooperation of both assembly and parliament and demand a much better governor than Cornbury, hopefully one appointed by the queen upon S.P.G. recommendation. With care, expenses might be reduced. Schoolmasters could be paid in kind—say, in broadcloth, buttons, and silk for suitably clothing men of their rank. Teachers might be enlisted in the Royal Navy and stationed near colonial shipyards and naval stores factories where children could work part time manufacturing sail cloth and rigging, the rest of the time learning to read and write.[21]

20. Colonel Heathcote to the Secretary, Manor of Scarsdale, New York, April 10, 1704, *S.P.G. Letter Books,* Series A, Vol. I, No. CLXXXII. The Colonel claimed the men opted Bible reading. See also Colonel Heathcote to the Secretary, Manor of Scarsdale, November 9, 1705, *ibid.,* Series A, Vol. II, No. CXVII; Colonel Heathcote to the Secretary, Stratford, January 1, 1707/8, *ibid.,* Series A, Vol. III, No. CLXXXVIII.

21. For the full development of this idea, see Colonel Heathcote's letters to the Secretary, *ibid.,* Series A, Vol. I, Nos. CLXXIV, CLXXV, CLXXXII; Vol. II, No. CXVII; Vol. III, Nos. LXXXVI, CLXII, written between June 1, 1704 and December 24, 1707. Also see Colonel Heathcote to the Secretary, Manor of Scarsdale, June 8, 1704, *ibid.,* Series A, Vol. I, No. CLXXV; Colonel Heathcote to the Secretary, New York, February 24, 1707, *ibid.,* Series A, Vol. III, No. LXXXVI; Colonel Heathcote to the Secretary, Manor of Scarsdale, December 24, 1707, *ibid.,* Series A, Vol. III, No. CLXII; Colonel Heathcote to the Secretary, Manor of Scarsdale, December 18, 1707, *ibid.,* Series A, Vol. III, No. CLXI; Colonel Heathcote to the Secretary, Manor of Scarsdale, December 16, 1706, *ibid.,* Series A, Vol. III, No. CLX. Heathcote's scheme for combining child labor and elementary instruction in a shipbuilding

To start with, of course, ministers and schoolmasters would have to ride beyond the settlements to reach isolated parents and their children, and be prepared to meet nonconformist resistance with a "soft and easy" means of instruction and conversion. In the beginning, too, only moderate academic progress need be contemplated, since in a domestic economy, few parents could spare their children's time beyond the fundamentals of catechism and copy book. Meanwhile, with employment enough for missionaries among white colonists, efforts to civilize Indians could safely be postponed. When time was ripe for such Indian missions, the S.P.G. would have to seek young men willing to live among the savages and learn their languages and peculiarities. In this, youth alone could endure the fatigue.[22]

These lay colonial office holders and gentlemen, unlike several of their Society co-members in Britain, hewed rigorously to the practical side of things, painting a markedly gloomy picture of colonial morality and leaning heavily toward legislative solutions to S.P.G. educational problems afield. Society functionaries specifically dispatched to survey the colonial mission situation were to arrive at similar judgments.

With that initial zest men show in missions newly undertaken, the Reverend George Keith, his traveling companion the Reverend John Talbot, and the bishop of London's South Carolina commissary, the Reverend Gideon Johnston added to home observations and colonial estimates their own appraisals of a North America awaiting S.P.G. edification.

Intimately acquainted with the vagaries of religious power

---

economy was by no means far-fetched. The master of Scarsdale had successfully contracted for the construction of frigates on previous occasions. Dixon Ryan Fox argues that the Board of Trade turned Heathcote's education scheme down since its encouragement of colonial manufacture contradicted contemporary British mercantile theory. See Fox, *Heathcote*, p. 154.

22. Colonel Heathcote to the Secretary, Manor of Scarsdale, New York, April 10, 1704, *S.P.G. Letter Books*, Series A, Vol. I, No. CLXXXII; Colonel Heathcote to the Society, New York, October 23, 1704, *ibid.*, Series A, Vol. II, No. XXXVIII; Colonel Heathcote to the Secretary, Manor of Scarsdale, November 9, 1705, *ibid.*, Series A, Vol. II, No. CXVII. For work among Indian tribes, Heathcote recommended Scottish candidates because of their alleged facility for learning foreign languages.

structure in Britain, and following extensive experience in colonial church and state affairs, Keith secured nomination as first S.P.G. missionary with orders to investigate and report on the state of the Church in America. Although he was constantly embroiled in controversy, his account, published in 1706 as the *Journal* lent further direction to an organization groping its way.

Following an eventful two-and-a-half-year colonial tour, Keith concluded that the greatest obstacles to the established Church abroad were Quakers, whom he loaded with epithets. As far as northern independency was concerned, he adopted a less severe, if condescending, stance. Under correct episcopal supervision, he maintained, a trained, solvent Anglican missionary force could salvage the main hulk of New England dissent and tow it back to the haven of the Church. This maneuver was to be expedited by means of educational plans arising from Keith's dismay at what he considered Harvard's theological deviations. The proposal was to send over from Oxford and Cambridge, England, a president and fellows to assume control at Cambridge, Massachusetts, and so guarantee New England youth an antidote to "poisonous" prejudices against the Church of England. Above all, Keith's orientation remained fixedly theological. He expended much time and energy disputing such concerns as the sufficiency to salvation of the light within.[23]

23. George Keith, *Journal* (London: Joseph Downing, 1706), *passim*. Having shifted his own affiliations from Presbyterianism through Quakerism, to Anglicanism, Keith felt he was in a privileged position to criticize his previous Quaker acquaintances. That his position was understandable is illustrated by Edwin Scott Gaustad, who remarked that "the well-ordered society preserves its stable position by keeping the lines of authority completely untangled and firmly in hand. If ultimate authority resides in God, then the rulers of society must be God's authentic Spokesmen; if the authority is the Bible, they must be its legitimate interpreters; if the authority is power, the control of that power must be wholly theirs.

"To any such neat boxing and compassing of the social order, the Quakers were a fearsome threat." See *Historical Atlas of Religion in America* (New York: Harper and Row, 1962), pp. 21, 22. See as well "An Account of the State of the Church in North America, by Mr. George Keith and Others," reprinted in The Protestant Episcopal Historical Society, *Collections* (New York: Stanford and Swords, 1851), pp. xv-xxi; Mr. Keith to Dr. Bray, Philadelphia, February 26, 1702/3, *S.P.G. Letter Books*, Series A, Vol. I, No. LXXXVIII; Mr. Keith to the Society, New York, November 29, 1702, *ibid.*, Series A, Vol. I, No. L; Keith, *Journal, passim*.

Filtered down through college, congregation, and school, the Church answers to these and similar questions were, in his opinion, to provide the basis for a colonial spiritual order. Social, economic, and political amelioration would follow as a matter of course.

Aboard the *Centurion* during Keith's 1702 voyage to America was ship's chaplain the Reverend John Talbot, destined to a quarter century of S.P.G. service terminating amid allegations of nonjuror[24] status in dismissal shortly before his death. Educated at Cambridge, England, and a previous visitor to Virginia, Talbot complemented Keith in first-hand knowledge of Church pursuits in Britain and America. But while many of his sentiments regarding S.P.G. responsibilities merely duplicated Keith's, a more convincing composite view of the colonial scene and its implications for the Society teacher emerges here.

For one thing, Talbot nurtured a continuing interest in Indian conversion. For another, his unsolicited eulogizing of New York Governor Cornbury and Virginia Governor Nicholson appeared to reassure the Society of its own wisdom in consolidating connections with strategically placed colonial officials. Furthermore, his descriptions of hundred-mile rides and saddlebags bulging with books for the dual purpose of comforting wilderness dwellers and serving Church interests reminded the S.P.G. about alternatives to bold frontal attacks on dissenting population centers like Boston or Cambridge. Even his preoccupation with the propriety of his own apparel revealed in Talbot a sensitivity to class structure typical of Cantabrigians abroad, and sharpened the issue of missionary stipends low enough to fit the Society budget yet high enough to command respect among materially minded proselytes. Schoolmasters, declared Talbot, proved especially susceptible to the privations of meager sub-

---

24. See Edgar Legare Pennington, *Apostle of New Jersey: John Talbot, 1645–1727* (Philadelphia: The Church Historical Society, 1938), pp. 66–72. Nonjurors were those Anglican bishops and lesser clergy who had sworn allegiance to James II and refused to do likewise to the new monarchy at the time of the Revolution Settlement of 1689.

sistence. Subscriptions of £20 colonial money barely nourished family men. Only good salaries could attract competent masters and rectify such scandals as Philadelphia "heathens" (that is, Quakers) having three schools "and the Christians not one." Nor need a well-paid teacher want for work. Doubling as deacon, he might very well read prayers and sermons, baptize and catechize children, visit the sick, and bury the dead.[25]

While Keith and Talbot described northern and middle colonial life, Commissary Gideon Johnston penned unrestrained letters advising S.P.G. officials about ways of improving life and advancing the Church cause in South Carolina. Johnston's initial impressions of inhabitants of Charles Town and vicinity matched for directness some of Keith's diatribes on Quakers. They were, Johnston protested, the vilest race of men imaginable. Two years later, however, and with the impact of a first look softened by progressive familiarity with local conditions, Johnston addressed the S.P.G. in what must surely be a classic of colonial reporting. Frank J. Klingberg has drawn attention to its salient features.[26] Johnston detailed the poverty of a new

25. Mr. John Talbot to Mr. Richard Gillingham, New York, November 24, 1702, *S.P.G. Letter Books*, Series A, Vol. I, No. LVI; Mr. Talbot to the Secretary, Philadelphia, September 1, 1703, *ibid.*, Series A, Vol. I, No. CXXV. In 1702 the governor of Rhode Island, who was not appointed by the queen, had been of little help to George Keith in his bitter disputes with Quakers. See George Keith, *Journal*, entry for August 6, 1702, p. 15. By contrast, royal nominees' instructions specified Church responsibilities. Lord Cornbury's orders included accountability for orthodox, public worship, church maintenance and construction, establishment of parishes, and consultation with the bishop of London on a variety of matters including preferment, discipline, vacancies, vestries, and taking holy orders. For instructions to Cornbury, see Samuel Smith, *History of the Colony of Nova Caesarea or New Jersey*, pp. 230–61, cited by Pennington, *Apostle*, pp. 11–12. For further elaboration of Talbot's views, see Mr. Talbot to Mr. Gillingham, Virginia, May 3, 1703, *S.P.G. Letter Books*, Series A, Vol. I, No. CXX; Mr. Talbot to the Secretary, Philadelphia, September 1, 1703, *ibid.*, Series A, Vol. I, No. CXXV; *ibid.*, Series A, Vol. I, Nos. LVI, CXIX, CXX, CXXV; Vol. II, Nos. XXIII, CXIV; Mr. Talbot to the Secretary, Burlington, June 30, 1709, *ibid.*, Series A, Vol. V, No. XIX; Mr. Talbot to the Secretary, Philadelphia, April 7, 1704, *ibid.*, Series A, Vol. I, No. CLXXXI; Mr. Talbot to the Secretary, Burlington, October 28, 1714, *ibid.*, Series A, Vol. IX, No. 40.

26. Mr. Johnston to the Lord Bishop of Sarum, Charles Town, September 20, 1708, *ibid.*, Series A, Vol. IV, No. XVII; Gideon Johnston to the Secretary, Charles Town, S. Carolina, July 5, 1710, *ibid.*, Series A, Vol. V, No. CLVIII. For an excellent introduction to this last, long letter, see Frank J. Klingberg (ed.), *Carolina Chronicle: The Papers of Commissary Gideon*

colony, greatly in debt, dependent on investments from abroad, circulating an inflated currency, and facing acute shortages of medicine, books, and household furnishings, not to mention luxury consumer goods. He told of growing resentment of regimentation and a reciprocal appreciation of spontaneity in sermon and prayer. He indicated an interest in schools and noted a fairly common ability to read. He spoke of community resolution to elect ministers by vestry or congregation vote, and of a parallel enthusiasm for shopping around from church to church in an effort to discover and appoint the best preacher possible. He also dwelt on the difficulty of keeping Church libraries well stocked.

To be sure, Johnston appeared frustrated. But at the same time the South Carolina commissary offered common-sense suggestions appropriate for those who, as Dixon Ryan Fox put it, sat in comfortable English libraries and planned provinces across the sea.[27] For instance, he maintained that local trade credit was not going to stretch indefinitely just to accommodate S.P.G. missionaries and their large families. Likewise, he echoed others' accounts in stating the wisdom of political intervention to ensure a strong Anglican hand in developing free schools. As for any high theory about empire benefits accruing from Indian education, Johnston made clear the futility of sending English teachers to the Indians so long as English traders set so miserable an example by their personal misbehavior and questionable methods of barter. Less attuned, perhaps, to changing circumstances abroad was his plea for increased Society intercession in the colonial custom whereby vestries selected ministers themselves rather than acquiescing to episcopal appointees. But his appeal for reconciling S.P.G. recruitment propaganda with the facts of colonial missionary life in the South was soundly based. The prospective missionary candidate, complained Johnston,

---

Johnston, 1707–1716 (Berkeley and Los Angeles: University of California Press, 1946), pp. 31–34. The letter itself is reprinted in the same work, pp. 34–63.

27. Fox, *Heathcote,* p. 98.

dreamed of a plenteous life. However, there were many disappointments. Poverty, debt, stifling heat, "fflux and ffeaver" belied the romance of the travel books and the calculated optimism of merchants standing to profit through missionary enterprise.

Enthusiasm often outstrips executive capacity. There is much comfort in getting things down in writing; certainly, authority and structure as embodied in and effected through the S.P.G. charter of 1701 were by all eighteenth-century standards the necessary points of departure for the S.P.G. adventure in American education. Conversely, a curious aspect of this massive undertaking was the discrepancy between Society planners' organizational finesse on the one hand and, on the other, perceptual aberrations regarding their own purpose and much of the advice they received from interested correspondents. Even making due allowances for the advantage of historical retrospection, one is struck by the Society's official insensitivity to forces acting against its best intentions. Indeed, without appreciating this tension between decision and execution, one cannot properly understand why, from the outset, the S.P.G. struggle to fulfill its charter expectations proved at times so exceptionally hard. To illustrate, no early executive problem proved so thorny as the basic matter of recruitment for S.P.G. work in America. Where, in fact, were the parsons and pedagogues? Although their parentage varied considerably, eighteenth-century Church ministers usually shared a common background of "public" or grammar school training, followed by education at an Oxford or Cambridge college. But education alone did not guarantee preferment. Neither did high birth; several sons of tradesmen rose to positions of Church status. Per contra, political skill proved essential to the ambitious. Furthermore, parsons of whatever degree shared common assumptions about the nature of promotion. Promising younger men served in lesser posts as lecturers, prebendaries, or librarians. Royal chaplaincies denoted rising fortunes, as did invitations to preach before parliament. Elevation to higher Church echelons frequently brought the incumbent to London, a cultural center soon to embrace Walpole's and Pitt's statesmanship, Blackstone's law, Fielding's novels, the paintings of Hogarth, Reynolds, and Gainsborough, Handel's music, Garrick's acting, Johnson's acid wit, Wedgwood's china, and Chippendale's furniture. It also put him in touch with the metropolitan bishop whose episcopate encompassed all North American colonies and who conducted affairs at home with pomp underwritten by revenues and perquisites in excess of £4,000 annually.[28] Inducements such as these certainly prompted many to remain in the promotional stream at home.

Thus, the question of who should educate the colonies persisted. On the one hand, endurance, imagination, education, experience, and maturity stood high on the list of requirements, as Dudley, Cornbury, Morris, and Talbot consistently argued. But on the other hand, here was the very formula for preferment in Britain. The principal clergy, contended one spokesman long after the Society's inception, were far too busy with their own stray sheep at home to set foot on colonial shores. Even past mid century, another frankly admitted that only those not occu-

28. An Oxford scholar, Bishop Richard Watson once accepted the Trinity Professorship of Chemistry although "he knew nothing at all . . . on the subject." As Norman Sykes puts it, he brought similar qualifications to the chair of divinity. See Norman Sykes, *Church and State in England in the XVIII Century* (Cambridge: Cambridge University Press, 1934), pp. 334, 335, 336. On the matter of the connection between birth and preferment, one notes that Richard Willis, dean of Lincoln, 1701, bishop of Gloucester, 1715, of Salisbury, 1721, and of Winchester, 1723, was the son of a journeyman tanner; Sir Leslie Stephen and Sir Sidney Lee (eds.), *The Dictionary of National Biography* (Oxford: Oxford University Press, 1959–1960), Vol. XXI, pp. 490–92. The offspring of a brandy and cider merchant. Thomas Newton rose to be bishop of Bristol in 1761; *ibid.*, Vol. XIV, pp. 403–05.

For a first-rate treatment of the cultural matrix of eighteenth-century British politics, see Basil Williams, *The Whig Supremacy, 1714–1760* (Oxford: The Clarendon Press, 1939), Chapters I, V, XIV, XV, XVI. When the London bishopric was worth £ 4,000 per annum, York was worth £ 4,500, Winchester £ 5,000, Durham £ 6,000, and Canterbury £ 7,000. See Sir J. Fortescue (ed.), *A List of Archbishops, Bishops, Deans, and Prebendaries in England and Wales, in His Majesty's Gift. With the reputed Yearly Value of Their respective Dignities, 1762*, to be found in *Correspondence of K. George III*, 6 vols., 1927, i, 33–44, cited by Williams, *Whig Supremacy*, plate I, after p. xx. See also Sykes, *Church and State*, p. 61. For comparative data, 1835, see *ibid.*, p. 409.

Library
I.U.P.
Indiana, Pa.
{ EDUCATING THE S.P.G. }
377.83 C125p
C.1   25

pied at home should face the dangerous voyage to and uncertain future of the mission field.[29]

For some, of course, the voyage was a necessity either of conscience or subsistence, and these commented on the hardships of removal from the center of their cultural and professional universe. Just getting started was bad enough. At London, Rye, Portsmouth, and Plymouth, outward-bound ministers waited in vain for royal bounties and Society advances. They watched ready cash dwindling as passage fares, porters' charges, lodging costs, and medical fees relentlessly mounted. They thought about unsafe, uncomfortable ships and unknown destinations.

According to others, arrival was worse than departure. Glebe land lay unworked. Places of worship lacked desk, pulpit, and bell. Communities abounded in ignorance. Savages menaced frontier settlers. The French harried the North and the Spanish the South. Ex-residents of quiet English parsonages rode to exhaustion or were drenched in canoes in an effort to reach scattered congregations, only to meet obstructive Quakers and Independents. Hazards to health, dignity, and reputation meanwhile pursued early missionaries even to the heart of populous colonial towns.[30]

So, to certain S.P.G. servants at least, appeared the mission field in aid of which a punctilious charter had evolved. Understandably, theirs was the classic problem of maintaining an altruistic outlook in an environment which reminded them time and again of their lowly status in the temporal order of things.

29. Joseph Wilcocks, bishop of Gloucester, *A Sermon Preached before the Incorporated Society for the Propagation of the Gospel in Foreign Parts* (London: Joseph Downing, 1726), pp. 22, 23; Anthony Ellis, bishop of St. David's, *A Sermon Preached before the Incorporated Society for the Propagation of the Gospel in Foreign Parts* (London: E. Owen and T. Harrison, 1759), pp. 21, 22.

30. Consult, for instance, Mr. Samuel Thomas to Dr. Bray, Rye, August 17, 1702, *S.P.G. Letter Books*, Series A, Vol. I, No. XXI; Mr. Honyman to the Secretary, Jamaica, Long Island, April 15, 1704, *ibid.*, Series A, Vol. I, No. CLXXXVI; Mr. Prichard to the Secretary, Mamoroneck, June 5, 1704, *ibid.*, Series A, Vol. I, No. CLXXX; Mr. Thomas to Mr. Hodges, Carolina, March 22, 1702/3, *ibid.*, Series A, Vol. I, No. XCV.

Intimately related to their own dilemma, too, was the more serious policy predicament of the S.P.G. itself. A rounded picture of North America was vital to the Society's long-range plans. Yet, the early missionary portrayal of the new world to some degree consisted of impressions of men least able to cope with it.[31]

The uncertainty which drove these first S.P.G. employees abroad to render such dismal accounts of their new surroundings drew from American nonconformists countercharges of deliberate distortion and produced a second major obstacle which the Society seems to have underestimated.

Some of these latter expressions of resentment found individual targets. George Keith was one. A former Quaker, Keith had upon occasion tangled with the Mathers, Samuel Willard, and other prominent New England Congregationalists. Increase Mather considered him nothing but an arrogant hypocrite. President Willard of Harvard added charges of personal affront and political intrusion. Former Quaker acquaintances repudiated Keith, their onetime leader.[32]

Quite apart from individual aversions, though, colonials of other persuasions feared a more sweeping failure on the part of S.P.G. envoys to grasp either the spirit or the statistics of colonial nonconformity. Cotton Mather once explained how his antecedents came into the wilderness to enjoy self-rule. That this extremely simple idea continued to elude the Society is

31. Strong feelings of homesickness characterize many letters. Not all lack of appreciation for natural beauty was a result of America's strangeness, however. As Norman Sykes has reminded us, "neither admiration nor understanding of the beauties of . . . scenery" were typical of eighteenth-century temperament. Such emotions awaited Wordsworth and the romantic revival. See Sykes, *Church and State*, p. 424.

32. Increase Mather, *Some Remarks on a late Sermon* . . . (Boston: 1702), cited by Ethyn Williams Kirby, *George Keith: 1638–1716* (New York: D. Appleton Century Company, 1942), p. 127; Samuel Willard, *A Brief Reply to George Keith* . . . (Boston: 1702), *ibid.*, p. 129; *An Account of the Life of that Ancient Servant of Jesus Christ, John Richardson* (London: 3rd edn., 1774), *ibid.*, p. 130; Caleb Pusey, *Proteus Ecclesiasticus* . . . (Philadelphia: 1703), *ibid.*, p. 134; *Penn-Logan Correspondence, Memoirs of the Historical Society of Pennsylvania* (Philadelphia: 1870), Vol. I, p. 179, *ibid.*, p. 139.

indicated in the younger Mather's *Diary*. Later entries expressed satisfaction at the S.P.G. defeating its purpose by sending to America inept ministers who brought shame on the Church of England. But earlier notations evinced more serious concern. In the South, Mather asserted, S.P.G. missionaries invaded churches well versed in Christianity but neglected plantations in spiritual need. As the Society opinion of the North was insulting, so was its presence in the South a danger worthy, in Mather's thinking, of dissentient counteroffensives including pamphlets and complaints to influential Anglican bishops.[33] Far, then, from being ripe for Anglican orthodoxy, American congregationalism as represented by its principal interpreter felt threatened but resolute.

Less vehement than Cotton Mather, other colonial dissenters expressed like objections to S.P.G. designs on America. A prominent example, Boston moderate the Reverend Benjamin Colman kept in touch with Anglican developments through reading S.P.G. anniversary sermons. White Kennett's 1712 dissertation with its statement that the Society had offended no one moved Colman to challenge the accuracy of S.P.G. missionary reporting. The Society, he insisted, was badly misinformed. Heathenish places in Virginia, Maryland, the Jerseys, Rhode Island, and the Narragansett settlement, he conceded, made up a "vast and waste Space" attending Society benevolence. But in towns where religious patterns were set, those appealing for S.P.G. assistance consisted more often than not of undisciplined, disgruntled Congregationalists spiteful over tax rates or the location of new churches. Such, according to Colman, had been the case of Braintree, Newbury, and Jamaica, and the Society's response sabotaged the Congregational interest as surely as it

33. Cotton Mather, *Magnalia Christi Americana*, Book III, Part i, Section vii, cited by E. L. Pennington, *The Reverend John Checkley* (Hartford: The Church Missionary Publishing Co., 1935), p. 1; Worthington Chauncey Ford (ed.), *Diary of Cotton Mather*, Vol. II: *1709–1724* (New York: Frederick Unger Publishing Co., [1911], entry for October 21, 1711, p. 120; *ibid.*, entry for December 23, 1711, p. 145; *ibid.*, entry for May 31, 1713, p. 212.

ignored areas where Anglicans might have done some good. Although his concept of more reliable informants—notably colonial bishops—could scarely have reassured his Congregationalist correspondent, Kennett readily admitted the probability of misinformation.[34]

In thus learning about how to put into practice the unique charter it had so recently obtained, the Society itself did not lack for teachers. On the face of it, realization of that exceptional mandate drafted by Thomas Bray seemed assured. It bore the royal signature. It brought to a focus of influence powerful and promising Church prelates. It gained the support of authoritative political and financial figures, liberal with their advice and generous with their subscriptions. It attracted the attention of visionaries with every imaginable scheme in mind for missionary accomplishment. And, some hoped, it even promised the unification of the American colonies through the return to Anglicanism of the bulk of colonial nonconformists.

It now appears certain, though, that in its quest for a viable impression of North America, the S.P.G. depended on contradictory accounts. English governmental figures stressed military affairs and trade. British reformers lacking American experience proposed utopian schemes divorced from colonial facts. Colonial Church laymen predicted moral ruin unless Anglicanism were more firmly established in their domains. From the start, Society missionaries clashed with non-Church interests and wrote disparagingly of them. Nonconformists, on the contrary, protested Society interference in their affairs. Understandably, the S.P.G. placed maximum confidence in official overseas reports as the best basis for formulating its over-all educational plans.

34. Carl Bridenbaugh, *Mitre and Sceptre: Transatlantic Faiths, Ideas, Personalities, and Politics, 1689–1775* (New York: Oxford University Press, 1962), p. 59; Benjamin Colman to White Kennett, Boston, November, 1712, cited by Ebenezer Turell, *The Life and Character of the Reverend Benjamin Colman, D.D.* (Boston: Rogers and Fowle, 1749), pp. 122–26; White Kennett to Benjamin Colman, London, September 15, 1713, cited by Turell, *Colman*, pp. 126–29.

In so doing, however, it arrived at an uncomplimentary concept of what a colonist was like, hence what it would take to teach him Church and empire orthodoxy. This image of a stubborn, unyielding, essentially inferior America was to drain three quarters of a century of S.P.G. educational energy.

II

EDUCATING QUEEN ANNE'S AMERICA

IN AUGUST, 1713, the S.P.G. introduced the convention of signing its minutes. Certain unsteady signatures indicated that by then charter membership was on the wane. Greatly increased, however, appeared the ebb and flow of transatlantic correspondence. With this rising tide of letters, moreover, there emerged during the first decade and a half of Society work parallel indications of mounting disharmony between procedural or administrative fiat and American teaching conditions.

Society instructions concerning the correct behavior of those it sent out to propagate the gospel were frequent, detailed, and rigid. For instance, the 1706 missionary instructions illustrate a tendency to formulate regulations designed to meet all possible exigencies, whether in England, on board outbound ships, or in America. Thus, missionaries were cautioned to lodge at bookshops, not taverns, when they needed occasional shelter. They were likewise reminded that ocean voyages would furnish opportunities for instructing those whose living conditions on shipboard would merit every spiritual comfort. Continued study in the field was to be each S.P.G. man's aim, to ensure sound knowledge of doctrine and ability to understand and debate the principal points of controversy. Once installed overseas, missionaries were to instruct parishioners in the sacraments, to teach heathens the necessity of revelation, to distribute tracts, lend books, and set up schools. Their stipends would amount to about £50 sterling.[1]

As further rules indicated, the distinction between minister and schoolteacher was based on status more than function. Schoolmasters' regulations on the whole appeared more elaborate than those governing missionaries. Yet, the instruments of education were in either case Bible and Prayer Book, and the ultimate aspiration teaching obedience and "disposing children to believe and live as Christians." Ideally, schoolmasters were to be in deacon's orders, but in any case their work and that of the ministers was expected to overlap in catechetical instruction and various minor church functions. The Society paid the teacher less than the minister[2] but saw the two roles as complementary.

In addition to the rules, there appeared in the *Journal* hundreds of entries confirming the unified nature of the work of S.P.G. parsons and pedagogues overseas. Both jobs called for sober, prudent men of good character and reputation. Efforts in either church or schoolroom required men of learning. No missionary could take up an American post without ordination, and no ordination was possible without a university degree. Furthermore, a missionary needed to satisfy the London bishop and the relevant S.P.G. committee that he was up to date both in his grasp of current issues and his ability to arrange this knowledge into appropriately worked-out sermons and well-selected readings.

In the case of schoolmasters, applicants were not numerous. The Society, moreover, moved with caution to avoid duplica-

---

1. Pascoe, *Two Hundred Years,* pp. 837–45. English curacies at the time averaged £30–40 sterling per year. Parochial clergy made up to £300 in a system permitting plurality. See Sykes, *Church and State,* pp. 206, 227.
2. Teachers received £10, £20, or at most £30 allowances. Missionaries often were paid £50 or more.

tion of its teaching services abroad. According to the *Journals,* those applicants that received consideration fell into one of two categories. On the one hand were men whose own education, though considerable, stopped short of a university degree. On the other were Oxford and Cambridge graduates. In the one case, a combination of necessity and preference tended toward extended service in the classroom. In the other, classroom became halfway house to pulpit. Hence, the more qualifications a pedagogue brought to his schoolroom the less likely was he to occupy it for long. Recognizing this fact, the Society turned more and more to the colonies themselves as sources of supply,[3] with the result that most of its schoolmasters and many of its ex-schoolmaster missionaries called America their home. Quite apart from the appalling loss of life among the latter bound either to or from ordination in England, the zeal of the former was often dulled by their receiving instructions from a society they had never actually confronted.

At the same time as it perfected its administrative structure at home and sharpened its ideas about the right sort of servant to propagate the gospel abroad, the S.P.G. arranged for metropolitan London to learn about England's responsibilities to its colonial possessions. It therefore instituted an anniversary sermon which served a threefold purpose. First, it enhanced the reputation of any Churchman who delivered it. Second, it reviewed Society work during the past year. Third, it stated what S.P.G. policy should be. Although attendance figures never were noted in the Society minutes, it is probable that St. Mary-le-Bow church was filled. At any rate, public notice of the event was traditionally given in the London *Gazette* and special invitations extended to the Lord Mayor and aldermen. Meanwhile, those who missed the occasion could read one of the three or

---

3. After a decade of activity, the Society still hesitated to send schoolmasters abroad purely on speculation. See *S.P.G. Journals,* Vol. II, entry for January 4, 1711/12, p. 148, #8; *ibid.,* Vol. I, entry for April 18, 1707, p. 285.

four thousand copies of the sermon subsequently printed,[4] and form opinions of what life in the American colonies was like. What is more, colonial dissenters eventually came across copies and were frequently shaken by what they took to be a wholly misleading account of their rights and life styles.[5]

Indeed, the composite picture of colonies and colonials drawn by the first dozen or so yearly appeals on the Society's behalf presented a dark spectacle. One preacher pitied the "many Thousands there are in our Plantations, whom, perhaps, the unhappy Necessity of their Affairs, or some other Reason, have sent abroad," to become "almost as rude and ignorant as to Religion, as the Very Heathens themselves." Another held that in some colonies, "nothing is pursued but Gain and Luxury," and that colonists "go from hence but ill instructed. . . ." Yet another lamented the "Looseness and Prophaneness" rampant in the New World. Several more referred to degeneracy, cruelty, or the "shameful, wicked Lives and Practices of the Generality

4. The archbishop of York, pleading overwork, was one of the few who asked to be excused. *Ibid.*, Vol. I, entry for December 17, 1703, p. 128, #1. Good reviews of the leading ideas of anniversary sermons have been written by Frank J. Klingberg, *Anglican Humanitarianism in Colonial New York* (Philadelphia: The Church Historical Society, 1940), pp. 11–48, and by Edgar Legare Pennington, "The S.P.G. Anniversary Sermons, 1702–1783," *Historical Magazine of the Protestant Episcopal Church*, XX (March, 1951), 10–43. See as well *S.P.G. Journals*, Vol. I, entry for January 29, 1703/4, p. 131, #1; *ibid.*, Vol. II, entry for February 12, 1713, p. 355, #12; *ibid.*, Vol. III, entry for March 4, 1714–15, p. 42, #7. The Society's decision in 1714–15 was to print 1,000 quarto and 3,000 octavo anniversary sermons. It is difficult to estimate how many readers this would supply. Some clue is provided by Addison, who allowed twenty readers to every *Spectator*. See No. 10, Monday, March 12, 1710–11, in N. Ogle, Esq., (ed.), *The Spectator* (London: George B. Whittaker, 1827), p. 46.

5. Following a 1726 resolution, the Society did not deliberately send controversial works abroad. As William Webb Kemp shows, however, many of the thousands of books and pamphlets distributed in America proved inadvertently to be provocative. Among these were numerous anniversary sermons, as, for instance, White Kennett's 1712 discourse. An escalation effect operative during the pamphlet wars of the period prompted S.P.G. missionaries to appeal for whatever publications would help them meet dissentient objection to their presence. Printed sermons featured prominently among such literature. See William Webb Kemp, *The Support of Schools in Colonial New York by the Society for the Propagation of the Gospel in Foreign Parts* (New York: Teachers College, 1913), p. 34, n. 26; p. 53, n. 129.

of Christians." Sermonists urged that ministers, churches, school-masters, schools, and libraries be furnished forthwith, and that those sent over as S.P.G. workers set retrograde colonists a better example.[6]

As well as directing their attention to white settlers, the anni-versary sermonists speculated upon a proper approach to teach-ing Indians and Negroes. Compared with the generally critical view of the behavior of white colonists, the concept of the North American Indian appeared sympathetic. Indeed, the savage's alleged nobility and rationality caught the imagination of many Londoners. In the eyes of the sermonists as well, the Indian combined dignity with pathos. He was the "noble savage" of Defoe's later work. But he was the "poor native" too, tricked by Spaniards and Frenchmen who used "Beads and Crosses as Hooks and Baits to draw out Things of greater Value . . . ," raised in ignorance, suspicious of yet another nation of white men professing Christianity but practising trickery, yet tractable withal when addressed in his own tongue and treated with humaneness.[7]

Equally deserving of Society instruction, the African slave also constituted a proper subject for early anniversary rhetoric. For one thing, it was his labor that accounted for such fortunes as supported S.P.G. efforts to teach him. Reason, too, dictated

6. An exceptionally optimistic message was delivered by George Stanhope, dean of Canterbury, *A Sermon* . . . (London: Joseph Downing, 1714), p. 29. For much less sanguine appraisals of colonial America, see William Stanley, dean of St. Asaph, *A Sermon* . . . (London: Joseph Downing, 1708), p. 4; Gilbert Burnet, bishop of Salisbury, *A Sermon* . . . (London: Joseph Downing, 1704), p. 19; White Kennett, dean of Peterborough, *A Sermon* . . . (London: Joseph Downing, 1712), p. 26; Joseph Williams, bishop of Chichester, *A Sermon* . . . (London: Joseph Downing, 1706), p. 23; William Fleetwood, bishop of St. Asaph, *A Sermon* . . . (London: Joseph Downing, 1711), p. 15; St. George Ashe, bishop of Clogher, *A Sermon* . . . (London: Joseph Downing, 1715), p. 20.

7. White, *Sermon*, p. 11; Stanhope, *Sermon*, p. 28; Ashe, *Sermon*, p. 21. The idea of the noble savage came early to the eighteenth-century scene. Ob-servers like Baron de Lahontan used the notion not as a humanitarian gesture but as a means of portraying "civilized" Europeans as social and moral de-generates. See his *Travels*, *Mémoirs*, and *Dialogues* published in 1703 and cited by Paul Hazard, *The European Mind*, trans. J. Lewis May (New York: The World Publishing Company, 1963), p. 13.

that conversion from idolatry to Christianity should follow more easily than in the case of colonists or Indians, since Negroes in servitude were "not in a condition to refuse whatever they [owners] demanded."[8]

Here, however, was no appeal to educate by force. On the contrary, teaching Africans was to stem from a spirit of "mutual trust and confidence." In fact, some bondsmen might thus be so well taught as to return to Africa to preach. As for that centuries-old question of the relationship between bondage and Christianity, the Old and New Testaments could supply authoritative answers. In the time of Abraham, human, not divine, laws altered a man's social status. His being a Christian by no means allowed a servant to claim liberty from his Christian master. What it did entitle him to was to be treated somewhat better than a beast. How else would God suffer heathens to be dragged yearly from Africa to serve Christians in America?[9]

During the first decade or so of its work, then, the S.P.G. made great progress at home in supplementing tight institutional organization with ready access to public officialdom, public purse, and public opinion. At the Atlantic community's outer rim, on the other hand, official and actual Anglican establishment proved to be things apart, as did theory and practice affecting the strivings of S.P.G. parson and pedagogue to rectify matters by teaching those colonists, Indians, and Negroes whose rhetorical counterparts had captured the fancy of a decade of anniversary sermon congregations.

A divergence of concern marked 72 Society missionaries and 15 schoolmasters active in Queen Anne's America and Society officials at London headquarters. When, for example, Gideon Johnston's letter with news of one hundred and fifty Charleston epidemic victims headed east, westbound by ship moved the

8. Williams, *Sermon*, pp. 20, 21.
9. *Ibid.*, p. 23; William Beveridge, bishop of St. Asaph, *A Sermon* . . . (London: Joseph Downing, 1707), pp. 20-21; Williams, *Sermon*, pp. 20, 21; Fleetwood, *Sermon*, p. 15; Burnet, *Sermon*, p. 27; Beveridge, *Sermon*, p. 20

secretary's stereotype about correct forms of address. When Francis Le Jau rendered accounts of the punitive mutilation of runaway slaves in the Carolinas, there came to him after a long pause a routine rejoinder about the "great inconvenience [of] . . . Ministers leaving letters of Attorney . . . and afterward changing the same powers . . . ." In exchange for tales of loss by fire in South Carolina, slander at Newport, Rhode Island, Lutheran gains among Dutch Reform settlers in New York, or piracy on the high seas, arrived standardized responses from secretaries pleading insufficient time to reply to any but the most urgent and elaborately expressed missionary requests. Nothing but the tersest of instructions ever appeared to survive the rush to catch a fleet always on the verge of sailing.[10]

Among thousands of American appeals addressed to Society secretaries, however, none expressed so eloquently the sorts of adaptation problems confronting S.P.G. teachers abroad as did those of John Urmston.[11] Admittedly, Urmston's situation in a sparsely settled new colony so different in climate and geography from his gentle home surroundings presented him with extreme difficulties. Certainly men like East Apthorp, who fifty years

10. The breakdown for missionaries active in America during Queen Anne's reign shows South Carolina, 14; North Carolina, 4; Virginia, 1; Maryland, 4; Pennsylvania, 11; New Jersey, 4; New England, 8; New York, 16. New York claimed 7 of those schoolmasters who corresponded with the Society at that time. Figures are based on recorded correspondence, *S.P.G. Letter Books*, Series A, Vols. I–IX. For a sampling of correspondence indicating differences of emphasis distinguishing field from "home" letters, see Commissary Johnston's *Notitia Parochialis*, list of mortality, May 10, 1711 to May 16, 1712, *S.P.G. Letter Books*, Series A, Vol. VII, pp. 463–68; Secretary to Commissary Johnston, April 29, 1712, *ibid.*, p. 472; Francis Le Jau to the Secretary, South Carolina, Parish of St. James, Goose Creek, February 20, 1711/12, *ibid.*, p. 395; The Secretary to Dr. Le Jau, November 30, 1713, *ibid.*, Vol. VIII, p. 452; Mr. Maule to the Secretary, South Carolina, April 4, 1711, *ibid.*, Vol. VI, No. CXXVII; Mr. Honyman to the Secretary, Newport, Rhode Island, October 19, 1711, *ibid.*, No. CLI; Mr. Haeger to the Secretary (translation), New York, n.d., *ibid.*, No. XXI; Mr. Dennis to the Secretary, Boochay, Near Goose Creek, S.C., August 28, 1712, *ibid.*, Vol. VII, p. 428; The Secretary to Mr. Maule, April 29, 1712, *ibid.*, p. 474; to Mr. Honyman, April 29, 1712, *ibid.*, p. 564; to Mr. Haeger, April 29, 1712, *ibid.*, Vol. VII, p. 261; to Mr. Dennis, November 6, 1712, *ibid.*, p. 483.

11. Urmston served the Chowan district from 1709 to 1720, incurred Society disfavor, and moved to Maryland where he perished in a fire in 1732. See Pascoe, *Two Hundred Years*, p. 850.

later appeared as Cambridge's outspoken S.P.G. missionary, were much more comfortably disposed toward their physical surroundings. Adaptation, though, consists in the main of innumerable compromises following comparisons with home customs. In this respect Urmston articulated the gamut of problems, a good many of them common to his S.P.G. contemporaries, regardless of their American location.

Translated from Essex, England, by way of Archangel, to settlements north of Chowan River, North Carolina, Urmston joined many of his missionary confrères in explaining the difficulties of fulfilling obligations. He detailed the ravages of ill-health brought on by subsistence "many days only on dry crust, and a draught of salt Water from the Sound." Athwart his pastorate loomed rivers such as were never seen in the old country, "from one, two, to six, twelve and fifteen Miles over." Beyond these, the precincts of Chowan, Perquimans, and Pasquotank together made up one vast circuit, 70 miles deep, and as many wide, outstanding for "the bad uses of the Roades, broken Bridges, over dangerous places, wet or Cold Weather in Winter, [and] . . . excessive heat" which in summer drove one "even to shifting in the woods for want of Air . . . ." Approaching outlying habitations was difficulty enough. Arriving at them could be yet more discouraging. Church buildings baked and blistered. Their doors swung agape on sagging hinges. Even worse, "all the Hoggs and Cattle flee thither for shade in the Summer and Warmth in Winter, the [sic] first dig Holes and Bury themselves these with the rest make it a loathsome place . . . ."[12]

Disheartening though such natural hardships proved to a South of England teacher, they tormented him not half so much as certain political, social, and economic characteristics of American colonial society in the more remote parts of the land.

12. John Urmston to the Secretary, North Carolina, July 7, 1711, *S.P.G. Letter Books*, Series A, Vol. VII, p. 366; *ibid.* The deep coastal indentations about Currituck, Albemarle, and Pamlico sounds doubtless made it difficult for a newcomer to distinguish river from sea or to estimate distances. See, too, *ibid.*, p. 368; *ibid.*, p. 374.

For one thing, the colonial assembly reflected a religiously heterogeneous population, made up of "a strange mixture of men in various opinions, and Inclinations, often Church men, many Presbyterians, Independents, but most Anythingarians." For another, confusion perplexed a colony claiming simultaneously two council presidents and a Quaker-sponsored deputy governor responsible to the politically beleagured Governor Nathaniel Johnson in Charleston. Lacking that political encouragement he took for granted in England, Urmston seemed to see a specter rising from days best forgotten. As he put it, "Olivers [sic] days came again."[13]

Besides these political contretemps, there existed other, more profoundly disturbing, aspects of colonial life. Granted, the parsons and pedagogues serving Church interests in England's lesser parishes rarely lived opulently. Frugal as their livings were apt to be, though, they seldom augmented incomes through manual work. In the Carolinas, however, it was sometimes different.

Urmston quickly perceived that his £30 sterling per annum from the S.P.G. plus whatever he might glean in perquisites would fail to provide a standard of living, and thus, of respect, worthy of a Churchman in the field. He rapidly discovered that his "necessities of life"—sugar, molasses, rum, cider, malt, hops, oils, spices, paper, ink powder, and hardware—might best materialize if missionary became planter. But such resourcefulness in North Carolina was a far cry from gentleman farming in Britain. This colonial blurring of social lines was humiliating enough when a Society envoy was merely driven "to work hard with Ax, Hoe and Spade" or "forced to Digg a Garden [and] raise Beans, Peas, etc." in full view of neighbors who "love to see new comers put to their shifts." When the desired outcome further depended upon multiple skills in a land where materially successful men were "generally Carpenters, Joyners, Wheel

13. *Ibid.*, p. 373; *ibid.*, p. 372.

Wrights, Coopers, Butchers, Tanners, Shoemakers, Tallow Chandlers, Watermen,"[14] or owned slaves who were, the dignity as well as the prosperity of the S.P.G. missionary lay in jeopardy.

It would be reasonable to suppose that what Urmston lost in physical hardship, dissentient opposition, and marginal subsistence he gained through association with a Church established in Britain and encouraged in the Carolinas by act of assembly. But Carolina parishioners seemed apathetic. They proved reluctant to ferry their teacher across the network of waterways crisscrossing his immense curacy. They countered his proposal for a central church with requests for churches and missionaries enough to allow each neighborhood ready access to the sacraments, hopefully at S.P.G. cost. Such fiscal responsibilities as were assumed by the most conscientious congregations reflected the limitations of colonial resources in some areas. Contributions might be paid in depressed currency. More often they took the form of such payment in kind as "two Barrells of Skins and the worst pieces of Lean Beefe."[15]

Facing a combination of poverty and parochial obstinacy, Urmston prayed that the "very good, and proper Act"[16] concerning Carolina establishment would in itself guarantee a solid foundation for the Church, proper deference for its missionaries and schoolmasters, and a corresponding increase in literacy among children and adults seeking the Anglican way. In theory the act looked promising. It laid out parish boundaries. It required the selection of twelve vestrymen per parish required to meet, within six weeks of the act's publication, to choose church wardens. These were empowered on behalf of the parish to buy glebes, build churches and parsonages, and supply clergymen approved by the bishop of London.

Unfortunately for Urmston, though, circumstances developed

14. *Ibid.*, pp. 366–67; *ibid.*, p. 367.
15. *Ibid.*, p. 369.
16. *Ibid.*, p. 373.

which counteracted North Carolina establishment legislation. To start with, Chowan territory was huge and difficult to traverse for vestryman and missionary alike. Intoxication, charged Urmston, interfered with vestry meetings. Urmston's own indigence reflected that of his congregation. Vestries had to economize. But when thrift prompted them to retain not ministers but readers who presented sermons from a book of homilies borrowed from their minister, Urmston had cause to doubt the efficacy of the Church Act.

A more serious problem confronted Urmston. He discovered that nothing in the Church Act ensured a minister's seat in his own vestry or approximated the Articles of Visitation whereby England's church wardens were bound to follow advice proffered by their rector. What commenced as more or less honorable negotiations between Urmston and vestrymen over local allowances for services rendered at last deteriorated into haggling about sums impossible to collect. Reciprocal coolness led to open antagonism, and at length to two exclusive interpretations of the act. For Urmston, "ye Minister sh.ᵈ allway's be deemed a Vestryman." For his vestrymen, "ye Minister hath nothing to do in Vestry."[17]

Harassed though Urmston appeared, it would be too easy to dismiss him as a caricature of the early Society emissary in a state of shock over the irrelevance of old habits in new places. Admittedly, North Carolina did not typify a more settled existence enjoyed in certain middle and northern colonies; nor did it receive in the long run a great deal of S.P.G. attention. Granted, Urmston adopted a more than ordinarily critical posture toward colonials standing between him and his execution of S.P.G. orders. Significantly, though, the secretary at the Society home office reminded him it was "particularly kind" of the S.P.G. to provide "the large allowance of £30 p. Annum."[18]

17. *Ibid.*, p. 375; *ibid.*
18. Secretary to Mr. Urmston, December 17, 1714, *ibid.*, Vol. IX, p. 309.

Evidently he was no stranger to the types of letters Urmston generally wrote.

Considered together, though, Urmston's letters supply an arresting commentary on men striving to reconcile set instructions with unexpected threats to personal integrity.[19] In this regard, S.P.G. schoolmasters clearly had the worst time of it. Adjuncts to Society missionaries, they taught children to read, write, and cypher in return for a stipend so meager that they sometimes requested payment in textiles for resale. Even then, theirs was a precarious task. Without the support of colonial dignitaries, progress appeared impossible.

Some were fortunate. Teaching at Rye, N.Y., Joseph Cleator enjoyed the patronage of Caleb Heathcote. In New York City, catechist Elias Neau earned for a time Governor Cornbury's favor. To the south, Benjamin Dennis drilled his pupils in the Ten Commandments, the Apostles' Creed, and the Lord's Prayer under Governor Nathaniel Johnson's sponsorship.

But others proved less lucky. Destitute to start with, Joseph Robinson never obtained the teaching post for which he petitioned. On Staten Island, Benjamin Drewitt and Simon Brown endured their classrooms one and four years respectively, Francis Williamson held out just over a year, Thomas Potts a year, and Benjamin Miller only two. Often, practising schoolteachers like New York's William Huddleston memorialized the Society for an allowance to augment a slender income from paying students. But even where succesful, such requests could prove self-defeating. The S.P.G. subsidized only those schools willing to teach poor students gratis. Wary of being identified with pauperism, many well-to-do parents thereupon withdrew their fee-paying children and sent them elsewhere or had them taught at home. For these reasons alone, S.P.G. schoolmasters often

---

19. In contrast to emotionally charged, subjective reporting characteristic of this correspondence stands a dispassionate objectivity typical of earlier Jesuit accounts of progress in North America. See R. G. Thwaites (ed.), *The Jesuit Relations and Allied Documents* (Cleveland: The Burrows Brothers Company, 1896), Vol. XXIII, p. 291; Vol. LII, pp. 99, 174, and *passim*.

elected farming, commerce, or the ministry[20] as more remunerative occupations.

Although they commanded better stipends than did schoolmasters, Society ministers from Boston to Charleston shared many of the same frustrations. Good political connections proved equally important to them. If anything, dissentient antagonism toward their work cut even deeper. On top of this, S.P.G. parsons found they had to reteach Low Church Anglicans such High Church traditions as kneeling at Holy Communion and providing Godparents at infant baptism. Beyond harassments like these, however, S.P.G. missionaries continued to prove especially vulnerable to the sheer size and novelty of their new world precincts. In 1702, for instance, George Keith narrowly escaped disaster when a squall snapped the Portsmouth ferry mainmast. Gideon Johnston found himself marooned "on a sandy Island" near Charleston and lingered there twelve days on end without "Meat and Drink or Shelter," only to drown nearby eight summers after his rescue. William Andrews braved summer "musckatoes," fall floods, winter snow, and spring "nights in the Woods . . . on a bear Skin."[21] This unaccustomed itinerary on such a wide scale

20. Even ministers driven by want to offer private lessons envied those spared such sidelines. One of them reported he "had been Oblidge [sic] . . . to yield to the Importunities of Some Gentlemen . . . to teach their Sons the Latin Tongue that I might save some part of my Salary to clear . . . Debts. . . . I cannot help submitting to this Drudgery . . . except the Society shall think fit to set me free by their more than Ordinary Benevolence." George Ross to the Secretary, Chester, Pennsylvania, May 18, 1713, *S.P.G. Letter Books*, Series A, Vol. VIII, p. 477.

21. The difficulty encountered by High Church Society missionaries trying to coordinate their efforts with Low Church colleagues and congregations has best been demonstrated by Professor Robert T. Handy, "The Anglican Heritage in America," a lecture delivered at Union Theological Seminary on November 11, 1966. See, as well, George Keith, *A Journal of Travels . . .* (London: Joseph Downing, 1706), entry for August 30, 1702, p. 36. Very much in character, Keith seized this close call with disaster as an opportunity to try to convert Quaker John Burden, who towed the disabled vessel ashore. For further details of missionary reaction to a vast new land, see Gideon Johnston to the Lord Bishop of Sarum, Charles Town, September 20, 1708, *S.P.G. Letter Books*, Series A, Vol. IV, No. XCVII, p. 308; Pascoe, *Two Hundred Years*, p. 819; William Andrews to the Secretary, Queens Fort by the Mohawks Castle, May 25, 1714, *S.P.G. Letter Books*, Series A, Vol. IX, p. 125.

did trigger one significant result, however. It greatly increased
the importance of books in the work of S.P.G. men. Indeed, in
the mass of S.P.G. correspondence, nothing arrests the eye so
much as the common craving for books and the ingenious arguments contrived to get them.

Looked at from the viewpoint of the Society missionary this
quest for books made good sense. Obviously, the Book of Common Prayer, seemingly never in sufficient supply, was pivotal
to Society progress. So, naturally, was the Bible. Psalters were
essential to the encouragement of music as a form of worship.
All these were relatively costly. Children who would master
them first needed hornbooks, primers, and shorter catechisms.
Adults desiring a deeper understanding of the scriptures expected
explicatory sermons which, in turn, High Church missionaries
conceived of as set pieces, worthy of delivery (and publication)
only after deliberate and prolonged composition[22] in a study
containing the best commentaries. Physically and, perhaps, spir-
itually distant from the Church, uncommitted colonials "of the
better sort" might also be "brought over" through access to the
standard Anglican apologies. The more fundamental tracts left
among humbler, albeit literate, folk completed the moral or the
spiritual message initiated during an S.P.G. parson's short visits
to outlying districts. In all likelihood they also provoked a few
nonreaders to learn how to satisfy their curiosity. So, probably,
did the printed Society sermons and business abstracts.

Accustomed to regular reference work in British parochial
libraries with their tomes securely chained down, Society men
abroad found they now needed their books in their saddle bags
as well as on their shelves. Books attracted men to S.P.G. service
in the first place. An allowance of books constituted part of an
S.P.G. stipend. Books provided the wherewithal for public dis-
putations with Independents as well as less-organized confronta-

22. Anniversary sermonists, for instance, received notice at least a month
prior to the appointed date of delivery.

tions with Quakers. The packaging and dispatching of books was an art unsurpassed even today.[23] Loss of books was an S.P.G. disaster. Disputed ownership of books provoked some of the most spectacular internecine arguments recorded in S.P.G. annals. Allegedly unfair distribution of books occasioned chagrin among S.P.G. employees. A book given was the mark of generosity. It was likewise the instrument of an S.P.G. strategist committed to redressing the balance of Church establishment at home with its minority status in America.

In circumstances thus different from those of the Society supporting them, but drawing on a veritable arsenal of books and pamphlets appropriate to their cause, S.P.G. parsons and pedagogues pressed on toward the realization of such educational theory as resided in the Society charter and standing orders or was developed in anniversary sermons. In practice, however, they were to encounter stiff resistance to their efforts to convert their colonial brethren.

If trial and error characterized initial Society educational work among colonists, logic attended its hopes for Indian enlightenment. Indian tribes, so the story went, were nations. Accordingly, English royal delegates were to seek out Indian rulers and convince them of the benefits of the Anglican version of the white man's alphabetic culture.[24] Quite apart from isolated atrocities or general warfare, though, two major obstacles blocked a standard European diplomatic approach to Indian proselytizing.

23. Excellent illustrations of libraries of chained books form a generous part of Central Council for the Care of Churches, *The Parochial Libraries of the Church of England* (London: The Faith Press Ltd., 1959). The use of books in debates is illustrated in Keith, *Journal*, entry for July 16, 1702. For accounts of book shipments, a most tangible aspect of the transit of civilization, see Edgar Legare Pennington, *The Beginnings of the Library in Charles Town, South Carolina* (Worcester, Massachusetts: American Antiquarian Society, 1935), pp. 6–7; Joseph Towne Wheeler, "Thomas Bray and the Maryland Parochial Libraries," *Maryland Historical Magazine*, XXXIV (September, 1939), 254–55.

24. The phrase is Marshall McLuhan's. See *Understanding Media: The Extensions of Man* (New York: McGraw-Hill, 1964, 1966), pp. 81–88.

One hindrance was that Society representatives established only ephemeral diplomatic connections. Inexperience compounded by language barriers accounted for these *faux pas.* As the Society's missionary at Albany, Thomas Barclay, intimated, "Hendrick the great [Seneca] Prince that was so honour'd in England cannot command ten men; the other three were no Sachems: How far her Maj.^{ty} and the Society have been imposed upon, I leave it to you to Judge."[25]

A second impediment lay in the fact that when Indian leaders could be identified they failed to match Society paradigms. They were not kings. They were not noble, naive children of the forest. They stood less vulnerable to the alleged wiles of the Jesuit than missionaries expected. They did not always thirst for that knowledge of letters and of God which S.P.G. teachers were eager to provide. Instead, they often appeared as polished orators in their own right, especially sensitive to the practical economic and political problems of power-balance thrust upon them by European intrusion. On South Carolina's borders, for example, Yammonsee chieftains noted the collision course of Spanish Catholic and English Protestant interests and found their best recourse the avoidance of close ties with either. They told Samuel Thomas via interpreter that they were too much in danger of Spanish invasion to attend to English instruction. Similar scepticism appeared northward. At a gathering in Albany, Canada's Praying Indian Sachem remarked that prior to his departure from New York no one had talked of Christian conversion. Why, he asked, should anyone bother about it now? In any case, he contended, the French had so adequately seen to the welfare of his soul that he saw no reason at all to impede what was essentially a trade meeting with talk of religion.[26]

Despite failure to reach them via their chiefs, Society ser-

25. Mr. Barclay to the Secretary, Albany, September 26, 1710, *S.P.G. Letter Books,* Series A, Vol. V, No. CLXXVI, p. 525.
26. Mr. Samuel Thomas to Dr. Bray, Carolina, January 20, 1702, *ibid.,* Vol. I, No. LXXXVI; Extracts of what was said by the Sachem of the Praying Indians of Canada . . . to the Commission of the Indian Affairs in Albany, June 28, 1700, *S.P.G. Journals,* Appendix A, May 19, 1704, No. XL.

vants continued to regard Indians with a mixture of alarm and fascination and to extend to them the fundamentals of English letters and Christian ethics. On the one hand, they little understood nations which laced up their babies on cradle-boards, shared their wives, consumed English rum or French brandy with equal relish, or carried the bones of ancestors along on the war path. On the other hand, they claimed to detect in the circumcision rites, legends of ancient floods, and Indian speech some latter-day echo of the ten lost tribes of Israel, debased, perhaps, yet in no sense abandoned by God.[27] In either case, they clearly warranted instruction. The difficulty was deciding how to give it to them. How, indeed, could nomads secure in their own oral tradition be taught reading or the sacraments?

Since its inception, the S.P.G. had tried to answer this question. Some officials recommended training a cadre of English interpreters through residence among Indians. Others proposed the reverse—teaching English to Indian youths living in colonial settlements. Several believed traders might be pressed into teaching missionaries and schoolmasters the Indian dialects appropriate to their location. A handful set about self-tuition. At least one hinted that Hebrew might hold the key to the communications problem.[28] Generally, though, two paths lay open. One brought the Indian to the English-speaking Society outposts. The other took the S.P.G. teacher into Indian-speaking territory. Rarely used was a third alternative leading Indian trainees to an education in Britain.

By and large, the first approach to teaching failed. Nomadic of necessity, devoted by nature, an Indian parent was suspicious

27. As A. T. Vaughan points out, this notion was current from the earliest days of Puritan settlement. See his *New England Frontier: Puritans and Indians, 1620–1675* (Boston: Little, Brown and Company, 1965), p. viii. See also Francis Le Jau to Mr. Chamberlayne, Goose Creek, February 1, 1709/10, *S.P.G. Letter Books,* Series A, Vol. V, No. XCVIII; Francis Le Jau to Mr. Chamberlayne, Goose Creek, January 4, 1711/12, *ibid.,* Vol. VII, pp. 394–95; Mr. Halliday to the Secretary, Elizabeth Town, July 13, 1715, *ibid.,* Vol. X, pp. 191–92; Robert Maule to the Secretary, Carolina, August 17, 1712, cited in *S.P.G. Journals,* Vol. II, October 10, 1712, p. 229, item 15.

28. Mr. Halliday to the Secretary, Elizabeth Town, July 13, 1715, *S.P.G. Letter Books,* Series A, Vol. X, pp. 191–92.

of what happened to his child in the Society church or school-room. Indian children arrived, to be sure, and the novelty of their presence ensured their inclusion on such *Notitia Parochialis* and *Scholistica*[29] as were forwarded to London. In Goose Creek and Charles Town, the Chowan settlement, Philadelphia and Radnor, New York, Newbury, Elizabeth Town and Boston there were always a few Indian boys and girls learning how to cut a pen, mix ink, read a prayer, and prompt their Society mentors to generalize to headquarters about "dull and mean" Savan-nocks, "honest" Floridas, "justice-loving" Yammonsees, "much-civilized" Mohawks, or simply "decaying nations." Many learned English. Many were baptized. Yet, a lack of permanence attended even the best efforts. When accounts of the Carolina Indian massacres started to arrive at Lambeth Palace, S.P.G. administrators and legislators alike joined their employees abroad in pondering the relevance of Christian instruction among pagans. Late in 1714, some of the romance that surrounded visiting sachems was beginning to wear thin.

By far the best recorded attempts at early S.P.G. Indian edu-cation tell of the second general route to enlightenment—that of penetrating his enclaves. William Andrews, who himself lacked the skill to talk to Indians in their own language,[30] arrived toward the end of Queen Anne's reign to work among the Mohawks. But years before he came these people had grown used to preachers. Throughout the late seventeenth and early eighteenth centuries, the Reverends Godfrey Dellius and John Lydius had taught a few Iroquois in Albany, the latter with the aid of S.P.G. books. At Schenectady, their compatriot, the Reverend Mr. Freeman, translated parts of the English liturgy,

29. These were standard reports giving particulars about church and school enrollment.

30. Andrews' reports to headquarters indicate the passion for order which numerous S.P.G. envoys displayed in the New World. After an exhausting Atlantic crossing, a twelve-day battle against contrary winds up the Hudson to Albany, and an encounter with snowbanks of exceptional depth, S.P.G. emissary Andrews arrived among his Mohawks only to advise the Society that they spoke a language "imperfect in Adverbs conjunctions interjections." See Mr. Andrews to the Secretary, The Queen's Fort near the Mohawk Castle, March 9, 1712/13, *S.P.G. Letter Books*, Series A, Vol. VIII, p. 147.

prayers, creeds, and Testaments into an Indian tongue. In 1704 Mohawks in Albany greeted S.P.G. missionary Thorougood Moore with a combination of enthusiasm and procrastination, the true nature of which drove him to conclude it would be better to teach his own countrymen. Such interested Mohawks as drifted in and out of that town for a time thereafter learned Christian fundamentals from garrison chaplain the Reverend Thomas Barclay. Then, on the strength of a highly-publicized (though in Barclay's opinion, scarcely representative)[31] Mohawk delegation to see Queen Anne, William Andrews arrived. Following a lull in the formal instruction for Indians, his advent should have been cause for both Mohawk and Society rejoicing. For a time it was. But soon frustration set in once more.

It was not that Andrews lacked material support. Fort Hunter was new. Its chapel contained communion plate, the gift of Queen Anne herself. The Mohawks raised a 20 by 30 foot log schoolhouse. An unprecedented S.P.G. salary of £150 a year enabled the Society's parson to make those generous gifts so important to Indian relations.

Just the same, Andrews faced two major problems. First the Mohawks who came to the chapel or sent their children to the new school wanted instruction in their own tongue. Andrews did his best. He attempted that "imperfect" language with its "words being generally so long & much to be supplyed by the Understanding of the hearer."[32] He submitted for Society printing whatever useful Mohawk manuscripts he could find. He retained two Netherlands interpreters who transformed his words into Dutch and Mohawk respectively. But Andrews' lack of language skills never permitted him exactly to determine what actually transpired in the classroom when John Oliver, the second of the interpreters, assumed command as Society schoolmaster.

The other hindrance to progress among Indians was less

---

31. Compare with a similar opinion, Mr. Barclay to the Secretary, Albany, September 26, 1710, *ibid.*, Series A, Vol. V, No. CLXXVI.
32. Andrews, see note 30 above.

readily apparent. In fact, when forty Mohawk boys and girls, some eighteen years old, first crowded the schoolroom, it must have been hard to distinguish between their quest for knowledge and their more material curiosity whetted by the lure of provisions for which they needed neither to trade nor to hunt. Initial enthusiasm at length exceeded staying-power, however. Although some acquired rudiments of reading and writing the Mohawk language phonetically spelled, few continued more than a month or two. Attendance fell to twenty. Then it dwindled to six. Significantly, the best, most persistent scholar turned out to be a young man too lame for the chase. Finally, some five years before the Society abandoned the Fort Hunter mission, its hard-working pioneer grammarian confessed his utter discouragement.[33]

Thus, Society parson and pedagogue struggled to carry out their tasks among culturally unreceptive Indians. Urged on by political rationales for the work, as well as by more humanitarian demands for improving Indian life, they accomplished little of lasting value in the early years of Society intervention. But as was now and again pointed out, the Indian, like the colonist, was easily distracted from a knowledge of letters, hence of the Gospel. In the Negro slave, on the other hand, Society men discovered a captive pupil. For this reason alone, hopes for his rapid tuition and conversion soared.

The S.P.G. parson in America needed slaves. When he could afford to, he purchased them. When he could not, he expected parishioners to supply them. Slaves powered Urmston's canoe through North Carolina's fresh and tidal waters. Slaves tidied Treadwell Bull's and Thomas Hassel's South Carolina dwellings. West Chester's John Bartow rewarded "my negro man" by baptism. At Rye, Robert Jenney returned thanks for service

33. This account of the S.P.G. Fort Hunter enterprise is based on documents cited by William Webb Kemp, *The Support of Schools in Colonial New York by the Society for the Propagation of the Gospel in Foreign Parts* (New York: Teachers College, 1913) and by John Wolfe Lydekker, *The Faithful Mohawks* (New York: The Macmillan Company, 1938), pp. 1–45.

by seeing to the moral duty of "my own negro slaves." In a word, missionary slave ownership was a colonial commonplace. So was private instruction of these slaves in reading and religion, according to practical as well as to humanitarian lines laid down in Society anniversary sermons. But, in 1710, when the corporate Society inherited Christopher Codrington's Barbadian sugar estates, it found itself to a considerably greater degree in "the unenviable position of having to practice what it preached."[34] Involved here was the Christian education not of a few handymen or housekeepers but a 300-strong slave force. The Society set about teaching these Negro workers en masse. Thereafter, S.P.G. missionaries were faced with convincing the generality of American mainland slavemasters to do likewise.

As in the case of Indian education, though, here was no mean task. Even in Barbadoes, the first S.P.G. teacher clashed with Codrington's manager over released time for slave instruction. In continental America, meantime, talk about teaching Negroes was liable to land an S.P.G. man in serious local trouble. For many colonial slaveholders were reluctant to enquire whether Christian status freed the slave. Particularly in the principal slaveholding colonies, vestrymen feared that English law read too vaguely on the matter. Admittedly, few ventured outright to deny a modicum of Christian mercies in exchange for obedience. And, in any event, such material care as did not stem from humanitarian motives frequently took the form of attention to expensive property. Still, both middle and southern colonies had for a long time resisted any implication that Christianity might alter Negro servitude. This was an old view.

---

34. John Urmston to the Secretary, North Carolina, July 7, 1711, *S.P.G. Letter Books*, Series A, Vol. VII, p. 366; Mr. Treadwell Bull to the Secretary, St. Paul's, January 20, 1714/15, *ibid.*, Series A, Vol. X, p. 91; Frank J. Klingberg, *Anglican Humanitarianism in Colonial New York* (Philadelphia: The Church Historical Society, 1940), p. 155; Frank J. Klingberg, *An Appraisal of the Negro in Colonial South Carolina* (Washington: The Associated Publishers, 1941), p. 32; J. Harry Bennett, Jr., *Bondsmen and Bishops: Slavery and Apprenticeship on the Codrington Plantations of Barbadoes, 1710–1838* (Berkeley and Los Angeles: University of California Press, 1958), p. 75.

Between 1664 and 1706, acts were passed or reinforced in Maryland, Virginia, North and South Carolina, New York, and New Jersey that in one way or another stipulated that for the slave baptism and freedom were related in no sense whatsoever.[35]

Society humanitarianism on the one hand and restrictive laws on the other meant that S.P.G. parsons and pedagogues were obliged to tread warily. Correspondence on the subject reveals a wide variety of local practice concerning the education of Negroes. Even by eighteenth-century standards, certain masters were cruel. A South Carolina master, for example, crushed apprehended Negro runaways in a coffin-like device with a stone-ballasted lid. In contrast to such extremes, some owners allowed much more leeway. For instance, Mesdames Haigue and Edwards rehearsed their own slaves in the Apostles' Creed, the Ten Commandments, and the Lord's Prayer. Many masters urged their Negroes to attend S.P.G. catechetical lectures. Some adopted a permissive posture. Daniel Bondet, S.P.G. minister at New Rochelle, told of a "Number of Negroes among whom some by hearing the instruction of their Masters to their Children have learned the principles of the Christian Religion." Still other owners allowed a half day, leaving for the slaves themselves the choice between learning their prayers or clearing and planting sufficient land "to clothe and subsist them and their families."[36]

35. Bennett, *Bondsmen and Bishops*, pp. 75–76. On the question of legal aspects of slaveholding, M. W. Jernegan cites Butts *v.* Penny (1677), 2 Levinz 201, in English Reports, LXXXIII, 518; Gelly *v.* Cleve (1694), 1 Lord Raymond 147, *ibid.*, XCI, 994; and the strong argument for the plaintiff that "in a christian [*sic*] nation . . .," Negro baptism "should be an immediate enfranchisement to them," Chamberl!ne *v.* Harvey, 5 Modern Reports 190, p. 191, see *Laboring and Dependent Classes in Colonial America, 1607–1783* (New York: Frederick Ungar Publishing Co., 1931, 1965), p. 216, note 10; *ibid.*, pp. 26–27.

36. Mr. Le Jau to the Secretary, Goose Creek, February 20, 1711/12, *S.P.G. Letter Books*, Series A, Vol. VII, p. 396; Mr. Ebenezer Taylor to the Secretary, St. Andrews Parish, S. Carolina, July 28, 1713, *ibid.*, Vol. VIII, p. 357; Pascoe, *Two Hundred Years*, p. 15; Mr. Bondet to the Secretary, New Rochelle, July 22, 1715, *S.P.G. Letter Books*, Series A, Vol. X, p. 198; "Instructions of the Clergy of South Carolina. . . .," Charles Town, S.C., March 4, 1712, *ibid.*, Vol. VIII, Part 2, item 4, p. 429.

Early records are full of accounts of Negroes learning to read, one so well that he began conducting marriages among his people using The Book of Common Prayer. Generally, though, no one minister or schoolmaster reported more than a handful of slaves, young or old, occupying benches or pews, mastering their alphabet, memorizing their prayers, or, occasionally, receiving the sacraments of baptism and communion. In New York City, on the other hand, there developed under the initiative of a Huguenot convert, Elias Neau, a program of Negro education that assumed considerable proportions and reflected the problems of slave instruction encountered by S.P.G. parsons and pedagogues throughout the American colonies during Queen Anne's reign.

Trader and lay catechist, Neau started in 1705 to teach on the strength of a license issued by Governor Cornbury but not bearing the bishop of London's endorsement. After a period of tension with Rector William Vesey of Trinity Church over the validity of the license, however, Neau persuaded the latter to encourage masters to send along their slaves for several hours weekly to learn the principles of Christianity in his house. After less than six months, some thirty-six owners, headed by Cornbury and Vesey, were sending a total of twenty-eight women and eighteen men to early evening classes, and it appeared for a while as though much larger accommodation, possibly Trinity Church itself, might eventually be required. But within a month attendance declined. Hearing the rumor that baptismal candidature was the first step to freedom, Neau quickly understood why only a dozen of New York's estimated 1,000 slaves continued to attend. Accordingly, he joined Vesey in pressing for legislation which, in 1706, publicly clarified the issue by assuring slaveholders that Christianity had nothing to do with liberty. The result was the tenfold restoring of Neau's lately dwindling enrollment.

Neau's account of how he responded to increased attendance

is rich indeed. When a hundred and more Negro catechumens arrived the following summer, he explained his plans to the Society. On Wednesdays, Fridays, and Saturdays these slaves, for the most part adults, crowded into a second-story chamber measuring 48 by 22 feet where they passed a two or more hour session seated on benches before an audience of white onlookers. When it grew too dark to read the words and "singing notes" of the English psalters or to follow the lines of catechisms, Neau lit candles and pursued his broader goal, which was "to give them an idea altogether spiritual of a Being infinitely perfect." Either the French trader was a superb teacher, or sufficient owner-observers attended to overawe the slaves. At any rate, Neau conducted a well-organized class. He said he detected a certain sharpness for imitation among his pupils, and capitalized on it by teaching, *memoriter,* the prayers and psalms which he read aloud, a verse at a time, eventually drawing the connection between the sound and the printed words. In this fashion, too, he helped newly arrived slaves with his own second language— English. He also encouraged singing, presumably by demonstration.

Yet, upon his own admission, education by emulation had its shortcomings. Admittedly, a few of his pupils earned baptism. But the rest, as well as the greater bulk of New York Negroes not in attendance, constantly exposed themselves to the indifference, scepticism, and bad example of owner and general populace alike in the fast-growing middle colony port. At the best of times, probably less than 10 per cent of New York's Negroes came to pray and sing in Neau's upstairs chamber. Then, after arson and murder during a 1712 Negro uprising, citizens cool toward his work turned upon him. They implicated his pupils. They maligned his school. They defamed his name and nationality. Despite backing from S.P.G. colleagues and Governor Hunter's own endorsement, Neau's work suffered. On common council order, Negroes without lanterns were peremptorily banned from the streets after dark. By denying illumination, masters thus thwarted Negro education. Neau's establishment reverted to its modest size of seven years before.[37]

It appears that this tension between Christian duty and ownership prerogative, so evident in New York society at the time of Neau's early enterprise, constituted a factor of American colonial life imperfectly understood at S.P.G. London headquarters. As the S.P.G. anniversary sermons stressed again and again, the Christian education of the servile Negro should have been less difficult than that of the nomadic Indian, as well as profitable in terms of reliable compliance with owners' commands. There arose hopes, as well, that colonial legislation guaranteeing continuing Negro bondage would facilitate Society educational efforts wherever slaves needed teaching. As in the case of the Indian program, though, S.P.G. enthusiasm in England failed to sustain its momentum in America. Unlike the Indians who lost interest, the Negroes maintained at least curiosity, and at most eagerness, over what the Society had to offer them. But no amount of British speculation or colonial legislation quite allayed a deep-seated American fear of Negro disobedience stemming from even minimal literacy. As a result, this felt threat to white security kept subsequent S.P.G. attempts to educate the Negro at the level of token gestures.

Assuming, nonetheless, that to settle the state of religion through a massive educational thrust was no mere inaugural slogan but the blueprint for a colonial duplicate of England's establishment, how did the discrepancy between the theory and the practice of the S.P.G. mission affect prospects of major successes in Queen Anne's time? Society hope to teach in North

37. In connection with the challenge of Negro education, one can turn to Carl Bridenbaugh, who uses the figures 3,900 in 1690 and 7,000 in 1720 as an estimate of New York's total population. Assuming the Reverend Neau's estimate of 1,000 New York slaves, *circa* 1706, to be reasonable, the magnitude of the task Neau was attempting may well be imagined. See *Cities in the Wilderness: Urban Life in America, 1625–1742* (New York: Capricorn Books, 1938, 1955), p. 143, note 1. For a generously documented discussion of Neau's early work, see Klingberg, *Anglican Humanitarianism*, pp. 124–36.

America sprang from high optimism and forceful planning. It depended on propaganda devices like subscription lists, annual abstracts of proceedings, and anniversary sermons. It benefited from lines of influence methodically extended into every walk of British public and private life. It also emerged from a sincere belief that colonists could be brought back to the Church, that Indians might learn religion, and that Negroes and their masters should share mutual humanity.

Working to forestall these hopes for achievement, on the contrary, was a cluster of circumstances detrimental to S.P.G. parsons and pedagogues striving in the American mission field. The first of these eventualities—the physical and, perhaps, emotional pressures of unaccustomed colonial existence—bothered homesick S.P.G. schoolmasters more than other Society servants overseas. At work between 1707 and 1712, Joseph Cleator at Rye, William Huddleston at New York, and Benjamin Dennis at Goose Creek, South Carolina, are cases in point. All three lived on the margin of poverty. Perhaps best off, Cleator started on a £20 Society grant, a local allowance, and a few shillings from the Church. In return for this, he taught "Sixty Scholars small Children Boys and Girls, not above eight" their catechism, apportioned his time among Rye, Mamaroneck, Bedford, and White Plains,[38] read Church prayers and morning and evening lectures in the absence of S.P.G. missionary the Reverend George Murison, and performed the office of Rye Church Clerk—in all, a very strenuous existence.

In New York, William Huddleston's concern was how to support a large family on a small income. The Society provided a shipment of books and £10 for one year. In fulfilling the conditions of his stipend, the New York schoolmaster managed forty or so pupils in competition with four other city schoolmen. His "altogether ignorant, rude, and unpolished" charity school children prepared for trade or business by learning how to read, write, and cast accounts while their teacher struggled to provide

38. Mr. Cleator to the Society, Rye, July 14, 1707, *S.P.G. Letter Books,* Series A, Vol. III, No. CLI, p. 385; Kemp, *The Support of Schools,* p. 125.

them with books and clothing and to negotiate a larger Society salary.[39]

Benjamin Dennis no sooner took up his Carolina post than he pitched from the saddle and broke his leg. As it mended, he managed during the winter of 1711 to teach eighteen scholars, and by summer he got about well enough to instruct eleven more. But for the arithmetic lessons and the catechizing he needed a schoolhouse.[40] He waited in vain for the building, for the replacement of books plundered in a French raid, and for funds to supplement the £3 colonial money he had gleaned in payment of several months' tuition.

The second impediment—nonconformist resentment at S.P.G. inroads—soon diminished the initial confidence displayed by Society men of whatever rank. Toleration was hardly a tenet of Puritan congregationalism. Since Anglicans were New England's dissenters, their activities were closely observed, even by moderates like Benjamin Colman. Reconnaissances like those of Caleb Heathcote and Rye missionary the Reverend George Muirson to Stratford in 1706 were greeted with threats and charges of intrusion. Resident ministers constantly found themselves in trouble. Braintree citizens accused S.P.G.'s Thomas Eager of swearing at and striking a fellow townsman. Francis Phillips of Stratford stood charged with wishing "to see . . . Governor Hunter Hung fifty Cubits high." Jamaica's S.P.G. missionary Thomas Poyer went to law (personally subsidized by Governor Hunter) over ownership of the town parsonage.[41]

39. Huddleston's opposition included Andrew Clark, a Latin teacher with 33 scholars, Cornelius Lodge with 20, John Stephens with 28, and John Bashford with 8. See Mr. Huddleston to the Secretary, New York, July 15, 1708, *S.P.G. Letter Books,* Series A. Vol. IV, No. LVIII, p. 202; Mr. Huddleston to the Secretary, New York, January 16, 1710, *ibid.,* Vol. VI, No. LI; Mr. Huddleston to the Secretary, New York, February 23, 1711, *ibid.,* Vol. VII, pp. 147–48.

40. Mr. Dennis' letter from Boochay near Goose Creek, February 26, 1711/12, *ibid.,* Vol. VII, p. 402–3; Mr. Dennis his letter to Mr. Chamberlayne, Boochay near Goose Creek, July 1712, *ibid.,* p. 427–28.

41. Glenn Weaver, "Anglican-Congregationalist Tensions in Pre-Revolutionary Connecticut," *Historical Magazine,* XXVI (1957), 274; Depositions concerning Mr. Eager, Boston, December 2, 1713, *S.P.G. Letter Books,* Series A, Vol. VIII, pp. 564–65; Archibald Dunlop's Deposition, New York, September 10, 1713, *ibid.,* pp. 277–78; A Copy of Mr. Poyer's first Petition to Coll. Hunter, Jamaica, October 27, 1710, *ibid.,* pp. 334–36.

Reaction in London, granted, was grave. Eager was permitted to resign in 1714. Phillips was dismissed. Poyer got word through Governor Hunter that "it behove the Clergy to be very Cautious of what Steps they made."[42] But no amount of official censure in the case of particular misbehavior altered the fact that more general impressions of the Society's real posture toward America could be gathered without waiting for local crises. In fact, colonists with cause to read abstracts or anniversary sermons were displeased to find they had been represented as rude, ignorant, luxury-loving degenerates.

The third hindrance—self-defeating quarrels within Anglican missionary ranks—likewise worked contrary to S.P.G. interests. In South Carolina the Reverends Richard Marsden and Edward Marston openly challenged the authority of their own Commissary, Gideon Johnston. Their French counterpart, the Reverend James Giguillet, shocked his S.P.G. colleagues by marrying a "rich and decrepit wife" and resigning his cure. Pennsylvania and Maryland missionary Jacob Henderson not only accused New York's Lewis Morris of employing Society minister to the New Harlem Dutch, Mr. Henry Beyse, for the exclusive free education of his own children, but also provided the Society secretary with the sweeping observation that "the Clergy (Generally Speaking) are not soe Industrious nor their Lives so Innocent, as those Imploy'd by the Hon.[ble] Society." In Pennsylvania missionary Robert Sinclair deplored the neglect of fellow missionary George Ross, who in turn joined associate John Humphreys to endorse the Society cashiering of Francis Phillips. At New York occasional differences between S.P.G. catechist Elias Neau and Trinity Rector William Vesey were eclipsed by the power struggle that pitted Society correspondent Lord Cornbury against S.P.G. itinerant preacher and sometime Indian teacher Thorougood Moore. Similarly, Rhode Island witnessed the forced entry, by followers of S.P.G. missionary Christopher

---

42. Pascoe, *Two Hundred Years*, p. 853; The Secretary to Mr. Phillips, August 21, 1713, *S.P.G. Letter Books*, Series A, Vol. VIII, pp. 319–20; The Secretary to Governor Hunter, July 2, 1712, *ibid.*, Vol. VII, p. 264.

Bridge, of S.P.G. missionary James Honyman's Newport church.[43]

The fourth related stumbling block—lack of a colonial bishop—left the question of intra-Societal discipline in turmoil. As surrogate bishop, for example, Commissary Johnston found himself in a perplexing position. Institutionally, he was doubly responsible to the bishop of London and the Society secretary. He could encourage promising colonial candidates for missionary work but could not ordain them. In the same vein, he could caution miscreants but not unfrock them. Upon his own admission, the stopgap superintendency connected with the role of commissary seemed to grow more and more into "a mere empty title." Lacking a bishop, and ignoring their commissary, S.P.G. men looked around for the best referee they could find to rule on differences of opinion. To a limited degree, the Society itself responded by adopting as its own the codified instructions to colonial governors and assuming their recipients would be capable of carrying them out. Lord Cornbury, for instance, in theory held jurisdiction which amounted to a commissary's and called for his ensuring that the bishop of London's instructions would at all times be observed.[44] But other com-

43. For an excellent treatment of Church disciplinary problems in the South, see Frank J. Klingberg (ed.), *Carolina Chronicle: The Papers of Commissary Gideon Johnston, 1707–1716* (Berkeley and Los Angeles: University of California Press, 1946), pp. 21, 61–62, and *passim; ibid.,* p. 101. Other local squabbles are revealed in Mr. Henderson to the Society, London, July 1, 1712, *S.P.G. Letter Books,* Series A, Vol. VII, p. 24; Mr. Henderson to the Secretary, Patuxentin, Maryland, April 1, 1715, *ibid.,* Vol. X, p. 284; Mr. Sinclair to the Secretary, New Castle, December 7, 1710, *ibid.,* Vol. VI, No. LVI; Mr. Ross and Mr. Humphreys to the Society, New Castle, April 28, 1715, *ibid.,* p. 141; Lord Cornbury to the Secretary, New York, November 29, 1707, *ibid.,* Vol. III, No. CLV; Mr. Moore to the Secretary, Fort Anne, August 27, 1707, *ibid.,* No. CXLIV; Mr. Bridges to the Secretary, Newport, February, 1707, *ibid.,* Vol. III, pp. 521–23; Mr. Honyman to the Secretary, Newport, December 17, 1707, *ibid.,* pp. 551–53.

44. It is interesting to note that since the highest-ranking Church official in America—the commissary—could not confirm, colonial Church members were always denied one office of their religion unless they went to Britain to receive the rite. Pascoe uses Cornbury's governor's royal instructions to indicate how certain episcopal functions were assumed by lay government officers in the colonies. See *Two Hundred Years,* p. 60.

mitments made it impossible for Cornbury to carry out these responsibilities.

Cornbury was not alone in his perplexity. In New England, Governor Dudley acknowledged letters "commanding" him to look into the Bridge-Honyman affair. South Carolina Governor Sir Nathaniel Johnson reported the exploits of that "Common Incendiary" Edward Marston who, it was said, insulted parishioners and affronted the government. Lieutenant-Governor Charles Gookin in Pennsylvania "Called Mr. Evans to account" for meddling in colonial politics beyond the reach of his office of Society missionary. New York Governor Robert Hunter likewise accepted Society "commands" and declared that he would "obey exactly such Directions" as might be sent, though he looked for moderation, not fanaticism, in an S.P.G. envoy. Virginia Governor Alexander Spotswood saw to it that S.P.G. itinerant Giles Rainsford received no Virginia parish until the Society granted him permission to quit North Carolina. And assuredly it was in anticipation of a governor's cooperation that the Society added to its congratulations to Governor Craven upon his appointment its injunction to see that Society missionaries and schoolmasters "behave themselves Agreeably."[45]

But at best, colonial governors regarded supervision of Society personnel as the merest fragment of their total responsibilities. Indeed, even when General Francis Nicholson rose from a Virginia governorship to the post of Commander-in-Chief in North America and agreed as well to submit comprehensive reports on S.P.G. "Missionaries, Schoolmasters &

45. Governor Dudley to the Lord Bishop of London, Boston, May 27, 1708, *S.P.G. Letter Books,* Series A, Vol. IV, pp. 113–14. That Dudley exercised his Church mandate uneasily at times may be deduced from his confession that "I cannot be at peace with Mr. Mather and his son, the [*sic*] pursue me every where, I must bear it as well as I can," *ibid.* For additional reactions from colonial governors involved in S.P.G. affairs, see South Carolina Council to the Society, February 13, 1707/8, *ibid.,* pp. 131–34; Colonel Gooking to Mr. Chamberlayne, Philadelphia, January 21, 1711, *ibid.,* Vol. VII, pp. 506–7; Governor Hunter to the Secretary, Gosport, March 4, 1709, *ibid.,* Vol. V, No. LXXII, p. 183; Governor Hunter to the Secretary, *ibid.,* No. LXXX, p. 199; Colonel Spotswood to Mr. Rainsford, Williamsburg, November 14, 1712, *ibid.,* Vol. VIII, p. 371; Letter from the Society to Governor Craven, n.d., *ibid.,* Vol. VII, p. 475.

Catechists" and their "Churches, Glebes, Parsonage Houses & Libraries," he doubted the adequacy of governors' surveillance to S.P.G. success. Along with a decade of parsons and pedagogues in America, and of Society members in London, he concluded that when it came to organizing a teaching force in the new world, commissaries, governors, and commanders-in-chief were totally inadequate. What was needed was a colonial bishop. At the end of Queen Anne's reign, however, chances of ever securing a colonial bishop looked slim. And, in a circuitous sort of way, chances were likely to become even slimmer to the extent that dissenting pressure groups exerted their influence upon parliament, a thing they were most likely to do in face of suspected S.P.G. intrusion into their colonial religious affairs.[46]

Society organization during its first fifteen years continued, then, to show that impressive facility for rational planning that marked the emergence of its 1701 charter. Coetaneous with Marlborough's stunning continental military successes, the S.P.G. approached its educational tasks abroad with all the thoroughness of a well-planned army campaign. In line with contemporary political notions about the value of cabinet unanimity, it worked out matters of policy in regular sessions attended by key members. Its fiscal dealings reflected the steady coordinating influence of the newly founded Bank of England rather than the more daring financial exploits of the older trading companies. Even its minutes embodied a tidy, self-assurance typical of an age when clubs and societies characterized English life, and club and society members found orderly frameworks for discussing and dealing with life's many problems.

46. As a matter of routine, S.P.G. missionaries were advised of promotions to the post of colonial governor. See for example Letter from the Secretary to Mr. Maule, November 6, 1712, *ibid.*, p. 353. Nicholson concluded, as did the majority of governors, that episcopal bishops in the colonies were essential; see General Nicholson to the Secretary, Boston, May 11, 1714, *ibid.*, Vol. IX, p. 353. Opponents of Church expansion took a different view. For an absorbing treatment of effective lobbying by well-organized nonconformity on either side of the Atlantic, see N. C. Hunt, *Two Early Political Associations: The Quakers and the Dissenting Deputies in the Age of Sir Robert Walpole* (Oxford: The Clarendon Press, 1961).

But, if sensitivity to the factors distinguishing a closed British from a more open colonial society be the measure, the Venerable Society failed in its preliminary effort to realize its charter. It failed to understand that tales of frustration and delinquency from abroad denoted not so much repeated missionary short-comings as certain peculiarities distinguishing American from English life. It failed, for instance, to grasp the difference between colonial dissent and colonial disloyalty. It failed to comprehend that through years of ineffective episcopal direction, at long range from London, American Church vestries had developed their own techniques and policies of appointing parsons and pedagogues which they were unlikely to relinquish, especially without a colonial bishop. It failed to appreciate the fact that to Christianize an Indian was to diminish his ferocity as a frontier ally, or that to teach a Negro was to threaten a planter. And, finally, it failed to notice that a full century had slipped by since Dale prescribed his Virginia laws about rank, and that in early eighteenth-century America defying colonial governors on a variety of issues was becoming unexceptional.[47]

Between Queen Anne's death in 1714 and the addition to Britain of France's North American empire in 1763, the Society was to continue its static program of teaching colonials to conform not just to the Church established by law but to a preconceived empire order as well. But it would prove inappropriate for a dynamic religious, social, and political scheme of things. As ever, books and other printed materials were to play a major part in the educational process, and it is to this medium that we now turn.

47. Professor J. A. Lauwerys has indicated that stated missionary intentions rarely matched results. See Brian Holmes (ed.), *Educational Policy and the Mission Schools: Case Studies from the British Empire* (London: Routledge and Keegan Paul, 1967), p. viii. In this instance, failure to realize the charter is not to be confused with tangible accomplishments in bringing church and school services to the colonies. For my assessment see Chapter VI.

III

LESSONS IN
PRINT

BETWEEN Queen Anne's death and the cession of New France in 1763, the S.P.G. printed extensively. In London anniversary sermons and Society abstracts regularly appeared under the Downing, Buckley, or Owen & Harrison imprint. In major colonial centers from Boston to Charles Town, missionary homilies and occasional pieces on current themes circulated widely. Prolific as literary innovator, the Society to a far greater extent adopted the role of book distributor. Emulating the interlocking organizations of Bray's Associates and the Society for Promoting Christian Knowledge, it set about acquiring and giving out books and tracts, and translating texts, all of time-tested Christian significance.[1] This S.P.G. interest in publishing was no passing fancy. Over-all Society expenditures rose from £3,119 in 1714 to £5,344 in 1763, and a good deal of this

---

1. In this respect, the S.P.G. was simply working within the context of eighteenth-century propagandizing. In England, freethinkers like Toland, Collins, Gordon, Wolston, Middleton, Tindal, Chubb, Morgan, and Annet flooded the market with pamphlets and learned works. A counterflood of brochures defending revealed religion kept eighteenth-century presses active. See Paul Hazard, *European Thought in the Eighteenth Century from Montesquieu to Lessing*, trans. J. Lewis May (New York: The World Publishing Company, 1963), pp. 59–62.

increase paid the printer. Quite apart from private bequests, C. F. Pascoe estimated that by 1757 no fewer than 13,000 Bibles, Prayer Books, devotional works, and smaller instructional tracts had been distributed by Society men. Here, then, developed a large body of printed matter calculated to remind colonists of empire as well as spiritual responsibilities. It also furnished sources from which many Englishmen gained their impressions of the colonial scene.

That this corpus of sermons, abstracts, observations, translations, and pamphlets reflected any Society response to changing religious, social, or cultural conditions in America, however, is another matter entirely. Not that S.P.G. missionaries had any reason to question the social and cultural premises upon which the writings they dispensed were based.[2] And in any case, the Society charter had made it perfectly clear that the S.P.G. task was to adjust the conditions of American colonial life to fit a Society pattern, rather than the other way round. What, however, were the conditions of colonial life? What, in the minds of Americans, distinguished New from Old World existence? What, in fact, inspired the thoughts and actions of a people which, in John Adams' view, underwent a "radical change in . . . principles, opinions, sentiments and affections" during the period here in question?[3]

To start with, the movement past mid-century of American colonial life legitimized to a hitherto unrealized extent the art of getting ahead. At a very fundamental, economic level, a labor shortage guaranteed at least menial work for all. No longer merely a question of self-defense against a hostile frontier, working with one's hands assumed an air of respectability, even

2. See Bernard Bailyn, *Education in the Forming of American Society* (New York: Vintage Books, 1960), p. 20.

3. Some accounts of the dynamics of colonial life include Bailyn, *Education;* Daniel J. Boorstin, *The Americans: The Colonial Experience* (New York: Vintage Books, 1964); Carl Bridenbaugh, *Cities in the Wilderness* (New York: Capricorn Books, 1938, 1955); *The Colonial Craftsman* (Chicago: The University of Chicago Press, 1950, 1964); Louis B. Wright, *The First Gentlemen of Virginia* (Charlottesville: Dominion Books, 1940, 1964); *The Cultural Life of the American Colonies* (New York: Harper Torchbooks, 1957, 1962).

dignity. American gentlemen[4] grew wealthy by trade, thereby finding the leisure to study writings of the Enlightenment. For Benjamin Franklin, an ideal education was one preparing a man for "any business, any calling, any profession." For dozens of Atlantic seaport towns, the tavern, not the church, was to gain ascendence as common meeting place for men of all ranks of society—"the most democratic places in the villages," as Carl Bridenbaugh puts it.

To this progressive justification of social mobility through labor, education, or opportunism was added regional differentiation. Immigrants of many nations arrived in America to fill a labor shortage. Colonial cities and settlements developed their unique atmospheres. A rural South assumed a tidewater as opposed to a back-country society and economy, both distinct from a commercial North with its network of villages and seaports. Dozens of colonial subsocieties, moreover, assumed local characteristics. For the five decades spanning the period from Queen Anne's passing to France's surrender of Canada, this fragmenting process deeply affected colonial American existence. Considered by some historians as the second city of the empire, Philadelphia developed a whole range of professions and crafts with their social clubs or societies. Indigenous propaganda organizations like the Society for the Propagation of the Gospel among the Germans in Pennsylvania were directly challenged by German newspapers proclaiming the special genius of German newcomers. The awakening preachings of George Whitefield, Theodorus Frelinghuysen, and Gilbert Tennent and the anti-Tory sermons of Jonathan Mayhew and Ezra Stiles encouraged the proliferation of religious sects, each with its special educational style and ambitions.

---

4. This is not to say that the ideal of gentleman merchant was exclusively American. As Hazard shows, periodicals like the *Tatler* and the *Spectator* argued in theory that the merchant had a better claim to the name of "gentleman" than did the courtier. See Paul Hazard, *The European Mind 1680–1715*, trans. J. Lewis May (New York: The World Publishing Company, 1963), p. 328. In practice, however, eighteenth-century Americans appeared less hesitant over the social consequences of labor.

Divisive though this fragmenting process could be, it was accompanied by a corresponding series of accepted ways of thinking and behaving essentially different from those deemed proper in mid-century England. For instance, schools and colleges established as a result of the awakening inspiration of George Whitefield and other fundamentalists needed to look to their particular sectarian requirements, and in so doing became highly responsive to local pressures, especially in cases where general school taxes superseded private donations. Widespread assumption of local or individual initiative became, in fact, the very essence of American culture, revered by later revolutionaries as much as caricatured by antagonistic Old World conservatives. American Anglicanism itself, although for the most part the religion of "wealth, fashion, and position," copied a Virginia style of vestry system which furnished parishioners with a degree of local control in Church affairs far greater than that obtaining in England. American science with its strong natural history bent brought together men of differing ranks and fortunes to compare notes on what they had found to be locally interesting or practically applicable. American craftsmanship, especially in the North, nurtured a sturdy middle-class of artisans able to come to terms with colonial laborers as well as colonial noblemen. American roads and an American press, meantime, made it increasingly convenient for colonists to compare findings on the solutions to the many problems confronting their daily lives.

The result of such a multiplication of clubs and sects and schools and ways of doing things, accelerated by relatively poor wartime communications with England until after the French cession, and by progressively improving intercolonial communications, was a persistent eroding of "the great law of subordination." Daniel Boorstin puts the case emphatically. No features of English society in the eighteenth century, he argues, were more valued than security and dependence. Security came from the assurance of living in a network of familiar and predictable relationships. The flavor of American life, he continues, was, conversely, compounded of risk, spontaneity, independence, initiative, drift, mobility, and opportunity.[5] And it was into this changing America that the S.P.G. introduced its sermons, abstracts, and occasional works, many of which proposed subordination as the key to accomplishment and tranquility in all human enterprises.

It would, of course, be foolish to suppose that by propagandizing establishment beliefs about church and state affairs the S.P.G. pressed a theory of subordination unique in eighteenth-century thought. Spurred by philosophes' attacks on miracles, the Bible, prophets, dogma, and the sacraments, and constantly alerted to heresies of one sort or another, English divines habitually warned against ill-advised change. In his *Alliance between Church and State* (1736) for example, Bishop William Warburton of Gloucester argued the need of close ties between essentially discreet ecclesiastical and governmental bodies, a thesis of interdependence later elaborated in his *The Divine Legation of Moses*. What Norman Sykes has called this "confident optimism concerning the correspondence between the establishment of England and the eternal order of the universe" was likewise reflected in Archbishop Herring's opinions on the matter. "Nothing in the world," he wrote, "is more contrary to my judgment of things than to make alterations in our establishment, of which in some sense the toleration act is a part; and what I am determined to stick to is the support of these two in conjunction. I think philosophy, Christianity, and policy are all against changes."[6]

---

5. Daniel J. Boorstin, *The Americans: The Colonial Experience* (New York: Vintage Books, 1958, 1964), p. 85.

6. For a clear discussion of such theological deviations as Antinomianism, Arminianism, Arianism, Pelagianism, Socinianism, and Deism, see Alan Heimert and Perry Miller (eds.), *The Great Awakening: Documents Illustrating the Crisis and its Consequences* (New York: Bobbs Merrill, 1967), pp. xvii–xxi. For other expressions of subordination as a social and political ethic, see Hazard, *European Thought*, pp. 83–84; Sykes, *Church and State*, p. 284; Herring to Hardwicke, 13 September, 1748, Add. MSS. 35598, f. 342, cited in Sykes, *Church and State*, p. 284.

Nor were such notions of subordination to due order foreign to New World nonconformity. Threatened by the theological and social disruptions of the Great Awakening, for example, American colonial preachers delivered solemn warnings against innovations likely to challenge church and state prerogatives. Charles Chauncy denounced an enthusiastic religious movement that had "promoted faction and contention," and he held that good order was the strength and beauty of the world. Civil rulers, he pointed out, ought to apply their authority to keep in check men who "insult their Betters, vilify their Neighbours, and spirit People to Strife and Faction." Children, he continued, should obey parents, who themselves should restrain and command offspring. Servants owed honor to masters, he went on, and masters needed to keep servants "within the Rules of Order and Decorum." Jonathan Mayhew, despite his later sermon against unlimited submission, defended New England Congregationalism against radical enthusiasm by demonstrating the unreasonableness of "chusing our religion by vote." Further, he resisted the inroads of atheism by adopting argument-by-design to praise a God who fashioned "the stupendous magnitude, the regular motions, the beautiful order, . . . the numerous worlds" of a Newtonian universe.[7]

Sometimes, too, entire institutions reacted against the menace of instability. In 1744 the president and fellows of Harvard formally castigated George Whitefield's threat to "Peace and Order." One complaint concerned the itinerant preacher's "monstrous Reflections upon the great and good Archbishop Tillotson," the Canterbury prelate whose sermons circulated in

7. Charles Chauncy, *Enthusiasm described and caution'd against. A Sermon* . . . (Boston: 1742), cited in Heimert and Miller, *The Great Awakening,* p. 243; Charles Chauncy, *Seasonable Thoughts on the State of Religion in New England* . . . (Boston: 1743), cited in Heimert and Miller, *The Great Awakening.* pp. 298, 300, 301; Jonathan Mayhew, *Seven Sermons . . . Preached at a Lecture in the West Meeting House in Boston . . . in August 1748* (Boston: 1749; reprinted London, 1750), cited in Heimert and Miller, *The Great Awakening,* p. 577; Jonathan Mayhew, *Christian Sobriety* (Boston: 1763), cited in H. Sheldon Smith, Robert T. Handy, and Lefferts A. Loetscher (eds.), *American Christianity: An Historical Interpretation with Representative Documents, Volume I, 1607–1820,* p. 387.

America among conformists and nonconformists alike. A second deplored the extempore manner of preaching with its implication of the superfluousness of study and planning. And a third hit at itineracy itself,[8] a manner of preaching quite out of keeping with organized congregations, "orthodox" or otherwise. Indeed, so often did mid-eighteenth-century pulpits on both sides of the Atlantic lend themselves to examining such questions as hierarchies, duty, responsibility, order, and subordination, it is no easy task to establish the singularity of S.P.G. persuasion up to the French cession of Canada. In one respect, however, the uniqueness of mid-century Society propaganda invites concession. As to frequency, variety, and predictability of the subordination theme, whether religious, political, economic, social, or (as was often the case) a mélange of some or all of these, it appeared to have no institutional counterpart in England or America. Thus, by constantly interpreting the S.P.G. charter, it provided a body of opinion as to where Society responsibilities lay at any given time; but it also assumed the function of a quasi-official voice for all English conservatives whose interests were conditioned by colonial American policy.

Considered as a whole, the anniversary sermons instigated soon after S.P.G. incorporation, and the abstracts of Society proceedings, usually bound and circulated with the sermons, continued up to 1763 as the most regular and reliable instrument of Society propaganda both in England and America.

In the case of the anniversary sermon, themes other than religious maintained a remarkable consistency. A recurring thesis was a mercantile theory of empire, and it was stated again and again by successive prelates at St. Mary-le-Bow. They used expansive terms such as "trade and riches," "mines of wealth," "temporal riches," and "honest commerce" in order to establish the central importance of trade in the colonies. Although

8. *The Testimony of the President, Professors, Tutors, and Hebrew Instructors of Harvard College, against George Whitefield* (Boston: 1744), cited in Heimert and Miller, *The Great Awakening,* pp. 347, 350, 351.

sermonists employed Biblical imagery, their over-all message was in harmony with the Marquis of Carmarthen's parliamentary query *"for what purpose were they [American colonists] suffered to go to that country unless the profit of their labour should return to their masters here?"* As one preacher had phrased it in earlier times, "if trade be lost, we are a ruined nation . . . and shall ourselves become slaves." Others stressed the same point. Should the colonist and his slave toil, they said, Britain would prosper. But should they be profligate, England might suffer. Later sermonists emphasized personal rather than national benefits. England's venturer and colonial planter, they argued, stood to reap the chief monetary rewards of overseas enterprise.[9] Accordingly, they above others should support the S.P.G., a society whose efforts would strengthen the mercantilism which created their wealth.

In addition to these economic observations, the Society anniversary sermonists elaborated upon the theoretical connection between territorial and religious expansion and showed that these two facets of colonizing also affected trade. England's honor, they pointed out, hung in the balance. Spain and France threatened. Thus menaced, England's power would have to be readied for an effort designed both to win an empire from the French in Canada and to "make distant countries accessible to missionaries."[10]

These authors of printed anniversary sermons made it clear that the commercial as well as the proselytizing potential of the American colonies was not to be reduced through haphazard notions about the sort of colonial society best suited to produce

9. For Carmarthen's view, see *The Parliamentary History of England,* XVII (London: 1813), 1208, 1209, cited in Richard B. Morris, *Government and Labor in Early America* (New York: Harper Torchbooks, 1946, 1965), p. 2. This theme of colonial productivity for England's benefit is especially well developed in William Fleetwood, *A Sermon* . . . (London: Joseph Downing, 1711), p. 22; Thomas Secker, *A Sermon* . . . (London: for J. and H. Pemberton. 1741), p. 15: Robert Hay Drummond, *A Sermon* . . . (London: Edward Owen, 1754).
10. Nicholas Clagett, *A Sermon* . . . (London: for J. and T. Pemberton, 1737), p. 25; John Hume, *A Sermon* . . . (London: E. Owen & T. Harrison, 1762), p. 16.

highest dividends. Sermonists envisaged the relationship of colonists with each other and with England as a union of strictly delineated components. Obligation, obedience, fidelity, and dependence were watchwords. Sectarianism was anathema. As one clergyman expressed it, every wise man would see and every good man lament the want of proper sanction and authority to enforce obedience.[11]

Politically, too, the picture sharpened. All ranks and orders were to operate under the authority of the reigning monarch, and since they were dependent on Britain, colonials would evince filial reverence to their remote mother country, source of colonial constitutions and policies. Most important, close colonial attachment to the crown was essential since the more loyal a subject was the more able and willing would he be to defend himself from the king's enemies encroaching upon colonial territory.[12]

On the social level, the concept of order was translated into terms of a ranked body of American colonials, a Negro slave class, a class of Indians whose precise position in the scheme shifted about, and a class of European immigrants requiring special attention. By inference from numerous complaints in the sermons about newcomers being lured away from honest industry by the effusions of backwoods, nonconformist ministers, their status as a productive, servile, working force appeared natural and desirable to the Society. Since their alleged susceptibility to irresponsible teaching about the unlawfulness of war[13] threatened not only the hoped-for dignity of a colonial Church of England but also the very existence of the colonies, conti-

11. *Ibid.,* p. 11.
12. Although this crown/colony relationship was often expressed throughout the period, the matter of responsibility for self-defense in face of French and Indian attack varied wtih the crises involved. The last question is typically discussed in Anthony Ellis, *A Sermon* . . . (London: E. Owen & T. Harrison, 1759), p. 29.
13. John Egerton, *A Sermon* . . . (London: E. Owen & T. Harrison, 1763), p. 18; Ellis, *Sermon,* pp. 29–30.

nental European immigrants were to furnish a laboring caste whose supposed unreliability would accordingly keep them inferior to British colonial workers, but whose race sustained them socially above both Indian and Negro.

Such, in brief, appeared lessons about an empire social order consistent with whatever profit motive of colonial expansion the Society professed at any given time. But working toward this optimum network of connections called for definite strategies deemed suitable for achieving such conformity as would further the economic, military, and social, as well as religious interests of Great Britain.

Again, financial considerations claimed high priority. It was argued, for instance, that masters could expect little productivity from heathen servants, or princes from atheist subjects. Conversely, Christianization of servants and slaves was shown to affect favorably their productive capacity. Not surprisingly, this pragmatic approach to colonial missionary work led to assumptions about sources of revenue for the S.P.G. itself. London, often called that "great opulent city," and its merchants, traders, and adventurers[14] stood most likely to profit; the metropolis and its entrepreneurs accordingly would be expected to do their share in financing Society work abroad.

This was not to say that S.P.G. missionaries and schoolmasters were to be sent to America to intrude. Quite the contrary. Missionaries were warned not to interfere with politics and the intricacies of colonial administration. Moreover, they were to be sent to colonial posts only upon request.[15] Persuasive tactics, the sermonists felt, would result in wider adoption of Anglicanism on the part of uncommitted colonists and perhaps nonconformists too.

14. See, for example, John Leng, *A Sermon* . . . (London: J. Downing, 1727), pp. 28–29; Joseph Butler, *A Sermon* . . . (London: For J. and P. Knapton, 1739), p. 22 and *passim*.
15. These ideas of nonintervention were well-developed in Thomas Haley, *A Sermon* . . . (London: Joseph Downing, 1717), p. 14; John Egerton, *A Sermon* . . . (London: E. Owen & T. Harrison, 1763), p. 16.

Parallel with this increasingly gentle reference to colonial dissent throughout the period there also ran a line of reassessment as to the proper objectives of S.P.G. benevolence. Since a connection was assumed to exist between orthodox religion and obedience to England, earlier sermons stressed directing the major effort toward English-speaking colonists, whatever their denomination. The same relative scale of priorities was still current in 1720 when it was reiterated that the Society should begin "with our own countrymen . . . going on from them to the meer heathens, whether native or slaves."[16] Past mid-century, though, this consistently-held idea began to waver. For one thing, reticence about intruding upon colonists gave way to frequent thought for Indians. Such sermons as those of 1758 and 1759 stressed that of all Indians, those converted by the S.P.G. proved militarily faithful to England. For another thing, there emerged a concern for Negroes, and in the case of both Indians and Negroes considerable discussion as to whether Christianization took precedence over civilizing or vice versa.

One must bear in mind that from the standpoint of their imagery and vocabulary, and in line with eighteenth-century sermons as a whole, these printed tours de force rang overwhelmingly Biblical in tone. Just the same, a cursory word count prompts one to remark how S.P.G. anniversary sermon rhetoric throughout the half-century period appeared linguistically suited to the religious/national/social ideas it expressed. Words like "rank," "order," "inferior," or "equal" pervaded the text. Closely allied was a range of abstractions referring to the relationship between parts and stressing degree, condition, subordination, conformity, obedience, submission, and self-denial. Imagery ran the gamut of metaphorical ingenuity. But after about 1740, prelates at St. Mary-le-Bow employed familial figures of speech with increasing frequency. Indeed, as Americans developed certain political and cultural self-sufficiencies,

16. Edward Waddington, *A Sermon* . . . (London: Joseph Downing, 1721), p. 23.

English anniversary sermonists reminded them more and more of the filial reverence owed a remote mother country. Unlike the anniversary sermons, the S.P.G. *Abstracts* were compiled from the Society's *Journals,* which in turn recorded discussions of S.P.G. news from abroad. As a form of promotional literature complementary to the sermons, they adopted a predominantly numerical assessment of Society progress abroad, couched in terms of bequests, legacies, new members, book distribution, missionary successes, developments and accounts in the Barbadoes enterprise, missionary lists, abstracts of the S.P.G. charter, membership lists, and specimen forms of legacy. In several respects, too, these tightly written summaries served as footnotes for the anniversary sermons with which they were usually bound. They underscored, for example, the close bond between commercial centers capitalizing on colonial expansion and potential sources of revenue for the Society work in America. They utilized, too, that characteristic familial turn of phrase that stressed the paternal nature of the British crown as well as the fraternal bond between an Englishman and his "poor Brethren in America."[17] In one sense, their more personalized, more localized, perspectives appeared well designed to attract further support. In another way, though, they provoked irritation. Nonconformist colonists continually came across them and objected to what they read.

Among these particulars, none attracted more attention than the question of preferential treatment in America which, in abstracted accounts to 1763, the Society presumed was its due

17. It is interesting to note that the term "success" shifted to "progress" in 1730 and to "pious labours" in 1738. The general patterns of the *Abstracts* is typified in *An Abstract of the Proceedings of the Society, 1726* and maintained throughout the period. Some, like the 1714 publication, spoke of extending the area of collection, radius ten miles about London and Westminster, to "such other *Capitals* and *Maritime* Places, which might probably be influenced by their Trade with other *Plantations,* to a more liberal Contribution . . .," see p. 26. Others, including that of 1718, were more precise, proposing Bristol, Plymouth, Whitehaven, Liverpool, Biddiford, Barnstaple, Exeter, and Newcastle-upon-Tyne as proper sharers with London of the burden of S.P.G. cost responsibilities. See p. 35. See also, *An Abstract . . .,* 1752, pp. 49, 50.

as missionary arm of the establishment. Some special provisions appeared innocuous enough. In connection with his work on the northeast side of North Carolina's Neuse River, for example, itinerant John Garzia laid before the assembly a supporting letter from S.P.G. Secretary Bearcroft, thereby gaining free ferry passage over all the rivers and creeks within a mission of some 9,000 souls. But on a more general scale, colonial moral and political support gave rise to corporate satisfaction reported in enthusiastic terms. At a given moment, to illustrate, grateful acknowledgments were returned simultaneously to those in high office furthering the S.P.G. cause—their Excellencies William Burnet, governor of New York and New Jersey, Governor Samuel Shute and Lieutenant Governor Wentworth of the Province of Massachusetts Bay in New England, his Excellency Francis Nicholson, governor of South Carolina, the Honorable Arthur Middleton, president of the South Carolina council, and the Honorable James Moore, speaker of the assembly. More pointed still seemed an earlier report that the enlarging of governors' royal instructions for New York forbade any binding court judgment prejudicial to the Church of England without appeal to the Crown Council, and that prosecution in the courts of chancery against Trinity Church's minister and wardens for arrears in rent were to stop, thanks to quit rents given up by ex-Governors Fletcher and Cornbury.[18]

Another disturbing aspect of S.P.G. *Abstracts* to many non-Church colonial readers was their ambivalence regarding American formal education and the insulting estimate of colonial society that they time and again revealed. In the one case— education—those charged with the job of compiling abstracts acknowledged the fact that some American colonists had access to good scholarship. King's College and the Philadelphia Academy, for example, they recognized as degree-granting institutions

18. *An Abstract* . . ., 1742, p. 53; *An Abstract* . . ., 1722, pp. 43, 44; *An Abstract* . . ., 1714, p. 27.

of acceptable standards.[19] But abstract editors more often contrasted the insufficiencies of colonial higher learning with the virtues of British universities,[20] touching on the "restless Spirit of Opposition but too visible in some of the Dissenting Teachers of Authority and Influence."[21] On the question of radical departures from either Church or dissenting styles of instruction, however, the precession abstracts reflected a wide area of unanimity. All concerned held in abhorrence the spirit of theological and educational amateurism allegedly permeating the Great Awakening.[22]

On this last count, all attempts at caution or compromise were tossed to the winds in favor of a rhetoric not dissimilar to the Keithian invective of Society pioneering days. One account lamented the infidelity and loose principles of a careless, luke-

19. In 1755 the Society named Mr. Winslow missionary to Stratford to succeed Dr. Samuel Johnson "who is *promoted* [italics mine] to be the President of the College for the Education of Youth in the City of New York," *An Abstract . . .*, 1755, p. 45. The same year, Mr. Barton produced for the S.P.G. "a Certificate from the Trustees, and from the Professors of the Academy of Literature and Useful knowledge lately erected at *Philadelphia,* that he had been more than two years employed as an Assistant in that Academy . . . [and was recommended] to the Society, as a proper Person for their Service," *ibid.,* pp. 52–53. Of the 213 S.P.G. servants active in the colonies between 1714 and 1763, twenty-four are also known to have held degrees from Yale and eleven from Harvard Colleges. Based on Pascoe, *Two Hundred Years,* pp. 849–56.

20. It was reported in 1754 that Samuel Seabury Jr. "had made as good Proficiency in Literature while in *America,* as *the present State of Learning there would admit of* [italics mine] and he was gone for further Improvement to the University of Edimburgh." In a recent exploratory piece, Professor Douglas Sloan has referred to this form of institutional name-dropping as the use of "symbolic authority." See Douglas Sloan, "Scottish Influence on Higher Education in Colonial America: A Bibliographical Exploration," (unpublished seminar paper, Teachers College, Columbia, 1967), p. 23.

21. See *An Abstract . . .*, 1762, p. 41. The reference is to Stratford, Connecticut.

22. Again, it must be stressed that objection to enthusiasm was not an exclusive S.P.G. trait but rather a reaction of old-line communions in both England and America. The warnings against awakening preaching by such men as Chauncy and Mayhew have already been noted. John Walsh points out that both Latitudinarian and High Church sermons in England during the 1720s, 1740s, and 1750s typically denounced enthusiasm. See his "Origins of the Evangelical Revival," *Essays in Modern Church History in Memory of Norman Sykes,* ed. G. V. Bennett and J. D. Walsh (London: Adam and Charles Black, 1966), p. 142. What strikes one about these S.P.G. observations is their comparative urgency and harshness, however.

warm people. Another elaborated on Dr. Samuel Johnson's Stratford letter telling of "travelling Enthusiastical, and Antinomian Teachers . . . who . . . so affright the People with their dismal Outcries, that their Bodies have been frequently affected with surprising convulsions, and Agitations . . . ." The same document echoed Mr. Punderson's shock at "Uncharitableness and Enthusiasm," as well as Mr. Colgar's lament about enthusiastic teachers being "found guilty of the foulest immoral practices . . . ," and Mr. Backhouse's regret at finding some of his old Pennsylvania rural acquaintances "grown giddy brained with Methodism." Subsequent summaries grew yet more intense in coverage and disparagement. The 1743 abstract made much of "wild doings" of "illiterate tradesmen," New England followers of George Whitefield, of Connecticut "Taylors, Shoemakers, and other Mechanicks, and even Women, Boys and Girls . . . become . . . Exhorters," of New Hampshire struggles against "the Contagions of Enthusiasm," and New York troubles arising out of Methodism and "a deep Tincture of Enthusiasm." Nor was awakening enthusiasm suffered easily, as terms like "Dissentions and Frenzies," "Extravagances and Confusions," the swarming of "Fanaticks [and] Ranters," and advice against "illiterate Exhorters, who ramble about the Country, and do all they can to seduce the People from Order and Decency"[23] continued to show throughout the period.

Thus did the home benefits of colonialism and the dangers of awakening enthusiasm supply the dominant propositions of the Society's official publications between 1714 and 1763. No doubt the infrequency of correspondence from any given colonial outpost, coupled with the S.P.G.'s dependence on commercially-oriented subscribers, led to the adoption of this inflexible doctrine of compliance to London-centered interests. Granted, insensitivity to changes in American ways of living might have

---

23. For details, see *An Abstract* . . ., 1738, pp. 39, 40, 43; *An Abstract* . . ., 1742, pp. 41, 44, 47, 51; *An Abstract* . . ., 1743, pp. 40, 42, 45; *An Abstract* . . ., 1752, p. 37; *An Abstract* . . ., 1760, p. 40; *An Abstract* . . ., 1762, pp. 39, 47.

been expected in direct proportion to proximity to the American Atlantic seaboard. Accepting this premise, one might expect from S.P.G. servants in the field sermons tempered by an appreciation of the growing diversification of colonial life as the eighteenth century approached the two-thirds mark. Such was not to be, however.

Unlike the annual Society homilies consciously designed for reviewing the S.P.G.'s past and mapping out its future, American sermons by Society missionaries evinced a freshness of topic stemming from the wide variety of occasions prompting their initial delivery. There were sermons preached before colonial assemblies, Church ministerial conventions, Masonic lodges, and troops awaiting embarkation. Other sermons commemorated the death of royalty, the demise of provincial officials, or the imminent appointment with the noose of condemned criminals. There were sermons deploring the decline of public morality and such possibly connected visitations as General Braddock's defeat and the folly of the '45 Jacobite rebellion in Scotland. Others urged the necessity of patriotism, colonial unanimity, wisdom at the polls, and the reciprocal duty of clergy and laity. There were sermons vindicating the celebration of Christmas Day, the sovereignty of revelation over reason, the power of Church commisaries over free-lance enthusiasts, the supremacy of free grace, the advantages of common prayer, and the duty of submission to authority. Yet, despite their extraordinary range of topic, style, and quality, these sermons echoed the collective sympathies of men clinging to order in a chaotically sprouting, individualistic society adopting piecemeal solutions to its many problems.

This yearning for order was reflected on many a printed page. It appeared as Aristotle's dictum that man was framed for society. It assumed the grammarian's style. Elsewhere, it showed as an astronomer's contemplation of "the Sun, Moon, and Stars, and all the Heavenly Orbs, so vast in their Bulk, so far in their

Distance, so large in the Compass of their Motions," yet all phased according to one confidence scheme. In one homily, it arrived as that insurance against extempore prayer, the Church form requiring "but a Capacity to read, nay, and scarcely that, for what is thus constantly used, will in a short Time, be treasured up in the Memory . . . and be ready upon every Occasion . . . ." In another, it came as a Masonic injunction to members to *"square* all their actions aright, and bring their passions upon a *level* with the excellent rules that are . . . laid down."[24] Most of all, it manifested itself in advice to colonial America to remember its duty to England.

On this last question, Timothy Cutler had shown the way some years prior to his resignation at Yale. Wisdom, he said, would teach men the ends of government, and government was to rest upon a justice vulnerable neither to "Entreaty, nor Flattery, nor Bribery, nor Friendship, nor Terror." With justice both the origin and dignity of power, those under rule would accordingly pay reverence to personal merit, character, and divine deputation. So, too, would they cheerfully contribute to the support of a government that it escape being despised at home or insulted abroad.[25]

This highly theoretical view of the rule of men came in for continued elaboration upon all solemn occasions. At Queen Caroline's death, for instance, Roger Price proved his candidacy for S.P.G. service by reminding New Englanders about the power of princes, and the divine right of kings deserving of prayer, obedience, and trust. But this consideration for the crown came

24. Timothy Cutler, *The Firm Union of a People Represented* . . . (New London: Timothy Green, 1717), p. 2; this sermon was preached before Cutler's conversion; George Pigot, *A Vindication of the Practice of the Ancient Christian* . . . (Boston: T. Fleet, 1731), p. 16; in arguing with Marblehead dissenters, Pigot led off with a technical broadside aimed at his adversaries' alleged ignorance of syntax; Timothy Cutler, *The Depth of Divine Thoughts* . . . (New London: Timothy Green, 1720), p. 13; Henry Caner, *Discourse Concerning the Public Worship of God* . . . (Newport: The Widow Franklin, [1748], p. 27; Arthur Browne, *Universal Love Recommended* . . . (Boston: J. and T. Leverett, 1755), p. 25.
25. Timothy Cutler, *The Firm Union* . . . (New London: Timothy Green, 1717), pp. 13, 17, 37.

unsteadily to disobedient children. As Arthur Browne explained to the doomed Penelope Kennedy just prior to her execution, not only parents but also masters or governors should see to it that families fulfill their role as nurseries of church and state by ensuring that children receive proper instruction. Later, Browne selected Proverbs 24, verse 21—"My son, fear thou the Lord and the King: *and* meddle not with them that are given to change"—as his text for deploring the '45 Scottish uprising. It is universally agreed, he insisted, that factions and divisions expose kingdoms to destruction, and that peace, safety, and security in a civil society are best secured when a right understanding exists between governor and governed. In the good old days of the Tudors, he continued, such harmony subsisted between four vital components—court, country, "our glorious Queen Elizabeth," and the people. But vice, he said, had got the upper hand and culminated in regicide, the Old Pretender's bid for the throne, the Gunpowder Plot, and now insurrection in the north. If only potential traitors could have been "expostulated with in this [Browne's] Manner," he exclaimed, the most barbarous of them would have trembled at the very prospect. But as it was, distances were prohibitive. All that remained for the Society missionary was prayer.[26]

As it turned out for S.P.G. preachers in America after Queen Anne's death, however, there were sufficient crises closer at hand to provide subjects for sermons on loyalty. French armies, French and Spanish privateers, cruel Indians, suffocating snows, iron frosts, epidemics, food scarcities, and new light enthusiasm furnished plenty of cause for self-scrutiny. Society parsons frequently drew upon such circumstances to illustrate their teachings.

James MacSparran demonstrated the evil consequences of arbitrary commanders and insolent inferiors. Men like Com-

26. Roger Price, *A Sermon Preach'd at the King's Chapel . . .* (Boston: S. Kneeland and T. Green, 1738), pp. 3, 8, 11; Arthur Browne, *The Folly and Perjury of the Rebelion in Scotland Display'd* (Boston: T. Fleet, 1746), pp. 3, 5, 7, 9, 14, 15, 16.

missary Alexander Garden at Charleston berated the impudence
of "inferiors" like George Whitefield, ill-disposed to recognize
the legality of his own suspension for disobedience. Upon a day
of general fasting, William Currie revealed to his Pennsylvania
congregation and afterward to his reading public the self-evident
truth that protection is "as truly due from the Government to the
People, as Obedience from the People to the Government," and
recommended an association of arms for mutual defense and
security. Samuel Quincy expostulated on the duty of submitting
to superiors, the reason being that without "Good Order and
Government" no society could last very long. James MacSparran,
making much the same point about Church office, once more
prefaced his theme with a denigration of parsons spreading their
self-styled talents too thinly.[27]

Even the titles of sermons indicated the disastrous results
likely to arise from lack of concerted efforts. In *Unanimity and
Public Spirit,* Thomas Barton at once deplored Braddock's defeat and extolled the virtues of patriotic dissentient preaching
about the rights of Britons and their effect upon New England's
readiness to defend itself. In *The Principal Marks of True Patriotism,* Thomas Pollen praised men eager to "fly to their country's
aid, instead of hiring to go in their room a set of vagabonds, who

27. James MacSparran, *A Sermon Preached at Naraganset* . . . (Newport:
1741), p. 13; Alexander Garden, *Take Heed How ye Hear* (Charleston: 1741),
p. 7 and *passim;* William Currie, *A Sermon Preached in Radnor Church* . . .
(Philadelphia: Benjamin Franklin and David Hall, 1748), pp. 11, 18; Samuel
Quincy, "The Duty of Giving No Offence Considered," in *Twenty Sermons*
(Boston: John Draper, 1750), Sermon No. 7, p. 108. In a passage deploring
individual advancement exclusive of system, James MacSparran wrote in part:
'tis obvious, what intollerable [*sic*] Confusion should inevitably be introduced into all *regular* Professions, should every Man, who judg'd himself
fit for an eminent Station, mount up into, and usurp it, before he was
admitted by competent lawful Authority. It's too natural for Man . . . to
think more highly of themselves [*sic*] than they ought to do. Every swag-
gering Soldier concludes he is qualified for a Commander; and every
opinionated Smatterer in Law, that he is equal to the arduous business of
the *Bench.* This Distemper is incident to men not only in *temporal* and
civil, but also in sacred and *religious* matters. . . . The Entrance into a
Dignity so great, an *Office* of Such Honour, and *Consequence* to the Souls
of Men, should be well guarded, to prevent the Prophanation of arbitrary,
promiscuous, and illimited Intrusions. See his *The Sacred Dignity of the
Christian Priesthood Vindicated* . . . (Newport: J. Franklin, 1752), pp. 3–4.

have neither property nor honor to lose, neither will nor power to fight . . . ." In *The Advantages of Unity,* Arthur Browne stressed that union and concord whereby "wise men may counsel and direct, men of learning may study, men of trade may get wealth, men of power may conquer and subdue . . . ." In *The Necessity of Reformation in order to avert Impending Judgments,* the same parson had construed the "wretched defence of Oswego" as God's punishment merited by a society whose moral character was enfeebled by luxury and, accordingly, "disqualified for laborious undertakings, or undergoing the difficulties and fatigues of war." Extreme optimism reflected in such titles as *Joyfulness and Consideration the Result of Prosperity and Adversity, The Felicity of the Times,* and *The Great Blessing of Stable Times* further drove home the point about rewards accruing from a proper regard for empire. The first of these employed George II's death as a datum line for a detailed blueprint of prosperous nationhood. The second expressed the "dependence which we ourselves, as Colonies, have on our Mother-Country," while the third proposed a combination of impartial justice, quiet and peaceable submission and obedience, allegiance to the crown, and comportment "according to your Several Stations," as the correct antidote for noxious "seeds of faction and disorder."[28]

When their focus was North America rather than empire, S.P.G. parsons still pleaded for a social unity made the more

28. Thomas Barton, *Unanimity and Public Spirit* . . . (Philadelphia: B. Franklin & D. Hall, 1755), p. xii; Thomas Pollen, *The Principal Marks of True Patriotism* . . . (Newport: J. Franklin, 1758), p. 9; Arthur Browne, *The Advantages of Unity* (Portsmouth: Daniel Fowle, [1758]), p. 11; Arthur Browne, *The Necessity of Reformation* . . . (Portsmouth: Daniel Fowle, 1757), p. 6. Author Henry Caner, concerned about colonial compliance, wrote in part:
  a nation is then said to be prosperous, when the Subjects of it are numerous and increasing, when its Limits are sufficient to contain and support them; when it has a flourishing Trade, the Ballance of which is greatly in its favour. . . . When the Subjects are quiet and peaceable, and obedient to their Rulers, content with their respective Stations, reverend to the Laws, and chearfully ready at all Times . . . to contribute to their [superiors'] Wealth, and to exert themselves . . . to defend their Happiness against all Invaders, whether they be domestic Enemies, or foreign Foes.
Joyfulness and Consideration . . . (Boston: Green & Russell, 1761), pp. 13–14. See also East Apthorp, *The Felicity of the Times* (Boston: Green & Russell, 1763), p. 4; Henry Caner, *The Great Blessing of Stable Times* (Boston: Thomas & John Fleet, 1763), pp. 7, 12, 17, 22.

necessary since people from all over the world were to populate the seaboard provinces. Brotherhood in common isolation supplies the main theme. In Newport, Rhode Island, for example, Thomas Pollen broached the subject of an America which "opens wide its arms to every nation under heaven . . . ." In Newbern, North Carolina, Michael Smith proved yet more explicit. "Nay indeed," he declared of compatriots, "two *Americans* tho' born in different Provinces, meeting in *Africa*, will think their being *American* a sufficient Reason for their uniting their Hands and Hearts." Midway, at Carlisle, Pennsylvania, Thomas Barton held forth to the detriment of Roman Catholicism, yet persuaded Provost William Smith of the College of Philadelphia to prefix a letter clarifying the relationship of a protestant priesthood with American society. "We are," urged Smith, "a People thrown together from various Quarters of the World, differing in all Things—Language, Manners and Sentiment. We are continually advancing nearer and nearer toward one another in our Frontier Settlements: and have here no *Ocean* . . . to serve between us as an impregnable Barrier.[29]

In imaginative predictions regarding the colonial future, East Apthorp emerged *victor ludorum*. His invocation for benediction embraced not only George III, the nobility, and the magistracy, but also the presidents, tutors, and students of Harvard College that they might emulate English universities "in virtue and useful knowledge." Speculating at length beyond the confines of his Cambridge, Massachusetts, parish, Apthorp indicated the extent to which the general peace of 1763 had rested upon colonial ingenuity. And what might such a colony not do to advance the well being of man kind! It would admit for ages settlers from Protestant countries of Europe. Its fertile land and just government would ensure personal enrichment and religious purity.

29. Thomas Pollen, Universal Love. *A Sermon preached in Trinity-Church, at Newport, in Rhode-Island, Before the Right Worshipful Lodge of Free and Accepted Masons* . . . (Boston: Green & Russell, 1758), p. 15; Michael Smith, *A Sermon Preached in Christ-Church, in Newbern, in N.C. . . . Before the Ancient and Honourable Society of [Free] Accepted Masons* (Newbern: James Davis, 1756), p. 12; William Smith, in Barton, *Unanimity*, p. xii.

While the "slavish African" and "effeminate Asiatic" bore tyranny's yoke, liberty and reason would make up for a hard climate. As for employment, agriculture and simple commerce would serve to "retard the corruption of manners and depravation of Religion, effects chiefly to be dreaded from an *iniquitous* and *excessive* Trade, and an inundation of wealth and luxury." Here was America, compliant asylum for the persecuted.[30]

What prompted S.P.G. men to attempt exposition beyond the ever-pressing demands of these formal sermons may never be known. Certainly, David Humphreys, for many years Society secretary, was close enough to available S.P.G. records to experience an urge to write Society history. And histories like the one he did write, and publish in 1730, were pertinent not just to the S.P.G. but likewise to such influential bodies as the Board of Trade, which drew on them to glean information useful for commercial and military strategy abroad, especially as it hinged on Indian affairs. John Wesley's Georgia *Journal* on the other hand constituted a much more intimate exercise in self-analysis. Started during his American missionary adventure, it was not available for the public until long after his return to England in 1738. James MacSparran's foreshortened survey of the colonies emerged after its author's vigorous, thirty-six year sojourn as Society parson overseas, perhaps as a substitute for an extended history which, however, never came to light. Published in Dublin in 1753, it seemed among other things to have been conceived as a deterrent to over-hasty British emigrants.

Whatever their motives for authorship, however, Humphreys, Wesley, and MacSparran attracted a great deal of attention with their respective works. The gist of what they had to say, however, could only have increased friction between England and her American colonists.

30. East Apthorp, *The Constitution of a Christian Church* (Boston: Green & Russell, 1761), pp. i, ii, iii; East Apthorp, *The Felicity of the Times* (Boston: Green & Russell, 1763), pp. 8, 9. Apthorp's statements would have satisfied British trade interests long convinced that over-developed colonial industry and commerce would adversely effect the British trade balance.

The Reverend David Humphreys' *An Historical Account . . .*, published by Joseph Downing in 1730, came as the first official S.P.G. history, examining the work of the Society from its 1701 charter to the year 1728. Humphreys entertained no doubts about his theory of history. Since the British American colonies were first settled for private gain, he argued, it was scarcely to be expected that provisions for religious or civil government would be suitable, especially since inhabitants there were of many denominations, most of them differing from the Church of England.

Fortunately, Humphreys continued, the providence of God raised up several eminent persons to rectify matters. The remainder of this superbly printed volume related how from 1701 to 1728 Anglican nominees made a massive educational onslaught upon impudent sectaries, vile ringleaders, wild Indians, subjugated Negroes, colonists lacking common humanity and decency, and those negligent of all religion—in short, those in America who did not to date subscribe to the tenets of the Church.[31]

Nevertheless, the book did serve to make clear how a philanthropic segment of British society had become increasingly involved in colonial affairs. It catalogued Sir Leolyne Jenkins' Jesus College fellowships founded in 1685 to supply naval chaplaincies or plantation missionaries. It documented Robert Boyle's establishing anti-infidel sermons by preachers willing to encourage commercial companies in their own provisions for propagating religion in foreign lands. It listed Charles II's 1679 allowance

31. David Humphreys, *An Historical Account of the Incorporated Society for the Propagation of the Gospel in Foreign Parts . . .* (London: Joseph Downing, 1730). For these and less flattering terms, see *ibid., passim.* The unpredictable style of the Humphreys work stems from the fact that his text consists largely of verbatim transcriptions of selections by many dozens of colonial correspondents. Apart from its choppy character and fanciful idea of American geography (see "A Map of New England . . . by H. Moll, Geographer, 1730," published as a folded insert, *ibid.,* center), what is truly remarkable about the account is the durability of its central contention that the S.P.G., brought tone to an otherwise barbarous land by a process of direct cultural transfer. In particular, Ernest Hawkins' *Historical Notices . . .* (London: B. Fellowes, 1845), C. F. Pascoe's *Two Hundred Years . . .* (London: S.P.G., 1901), and H. P. Thompson's *Into All Lands . . .* (London: S.P.C.K., 1951) assume the same posture for the same cause.

of a Church in dissenting Boston, William and Mary's 1691 chartering of the Williamsburg college that was to bear their names, and the expediting of episcopal commissaries, particularly James Blair and Thomas Bray, to America's mainland as principal steps leading to the eventual chartering of the S.P.G. in 1701.[32] Province by province, it assessed the population, the state of religion and education, the impact of Society preachers, teachers, and libraries, the commercial as well as the spiritual benefits of Negro and Indian instruction, and the ever-present menace of French Catholicism.

Yet, in spite of its protestation that the S.P.G. sent missionaries only upon local request, Humphreys' history left no doubt about future Society ambitions. The settling of the Church of England in the colonies, he concluded, was an excellent work scarcely requiring words to recommend it to a Christian. This goal was of particular significance, he insisted, "if it be farther considered, that numerous posterity of the present inhabitants will derive their knowledge of the true Christian Faith, from the labors of this Society; when those vast tracts in America, now waste deserts and wilderness, may, ages hereafter, become cultivated and fruitful countries, covered with cities and towns, and filled with nations of Christians."[33]

Written from the perspective of one lacking colonial experience, the Humphreys work, for all its criticism of colonists, managed to maintain theoretical aloofness. Conversely, John Wesley's *Journal from October 14, 1735, to February 1, 1737–8* recorded the miseries of a strong-minded visionary pitting his will against the vagaries of an experimental utopia, blueprinted in London, to use Daniel Boorstin's phrase.[34]

32. For some reason, Humphreys minimizes the work of Dr. Bray in drawing up the charter and pressing for its royal ratification, giving the laurels to Dr. Stanley, then archdeacon of London. See Humphreys, *Historical Account,* p. 13. Subsequent writers, including both Hawkins and Pascoe, have restored Bray to the position of chief inspirer.
33. See Chapter III, "The People in the Colonies very desirous of Ministers of the Church of England. Requests from Congregations of People in each Colony," *passim; ibid.,* p. 132.
34. Boorstin, *The Americans,* p. 80.

According to the *Journal,* John and Charles Wesley embarked at Gravesend on October 14, 1735, bound for Georgia "to save our souls." On Friday, the following February 6, 1736, "about eight in the morning," they set foot on American ground.[35] During the intervening fifteen adventurous weeks at sea, John Wesley disciplined himself to scant food, an eighteen-hour workday, the study of German in order to be of service to Moravian emigrants, and the facing with composure of giant waves constantly sweeping the decks.

Once occupied in his Georgia parish, Wesley exemplified the uncompromising Churchman determined to regularize the less-precise religious habits of a largely experimental trusteeship colony. In so doing, he took in stride the physical hardships of exposure in Georgia's woods and swamps. But the punctilio of his requirements concerning Church rubric constantly brought him into conflict with less intense Churchmen. Accordingly, parish children of parents averse to baptismal dipping remained unbaptised or received the sacrament from others. Similarly, parishioners omitting prior notification of the curate regarding their intention to take holy communion were denied a place at the Lord's table the following Sunday. On the latter count, the perfectionist Wesley incurred the grave displeasure of influential residents and at last fled the colony after less than a year and a half in the mission field.

Apart from the brevity of the interlude related in John Wesley's Journal, its most arresting feature was the counterpoint of objectivity and introspection measuring its pages. Thus, Wesley's observations on the wholesomeness of barbecued bear's meat preceded his "utter despair" of success in Frederica. So, too, did the journalist's review of his apprehension and trial for political interference counterpoise his struggle with the broader personal problem—whether God was bidding him return to England. As things transpired, Wesley was to leave Georgia, but not

35. See John Wesley, *The Journal from October 14, 1735, to February 1, 1737–8* (Grand Rapids: Zondervan Publishing House Edition, n.d.), p. 17 and *passim.*

before a most careful scrutiny of the would-be silk colony as a whole, its latitude and climate, its pine barrens, oak lands, swamps, and marshes, its towns and settlements, as well as its Indians. Yet, after his returning ship had passed the Lizard, skirted Beachy Head, and tied up at Deal, Wesley concluded that "I who went to America to convert others, was never myself converted to God."[36] As his *Journal* reminded generations of colonials to come, Wesley's Georgia was a place to put one's life in jeopardy—the end of the earth which provided sufferings calculated to reconcile a lost soul with an offended deity. Here was poor propaganda for an infant colony. Here, too, was scant advertisement for the S.P.G. that subsidized his journey but was never mentioned in the *Journal*.

Were one to justify Humphreys' historical caricatures by invoking his lack of first-hand experience in America, or attribute John Wesley's pessimistic account to unforeseen personal circumstances, one might reasonably have anticipated a more sanguine portrait of a growing, changing America at the hands of a man who grew along with S.P.G. missionary service for nearly four decades. James MacSparran, S.P.G. parson of Narragansett, was such a writer. But his *America Dissected* (1753), a metaphorically appropriate title for a work claiming to lay bare the sinew, nerve, and bone of American colonial life, had few compliments for an adopted country.

To be sure, MacSparran conceded the material benefits which, under mercantile economics, provided England with returns for investments. Georgia's projected silk economy, if not hugely productive, would at least relieve England of ne'er-do-wells. Carolina indigo and pork fell something short of excellent, but

36. *Ibid.,* p. 44. Wesley expected little justice from a jury including "one . . . Frenchman, who did not understand English, one . . . Papist, one . . . professional infidel, three Baptists, sixteen or seventeen other Dissenters; and several others who had personal quarrels against me, and had openly vowed revenge," *ibid.,* p. 56; *ibid.,* pp. 59, 61. Drawing his information second hand, Wesley held slim hope for savages lacking letters, religion, laws, civil government, or kings. His general assessment was of "gluttons, drunkards, thieves, dissemblers, liars," who were "implacable, unmerciful; murderers of fathers, murderers of mothers, murderers of their own children," *ibid.,* pp. 66, 75–76.

its rice and turpentine vied with the best. Virginia and Maryland supplied all Europe with top-grade tobacco, and the former with a governor's sincere worth £3,000 sterling. Pennsylvania exported flour, as did New Jersey and New York. Connecticut added its timber products and Rhode Island its livestock, pacers, ships, and fish, together with its ready market for English manufactured goods. New Hampshire furnished masts, yards, spars, and oars, thereby proving its crucial value to a nation seeking dominion of the seas. Massachusetts, with its Irish settlements on the French frontier, stood as barrier in time of war. Maine also received its quota of Irish settlers scattered along the French-Canadian border and promised to contain more, although not of any wealth. In fact, MacSparran insisted, it was the wealthy who suffered the greatest hardships of emigration. What was needed were those with nothing to lose, for "he that lies on the ground can fall no lower; and such are the fittest to encounter the difficulties attending new settlers."[37]

In addition to these comments, MacSparran proffered his views on where he thought the colonies stood with respect to establishment. Here, too, he looked on the bright side. Provincial law, he explained, bolstered Church of England security in such colonies as Georgia, the Carolinas, and Virginia. And under MacSparran's interpretation the Union Act of parliament established Anglicanism in all his Majesty's foreign dominions, regardless of strong feeling and behavior to the contrary in New England, and lukewarm practice elsewhere. At all events, Narragansett's S.P.G. parson acknowledged the credit side of the colonial ledger, although not without craving "a little rest in Europe,"[38] or perhaps even eventual settlement there once more.

In his assessment of mid-century American puritanism, American education, and American morals, on the other hand,

---

37. James MacSparran, "America Dissected, in Sundry Letters from a Clergyman there," in Wilkins Updike, *History of the Episcopal Church in Narragansett, Rhode Island* . . . (New York: Henry M. Onderdonk, 1847). (Originally Dublin: S. Powell, 1753), pp. 500, 520.
38. *Ibid.*, pp. 488, 514, 527, 530.

MacSparran appeared disdainful. With ill-concealed disapproval, the Narragansett Society preacher charted the course of puritanism from Elizabeth's day to his own. As to the character of Independent teachers, the dissector scarcely contained his condescension. Those who had undertaken to draw their picture, he stated, represented them as "noted for enthusiasm, and those affected inspirations, which for the most part begin in folly, and often (if not always) end in vice." Some pens, he continued, distinguished them for a grave hypocrisy, phlegmatic stiffness, and sacerdotal tyranny; and the laity, for "formality and preciseness," and for covering over ill arts and acts with a cloak of religion. Yet, he went on, such a representation was over-harsh. The introduction of Anglicanism and the intermixture with Europeans, he contended, would probably improve the complexion of New England nonconformity.[39]

Although he had taught such later eminent men as President Clap of Yale, MacSparran considered provisions for formal, higher education in America very slender indeed. What concerned him most was the proliferation of small colleges rather than the establishment of one general university as a means of advancing learning. Williamsburg, he pointed out, boasted "a small college." Philadelphia featured "a little academy" and New Jersey "a little college." New Haven sported a college with seventy or more students, a fellow or two, and President Clap. New Cambridge had "one college . . . and many petty, ill-taught grammar schools" which nonetheless were an aid to politeness over and above that of most colonial places. New York, too, was busy with a subscription in aid of "a little college." But, MacSparran believed, "the multiplication of such small seminaries" was not in the best interests of scholarship. Their endowments would be too small, he argued, and their libraries far below the acceptable standards of well-stocked European institutions.[40]

39. *Ibid.*, pp. 503, 504.
40. *Ibid.*, p. 500.

With respect to colonials as a whole, S.P.G. parson James MacSparran held no reservation whatsoever. Georgia consisted, in his opinion, of the sweepings of London's streets. South Carolina men appeared "gay and expensive" and their fellows in North Carolina rude, illiterate, irreligious and profane, immoral, and disorderly, having "degenerated into a state of ignorance and barbarism, not much superior to the native Indians." Virginians seemed a less ruthless lot whose gentry in coaches and lower people on horseback rode as much as thirty miles to church; but their dregs, and those of next-door Maryland, were so inferior as to evince MacSparran's doubts even of the efficacy of capital punishment as a counter measure. Pennsylvania, New Jersey, and New York inhabitants cut a rather better figure according to MacSparran. On the contrary, Rhode Islanders, upon MacSparran's arrival among them, made up a "field full of briars and thorns, and noxious weeds, that were all to be eradicated . . . ," rude and illiterate, lazy and greedy of gain.[41]

Significantly, Humphreys, historian-critic of the Society's early years abroad, never left England for America. John Wesley, S.P.G. missionary to Savannah, quickly returned to continue his work at home. Even MacSparran, so long absent, now and then expressed a desire for respite in Britain. Like so many of their S.P.G. contemporaries, these men were convinced of the economic and cultural domination of England over her colonies. Their respective narratives, glorifying king, Church, and empire, extended in historical form what S.P.G. sermons and abstracts

41. *Ibid.,* pp. 486, 488, 480–90. "Believe me, Sir," wrote MacSparran, "wherever distinction of persons is decried, . . . confusion will follow; for levelism is inconsistent with order, and a certain inlet to anarchy. . . ." *Ibid.,* p. 490. "As hanging seems to be the worst use men can be put to," wrote MacSparran about some settlers,
> it were to be wished, that a period were put even to the transportation of convicts from England and Ireland, to Virginia and Maryland.
> Though some of these felons do reform, yet they are so few that their malversation had a bad effect upon the morals of the lower class of inhabitants; great pity therefore, it is, that some punishment worse than death or transportation could not be contrived for those vermin; and sure, some hard drudgeries might be found out, which idleness, the inlet to their villanies, would dread more than hanging or transplantation . . . *ibid.,* p. 491. See also *ibid.,* pp. 511, 515.

were already repeating. Until Christianity and Anglicanism were synonymous in America, they warned, colonists could never be other than an inferior breed, incapable, even, of supplying Britain with the commodities which, as hub of empire, were her due. Nor did alternative forms of these lessons in print offer a much-changed posture over the nearly five decades between Queen Anne's death and French surrender in the St. Lawrence Valley.

Although the sermons, abstracts, and histories examined thus far occupied a prominent place in Britain's S.P.G. and parochial libraries, and circulated abroad as well, they by no means exhausted the publication options open to the Society in its educational task. In selecting printed works deemed productive in convincing Americans of a correct subordination to an empire order, the S.P.G. and its agents abroad also made considerable use of translations, tracts, and standard works.

First in priority were quantities of French Bibles and Prayer Books earmarked for French sympathizers in New York, New Rochelle, and the Carolinas, together with French editions of the *Annual Report* put out by the Society. Then, a 750-copy edition of the Church Liturgy in English and Low Dutch prepared by Vandereyken, reader at the Royal Dutch Chapel at St. James, and printed by Crellius in Holland, saw distribution among Low Country settlers in New York Province. Following the deliberate Society destruction of the entire edition of a Socinianized Prayer Book in 1716, Nucella and Coughlan prepared a safe replacement which did yeoman service. In addition, a 1,500-copy printing of a German Prayer Book, the work of the Prussian king's chaplain, J. J. Ceasar, and the bishop of London (at the latter's expense), provided a fixed form of worship for New York Palatines and Virginia Germans.

Eventually recognizing the Indian's reluctance to abandon his own language, the Society provided for several editions suitable for missionaries attempting to learn supposedly ungrammatical native dialects. These included Cornelius Bennet's Narragensett *Vocabulary and Nomenclature* for missionaries and schoolmasters, together with multiple editions of works for special use among the Mohawks. Prominent among the latter were T. Barclay's and W. Andrews' *Horn Book, Primer, and Prayers* (New York: 1714), and L. Clausen's *Portions of the Prayer Book with Family Prayers and several Chapters of the Old and New Testaments* (New York: W. Bradford, 1715), which thickened through four editions to a postrevolution volume of 511 pages and nineteen illustrations.[42]

With the gift of tongues a forgotten miracle of Old Testament antiquity, here at least were some provisional solutions to serious communications handicaps detrimental to the Society's ultimate charter-fulfillment—a Church ministry abroad working in the context of an established colonial social hierarchy. This last consideration, although implied in the sermons and abstracts, confronted in S.P.G. histories, and taken for granted in the translations, reached its peak of directness in the standard works which the Society recommended for colonial use and shipped whenever it could afford.

As the S.P.G. *Journals* indicate, most of the more permanently bound books selected for colonial edification were destined for parochial libraries for the use of missionaries and people of rank. Ephemeral pamphlets and tracts, on the other hand, were broadcast. The standard titles furnished raw material to be assimilated and reworked for Society missionary sermons. But the lesser pamphlets saw direct use among the minimally literate prevented from regular Church attendance and access to major reference books. As Archbishop Wake had phrased it before the Glorious Revolution, "books should be scattered abroad upon Pedlers [*sic*] Stalls, and thence come into the hands of common People, for the increasing of Knowledge

42. Pascoe, *Two Hundred Years,* pp. 800, 813.

and Piety, rather than be solemnly laid up and buried in the Libraries of the Learned."[43] What is immediately evident from the most cursory glance through the expendable printings, however, is the kind of "Knowledge and Piety" the archbishop had in mind and the S.P.G. thought was appropriate for colonial consumers.

Of paramount importance, for instance, appeared the entire question of social stratification and its implications for education and civil government. In his *The Christian Monitor* published in 1686 and regularly included in S.P.G. mid-century book lists, Archbishop Wake warned poor people against envying their betters. He also urged landlords and gentlemen to put tenant children to school, on the assumption that solid knowledge made men humble and meek, quiet, peaceable, and obedient to magistrates and ministers.[44] William Stanley proposed contentment as the cardinal virtue. As he phrased it in *The Faith and Practice of a Church of England-Man,* a 1688 publication highly regarded by the Society, "in every Government or Body of men that live together, there must needs be a great variety of Employments, some higher, some lower, some more, some less honourable, yet the meanest, if honest, are both useful for the goods of the whole, and may be lawfully managed by a Christian." As for the form of government, monarchy dependent on God's appointment, rather than on the people's choice, presented the highest mode "best fitted for preventing Factions and Divisions."[45]

Other authors emphasized different aspects of the same question. In his *A Kind Caution to Prophane Swearers* Josiah Woodward justified the law establishing a sliding scale, according to rank, of fines for profanity. In *A Dissuasive from the sin*

---

43. Archbishop Wake, *The Christian Monitor* . . . (London: Samuel Tidmarsh, 1686) [2nd. edn.], p. 4.
44. Ibid., pp. 43, 53.
45. William Stanley, *The Faith and Practice of a Church of England-Man* (London: Walter Kittilby, 1688), pp. 142, 125, 139. Note that pocket editions and large type account for high pagination.

of Drunkenness he offered as a principal argument against inebriation the contemptible behavior of men of rank in sight of servants and inferiors. Similarly, in his *A Disswasive from Gaming* he deplored the ruination of masters by indolent apprentices, and the creation of an upper class "too lazy to work, too proud to beg." In several of his other pamphlets he urged submission to commands at sea (however imperious), uncomplaining payment of customs duties, and strictest military obedience.[46]

The anonymous author of *The Husbandman's Manual* delivered much the same message, phrased in the traditional image of the apiary. They say, related the writer, that every hive is a pattern of a well-governed commonwealth and that

there is the King, the Nobles, and the Commonalty, acting all in their several Places, and the meanest doing their Duty, with as much Chearfulness as the greatest: There are no Murmurers or Complainers amongst them; no Schismaticks nor Separatists: but all unite their Powers for promoting one common Interest. And truly, this is the Way to prosper and flourish.—Would to God we Men were but as wise, either in Church or State.[47]

Quite apart from these general theories of social articulation between rigidly stratified levels of human importance, the tracts found suitable for S.P.G. distribution abroad also elaborated on

46. Woodward's tariff stood at a shilling for day laborers and common soldiers and sailors given to swearing. Every other person "under the Degree of a Gentleman" forfeited two shillings, with people thereabove fined five shillings. Josiah Woodward, *A Kind Caution to Prophane Swearers* (London: F. C. and J. Rivington, 1812 edn.), p. 10, in S.P.C.K., *Religious Tracts Dispersed by the S.P.C.K.* (London: F. C. and J. Rivington, 1815), Vol. XII; *A Dissuasive from the sin of Drunkenness* (London: F. C. and J. Rivington, 1812 edn.), p. 11, in S.P.C.K., *Religious Tracts; A Disswasive from Gaming* (London: F. C. and J. Rivington, 1811 edn.), p. 7, *ibid.;* Woodward's other pamphlets included his *The Seaman's Monitor* . . . (London: F. C. and J. Rivington, 1812 edn.), p. 43, *ibid.,* Vol. XIII; *The Soldier's Monitor* . . . (London: F. C. and J. Rivington, 1810 edn.), p. 7, *ibid.*

47. Anon., *The Husbandman's Manual* . . . (London: F. C. and J. Rivington, 1811 edn.), p. 47, *ibid.,* Vol. XI. The simile was sustained in aid of a vastly different conclusion to the 1705 publication attributed to Bernard de Mandeville and entitled *The Grumbling Hive, or Knaves Turn'd Honest.* This fable intimated that individual vice could conceivably add up to social virtue. See Paul Hazard, *The European Mind 1680–1715,* trans. J. Lewis May (New York: The World Publishing Company, 1963), pp. 290–91.

the special benefits of Anglicanism. Many showed the logical
connection between family and public worship on the one hand
and education on the other, admonishing fathers to question
their children, masters their servants, on main themes of Church
sermons, and to provide good books for Sabbath study. Some
outlined principal features of Church organization, its triad of
bishops, priests, and deacons, its subservience to the crown, and
the spiritual and political dangers of separating from it. Companion pieces stressed the fact that there were better roads to
knowledge for gentlemen Anglicans than hawking, hunting, and
drinking.[48]

Two treatises in particular went into considerable detail regarding educating children in Church affairs. In one of these,
"The Church Catechism Explained," William Beveridge provided a step-by-step procedure for ensuring knowledge of the
Church Catechism. Curates, he contended, were publicly to
examine neophytes. All "fathers, mothers, masters and dames"
were to "cause their children, servants, and apprentices" to
learn. But this would take time. Apprentices took seven years
to arrive at an understanding of the mystery of their trade—
religion would require no less. Repetition might serve to imprint
the words on their minds, but understanding would follow ability
to sound the words. And even with reading as the initial goal,
there were "several parishes in the country where there are few
or none of the parishioners that can read . . . much less that
will teach others to read. . . ." This, according to Beveridge,
would in turn require deacons to re-establish their ancient role

48. Wake, *Monitor*, p. 38; Stanley, *Faith and Practice*, pp. 5, 7, 8. Stanley
proposed religion, law, history and chronology, description and geography,
mathematics, geometry, arithmetic, astronomy, navigation, surveying, architec-
ture, fortification, military art, natural and experimental philosophy, anatomy,
"herbs" and "physick." These were in no sense adornments but rather subjects
to be put to use. Religion was, of course, prerequisite to serving God. Law
furnished a basis for jurisdictional duty. History, geography, and chronology
served to widen one's understanding of common news and of the world's relations and transactions. Mathematics and science sharpened man's reason, and
anatomy, herbs, and physick put him in a position better to help his neighbors,
his children, and his family. Stanley dismissed excuses for not learning, indicating that there were available plenty of books dealing with these subjects
in English. *Ibid.*, pp. 161–64.

of not only caring for the poor but also instructing the ignorant. As teachers they would also learn, thereby meriting promotion to the higher order. Meantime, catechetical schools were to be set up to complement the services of existing grammar and charity schools by teaching the catechism "as well as . . . any other science, art, or language . . . ."[49]

On the subject of charity schools, White Kennett also reminded young beneficiaries about the blessings and responsibilities of Anglican instruction. Fourth in importance behind reason, Christianity, and infant baptism, said the prelate, was being sent early to school. Education, he showed, in his *The Christian Scholar,* refined an otherwise wanton spirit. It prevented loitering at home, in the streets, or about marketplaces. It "taught to know the wonderful Invention of Letters; that thou canst spell Syllables, and read whole Sentences, and so canst find out the Sense of Man, and the very Will of God . . . ." It taught respect for parents. Above all, it developed obedience to teachers willing to demonstrate the good use of reason and religion, "to give the *Line upon Line,* and Precept upon Precept; to suggest, to explain, to repeat over and over; to exercise their own Patience in condescending to thy Capacity, and making Allowances for a thousand of thy Infirmities," thus not only guaranteeing knowledge but also ensuring "Modesty and Respect to their Betters"[50] on all occasions.

Thematically a far cry from Franklin's education for "any calling," and couched in a rhetoric quite out of tune with an increasingly spontaneous America, these tracts and pamphlets, so widely scattered over the fifty or so years here in question, delineated the Society's recommendations for ensuring conformity. A single work, rarely missing from S.P.G. booklists and often the Anglican's only self-owned supplement to the Bible

---

49. William Beveridge, "The Church Catechism Explained," in *The Theological Works of William Beveridge, D. D. . . .* (Oxford: John Henry Parker, 1844), Vol. VIII, pp. 8, 15, 130–34, and *passim.*

50. White Kennett, *The Christian Scholar . . .* (London: F. C. and J. Rivington, 1811 edn.), pp. 7, 29, 42, in S.P.C.K., *Religious Tracts,* Vol. VI.

and Book of Common Prayer, embodied, however, the collective mood and message of sermon and abstract, history and pamphlet. This was the ubiquitous *The Whole Duty of Man,* a basic literary target for any Anglican child who ever learned to read.

First published under Cromwell, *The Whole Duty of Man* passed through numerous editions and arrangements appropriate to the times.[51] This original Allestree catalogue of human shortcomings developed predominantly religious themes in each one of its several printings. Nonetheless, the social implications of much of its commentary upon man's frailty explains its centrality in the over-all S.P.G. cause in the American colonies as the eighteenth century wore on.

Few pages of this tome can be turned without some reference to class distinction. Worldly wealth, declared the author, adds nothing to the true worth of a man. Contentedness, he continued, makes for social stability since the ambitious man dislikes his present condition and seeks a higher one. In indicating these distinctions between men, apparel serves admirably, he went on, for since God has placed some above others, dress should hence match station.

Complementary to this basic appeal for submission to one's lot appeared a second line of argument outlining the directions in which man's duty reciprocally lay. To the supreme civil magistrate (the king), duty, obedience, and tribute are due, said Allestree, as to pastors and natural parents, irrespective of unkindness on their part. By the same token, parents must educate their children both as to their eternal well-being and to their ultimate employment. Servants, he insisted, owe masters obedience, fidelity, submission to rebuke, and diligence; masters

51. As J. Worthington pointed out in his 1744 edition, the old version was fundamentally aimed at improving morals before atheism and deism threatened the foundations of Christianity itself. See *The New and Complete Whole Duty of Man* . . . (London: for Alex[r] Hogg, [1744]), p. ii. This work was formerly attributed to Dorothy Lady Parkington or Richard Sterne, archbishop of York. See British Museum, *General Catalogue of Printed Books to 1955* (New York: Readex Microprint Corp., 1967), Vol. 7, p. 1010, Col. 162.

owe justice, admonition, good example, means of instruction, moderation in command, and encouragement in return. But, Allestree contended, the decay of Christian piety begets dissention both in families and states. Broken households are bad enough, but "the *spoils* of a broken Kingdom will afford something worth the *scrambling* for: And nothing more fit to *break it* than a pretense of Religion, which like the *stone* that smote *Nebuchadnezzar's* Image, has shivered the most goodly Monarchies."

But submission coupled with mutual responsibilities between high and low in no sense diminished the happiness of either, according to Allestree. Indeed, the condition of ruler and ruled alike had its compensations. Gentlemen of education, wealth, authority, and reputatioin need never take into their hands the spade or hammer, to work as farmers or mechanics. Alternatively, their advantages are held in stewardship for the better regulation of a less fortunate man. The latter, though, often has more real pleasures than the rich, for "his labour helps him to a more poignant, a more savory sauce than a whole College of Epicures can compound. His hunger gives a higher gust to his dry crust, than the surfeited stomach can find in the most costly, most elaborate mixtures . . . ." His many afflictions are a benefit in disguise in that they awaken repentance, sharpen guilt, incite compassion, and improve devotion. Thus, for the poor, resignation is the short way to serenity.[52]

So ran these S.P.G. lessons in print. In Britain they attracted a domestic readership eager to learn about colonial America. In America they drew the attention of nonconformist as well as Anglican. Society men in the field added occasional pieces of their own, refurbishing the old arguments, reenforcing the

52. Richard Allestree, *The Works of the Learned Author of the Whole Duty of Man* (Dublin: for P. Dugan, 1723), pp. 44, 49, 62, 85–89, 90, 98–100, 264, 317, 320; *The Art of Contentment* (Dublin: W. Helme, 1723), p. 17, in Allestree, *Whole Duty; ibid.,* pp. 32–38, 50.

principal points, updating the American issues, and expanding in essay, dialogue, discourse, or "letter" on matters which in church they might find scant time to deliver. The question remains, to what avail?

It is doubtful if, up to the S.P.G.'s activities in mid-century North America, the printing shop had ever been so important a part of missionary enterprise. From the standpoint of the Society, moreover, there was reason to be proud of the results. In a land where parsons and pedagogues needed to travel far and wide, the printed page ensured a much more extensive involvement in Church affairs of otherwise isolated people. The establishing of modest, permanent libraries made   tolerable otherwise intellectually barren mission assignments by keeping Society representatives in touch with their previous education. In church, sermons depending upon these printed works told not only of the excellence of Anglican Christianity but likewise of that well-ordered political and commercial unity founded on divine right of kings and the corresponding exploitative notion of a slave-based colonial order. In school, meantime, pupils were able to read not just about their duty before God, but also of their places in an ideal society with very rigid class boundaries.

But from the colonial, and particularly the colonial dissentient perspective, the mixture of condescension for colonial ways and of Anglican ecclesiastical imperialism gave many Americans every incentive to resist Society inroads, no matter how altruistic the motivation nor how legal the S.P.G. charter. Throughout a period when Americans applied their industry in the hopes of achieving social and material standing, S.P.G. rationalists continued to look on the Atlantic provinces as guarantors of Old World power and ease. This attitude was articulated through continuing references to colonial subservience as well as by a commonly expressed yearning on the part of British-born Society men to return to their birthplaces. During a time when American arts and crafts were assuming characteristics of their own, when

American trade and commerce was on the increase, and when American colleges and schools were capturing the imagination as well as the support of patrons on both sides of the Atlantic, S.P.G. parsons and pedagogues filled their printed pieces with comparisons between a well-ordered mother country and an indolent, presumptuous child colony. As Americans moved toward a more flexible society, its parts interacting with increasing frequency and vigor through improved transportation and such communications media as newspapers, the S.P.G. pressed its message of a predetermined scheme of things—in Church services, transatlantic political and commercial dealings, military obligations, and community intercourse.

The educational consequences of this collision course of conservative and liberating ideas boded ill for the S.P.G. Low Church Anglicans in America did not always take kindly to S.P.G. rigor regarding Church rubric, ecclesiastical law, or personal conduct. American middle class aspirations as embodied in Franklin's notion of self-education for personal advancement failed to blend with S.P.G. printed messages of a tighter subservience for social stability. Colonial enlightenment abstractions such as progress, liberty, or happiness—abstracts which aided Jefferson to devise his own subtle combination of naturally talented aristocracy and political democracy—proved antithetical to the Society's tenacity to a progressively tighter colonial rein.

This is not to say that there existed no common ground of agreement between the Society and the American established order it apparently menaced. Even *The Whole Duty of Man* with its Anglican, royalist tone took its place on New England as well as Virginia shelves, although, as Louis B. Wright pointed out, Cotton Mather used to sneer at the breadth of its title. For that matter, the same sort of patronizing attitude toward the New World characterizing S.P.G. announcements marked communications between dissenting deputies of an earlier day and their associates in America. And patriot ministers like Mayhew,

Langdon, Duché, and Zubly could speak of social stratification, although their themes had to do with the reduction of taxation and the attainment of liberty.[53]

The fact remains, however, that the principal body of S.P.G. argument emanating from British and colonial presses quite failed to reassure colonial nonconformists of Society disinterestedness in proselytizing all North America. In fact, American dissenters reacted early to Society publications and maintained a steady crosscurrent of counter arguments lest the educational welfare of their congregations should suffer contamination by inappropriate reading material.[54] To cite just two of the many efforts along these lines, Noah Hobart's 1747 *Ministers of the Gospel* linked Anglicanism with irreligion and profanity, and Jonathan Mayhew's 1750 *Discourse Concerning Unlimited Submission* warned of High Church designs and made its author a new colonial champion of religious liberty. In the meantime, Boston and New York newspapers became a battle ground for brisk exchanges over the question of the S.P.G. role in pressing for a full American episcopacy.

Thus, the bulk of the S.P.G.'s lessons in print pointed to the benefits of reducing man's every endeavor to a clearly defined human hierarchy depending for its effectiveness upon unswerving subservience of each member to his immediate superior. As the period 1714–1763 progressed, however, the colonial mood turned out to be one either ill-disposed or unequal to such precise articulation. Accordingly, the ultimate attainment of the Society's vision of an America responsible in every sense to an established British order would depend on the virtuosity with which it could educate the colonial population.

53. *The Cultural Life of the American Colonies, 1607–1763* (New York: Harper and Row, 1957, 1962), p. 137; Bernard Lord Manning, *The Protestant Dissenting Deputies,* O. Greenwood, ed. (Cambridge: Cambridge University Press, 1952), *passim; The Patriot Preachers of the American Revolution with Biographical Sketches, 1776–1783* (Printed for the Subscribers, 1860), pp. 31, 65, 77, 115.

54. For an excellent treatment of dissentient organization for disseminating printed material as antidote to S.P.G. publications, see Carl Bridenbaugh, *Mitre and Sceptre* (New York: Oxford University Press, 1962), Part One.

But, as has been shown, the lessons in print fell short of convincing large and influential bodies of colonial adults about the virtues of the well-ordered life the Society had in mind. The only S.P.G. alternative was to bring up generations of youth in the way they should go, at the hands of missionary-pedagogues. We next examine this aspect of the S.P.G. adventure in American education.

IV

CLASSROOMS FOR THE COLONIES

THE FUNCTIONAL boundaries separating S.P.G. missionary, catechist, and schoolmaster were never established with undue rigidity. But the tendency of degree-holding Society school-teachers to aspire to the minister's or catechist's post, while their less-educated counterparts contemplated year after year of marginal subsistence and classroom grind, gave rise to serious problems of quality and continuity in the S.P.G. classroom operation.

From the missionary's viewpoint, the level of importance of each teaching emissary must have appeared obvious. Considering the great amount of time and effort required of a missionary bent, for example, on the formal preparation of sermons, the delegation of catechetical instruction was essential, and its neglect by delegates was one of the most exasperating shortcomings conceivable to the S.P.G. parson. So, in the eyes of the Society at least, the catechist who frequently instructed very large numbers of Negroes, apprentices, and poor children also outranked the schoolmaster and received pay in proportion.[1] So it came about that S.P.G. schoolmasters whose predominant task was to teach children the three R's together with religious and social conformity were themselves most vulnerable to personal instability, professional frustration, and quasi-poverty.

Even making due allowances for eighteenth-century petition-writing as a fairly routine form of address, the plaints of pre-Stamp Act Society pedagogues regarding their livelihoods are arresting. Indeed, it was their common practice to base a plea for more money not so much on school services rendered as upon the charity due a hungry man. As a schoolmaster's family increased, so did his requests for further aid. Some schoolmen, like Staten Island's Nicholas Barrington, Albany's John Beasly, Chester's James Huiston, or Providence's George Taylor, wrote apologetically about their pinched circumstances and many children. But others rendered moving accounts of ill wives and hungry youngsters. Daniel Denton, schoolmaster at Oyster Bay in the 1720s explained that seven small children and a "weakly woman . . . not brought up to hard usage" made demands which £10 per year could not meet. Walter Hetherington of Trenton, New Jersey, requested a teaching post that would put him beyond the fear of destitution. George Taylor, Providence pedagogue, fretted over what might become of his wife and six small children should dissenters withdraw schoolchildren. The Reverend Thomas Morritt, sometime Charleston grammarian, asked to return to his native England for the sake of a fatigued wife, only to relent three months later "because my Wife was with Child." Most harassed of all, William Huddleston, New York Charity

1. Elias Neau claimed to have handled upward of eighty-five New York Negroes, mostly adult, between April and December, 1719. See Elias Neau, "List of Negroes Taught Since Reinstatement," *S.P.G. Letter Books,* Series A, Vol. 14, p. 141. Thomas Bradbury Chandler spoke of forty and up. See T. B. Chandler to the Secretary, Elizabeth Town, May 27, 1748, *S.P.G. Letters,* Series B, Vol. 17, No. 123. The *S.P.G. Abstracts* indicate catechists receiving from £40 to 50 sterling, the schoolmasters from £5 to 20 per annum, throughout the period 1714–1763.

School master, spent on his large family more than he earned and was detained for debt in the City Hall.[2]

Admittedly, Society pedagogues had every reason to fear for their financial future. For one thing, they constantly worked in conjunction with catechist and missionary colleagues commanding as much as five times their allowances. For another, consumer commodities were dear. The Society recorded Savannah beef at 28 shillings the barrel, pork at £2, and sugar nearly as much, prices calculated to impoverish the schoolteacher, who generally lacked the productive capacity of his missionary brother enjoying glebe land as a provision in excess of S.P.G. salary or church perquisites. Furthermore, news concerning better-paid counterparts of other places and persuasions reminded Society pedagogues of their own mean circumstances. From home base, meantime, came little comfort. In 1716 the secretary assured William Huddleston that his £15 stipend was relatively good in a province supporting thirty-three schoolmasters at about £10 each.[3]

But a decade later Timothy Cutler showed how things were done in the North. Boston, he declared, boasted a public grammar school at either end of the town, the one dividing £100 between master and usher, and the other paying the entire £100 to one man. In addition, three public writing and cyphering

2. Daniel Denton to the Secretary, n.p., February 17, 1729, *S.P.G. Letter Books*, Series A, Vol. XX, p. 384; "Petition of Walter Hetherington of Trenton in West New Jersey," August 21, 1742, *S.P.G. Letters*, Series B, Vol. XI, No. 175; George Taylor to the Secretary, Providence, May 1, 1741, *ibid.*, Series B, Vol. IX, No. 50; Thomas Morritt to the Secretary, Charles Town, April 6, 1726, *S.P.G. Letter Books*, Series A, Vol. XIX, pp. 312–14; Thomas Morritt to the Secretary, Charles Town, July 8, 1726, *ibid.*, Series A, Vol. XIX, pp. 318–24; "Mr. Huddleston's Petition to Genl Nicholson," May 11, 1714, *ibid.*, Series A, Vol. IX, pp. 212–13; Mr. Huddlestone to the Secretary, New York, November 27, 1714, *ibid.*, Series A, Vol. X, pp. 165–67. Members of the Church hierarchy were not immune to such *apologia*. Richard Watson, absentee bishop of Llandaff, justified his farming activities in the English Lake District as being the only means of ensuring "a moderate provision for eight children." R. Watson, *Anecdotes*, ii, 118, cited in Sykes, *Church and State*, p. 372.
3. "Savannah Price Current," *The Georgia Gazette*, Thursday, April 25, 1765, p. 3, in *S.P.G. Letters*, Series C, Vol. VIII, No. 52; The Secretary to Mr. Huddleston, London, April 23, 1716, *S.P.G. Letter Books*, Series A, Vol. XI, p. 367.

schools furnished three masters with £100 and a rent-free house each. Undoubtedly Mr. Edward Mills, Boston's S.P.G. teacher, compared his own £15 allowance for offering grammar, writing, arithmetic, the Church catechism, and "yᵉ Divine right of episcopal ordination and the Invalidity of that by Presbyters,"⁴ and may well have found it petty. Small wonder S.P.G. pedagogues turned their hands to other things in an attempt to provide bread.

Granted, some such auxiliary activities contributed directly to the Society's broader educational effort. Several men, like Joseph Cleator and Samuel Purdy at Rye or John Bartow and William Forster at Westchester, served respectively as clerk to the Church, town clerk, clerk of the mayor's court, and clerk of the county, each for a modest fee. But other subsidiary occupations took S.P.G. practitioners further afield. Some farmed. Others, involved in business, subcontracted some or all of their classroom responsibilities, not always with Society knowledge. At Rye, New York, Samuel Chubb claimed to have labored a dozen years for a blind Joseph Cleator who nonetheless drew his £15 Society grant. "One beats the Bush," exclaimed poetaster Chubb, "and another Catches the Hare, which to make a Rime I think Unfare." William Forster always retained a substitute when absent on business from his Westchester school. Both Samuel Purdy and Joseph Browne made yet more permanent arrangements. Purdy admitted that he "took care, when I have not attended my self [to] have at a Considerable Charge imployed Such Masters as are more capable and now keep a Young Scholler [sic] educated at New Haven, in my house, whom I maintain chiefly at my own cost that the school may be well tended . . . ." Brought up a saddler, Browne, according to reliable sources, employed Mr. Silby who on the whole

4. Timothy Cutler to the Secretary, Boston, October 10, 1727, *S.P.G. Letters*, Series B, Vol. I, No. 227; Edward Mills to the Secretary, Boston, November 1, 1721, *S.P.G. Letter Books*, Series A, Vol. XV, p. 143.

seemed to Stratford townspeople more acceptable than Purdy both for his learning and his diligence.[5]
It is probable, too, that many S.P.G. pedagogues engaged in yet more specialized adjunct activities. Besides his classroom and county clerical occupations, Westchester's William Forster is known to have practised "Surgery and other Employments," leading him at length to relinquish the school altogether. Also preoccupied, Nicholas Barrington, Richmond Town Society pedagogue and clerk of St. Andrews Church there, finally quit his £10 schoolmastership to seek his fortune in New York City by proffering the public there an ambitious private school program, while at the same time writing "for Gentlemen between Schools, Bills, Bonds, Indentures, Leases, Deeds of Sale, Wills, etc., at very reasonable Rates." In Jamaica, New York, Edmund Willett kept a small shop "chiefly tended by my Wife." Oyster Bay's Daniel Denton operated a tavern and brew house, although he branded as false the allegation that when their schoolmaster tended his barrels Oyster Bay children were left to shift for themselves. Industrious these men no doubt were. But in face of colonial necessity, many took liberties with a standing order which coupled industry with "Attendance at proper School-Hours."[6]

If simplicity of instructions alone had been the key to Society

5. "Samuel Chubb's Petition," Rye, n.d., 1733, *S.P.G. Letter Books,* Series A, Vol. XXIV, pp. 447–48; Mssrs. Vesey, Jenney, Wetmore, and Stoupe to the Secretary, Westchester, August 28, 1734, *ibid.,* Series A, Vol. XXV, p. 30; Samuel Purdy to the Secretary, Rye, December 30, 1747, *S.P.G. Letters,* Series B, Vol. XV, No. 116; Samuel Johnson to the Secretary, Stratford, December 2, 1751, *ibid.,* Series B, Vol. XIX, No. 49.
6. "Petition of Church Wardens and Vestrymen of St. Peters Church and Principal Inhabitants," Westchester, September 5, 1744, *ibid.,* Series B, Vol. XIII, No. 336; Unidentified colonial newspaper clipping enclosed in Nicholas Barrington to the Secretary, New York, December 19, 1752, *ibid.,* Series B, Vol. XX, No. 73; Edmund Willett to the Secretary, Jamaica, October 15, 1738, *ibid.,* Series B, Vol. VII, No. 121; Daniel Denton to the Secretary, Oysterbay, September 3, 1731, *S.P.G. Letter Books,* Series A, Vol. XXIII, pp. 340–41; "Instructions for Schoolmasters employed by the Society, 1706," in Pascoe, *Two Hundred Years,* p. 844.

accomplishment abroad before cessation of French hostilities, schoolmasters might have performed flawlessly. Goals were clearly stated. The objective was the instructing and disposing of children to believe and live as Christians. To this end, boys and girls should learn to read the Bible and memorize the Church catechism. At the same time they were to acquire such skills in writing, calculating, and good manners as would fit them for useful employment. Working carefully with available resources, the S.P.G. made every effort to achieve its objectives. Certain teachers embarked in Britain, eager for an adventurous assignmnt. Others, of colonial parentage, arrived in their classrooms from trade, from service at sea, or from one or another of the colonial colleges. Some had short careers; others stayed on two decades or more. Between 1714 and 1763, at least sixty-five schoolmasters and catechists plied their trades, thirty-seven of them in New York Province, eleven in New England, six in New Jersey, six in Pennsylvania, three in South Carolina, and two in Georgia.[7] To begin with, as few as a half dozen toiled along the entire seaboard. Never more than seventeen drew S.P.G. stipends at once. As a measure of missionary commitment, however, the numbers were quite impressive.

Despite their fairly wide scattering about the colonies, though, the S.P.G. schoolmen commanded more attention as individuals

---

7. *Ibid.,* pp. 844–45. Qualifications of British-born schoolmasters and catechists included bachelors' degrees from Trinity College, Dublin, education at the free school in Durham, at St. Paul's School, London, and at sundry writing schools. The best qualified colonial schoolmasters took B.A.'s at Harvard, Yale, or Philadelphia. Some authorities long continued to regard American degrees with misgivings. Philadelphia Churchmen wrote of Yale-trained William Sturgeon that "considering his youth and the stinted Education given in the American Colledges [*sic*] he discharges extremely well the Offices of his Function." See Vestry and Churchwardens, Philadelphia, April 25, 1749, *S.P.G. Letters,* Series B, Vol. XVII, No. 145. See also *supra,* p. 87, note 20. In no instance, though, do the records indicate a Bachelor of Arts making a career of schoolteaching for the S.P.G. Some worked over protracted periods as catechists, but most took holy orders and served the Society as missionaries. For further indications of career length, see John Calam, "Parsons and Pedagogues" (unpublished Ph.D. dissertation, Teachers College, Columbia University, 1969), Appendix D.

than did their schools as institutions.[8] As a result, their slim incomes together with community caution in these matters made the schoolhouse something of a rarity for the S.P.G. pedagogue and left him to get by as best he could in rented chambers or in a room of his home, should he be fortunate enough to own one. Even allowing for unreliable reporting, a glance at attendance figures renders some small impression of what it must have been like to tackle three-dozen catechumens in a stuffy upstairs compartment on a sweltering Charleston afternoon in August, or to keep going with firewood at fifty shillings a cord among two-score Stratford, Connecticut, novices huddled about an obdurate stove in a small stone house bearing the full brunt of Long Island Sound's boldest February blast.

School houses, whether just planned, partially constructed, or entirely built and in use, prompted letters of special pride and relief, indicating the sort of community cooperation in such affairs which theoretically Society-nominated masters and modest S.P.G. stipends were designed to elicit, not to underwrite *in toto*. William Morritt envisaged at Charleston an establishment "not to be parralled [*sic*] in America," and requisitioned "a School House built without yᵉ dwelling house—otherwise I shall daily run yᵉ risque of having my things broke & abused & that yᵉ boys will be crouded so much in yᵉ hot Season that yᵉ School will be insupportable." William Forster enjoyed a comfortable winter in a new Westchester edifice large enough to seat sixty scholars. Joseph Browne and Samuel Purdy told respectively of school building progress at Stratford and the finished product at Rye, as did missionary Ebenezer Punderson of the North Groton structure. Joseph Hildreth, New York schoolmaster, described the Charity School building made possible through subscriptions authorized by Governor George Clinton. It was to be, he said,

8. A large and unusual exception was the Society Charity School at New York. Carl Kaestle has noted a shift from identifying education with a master to identifying it with an institution over the pre-Revolutionary period in New York, and has shared his findings with Professor Lawrence A. Cremin's seminar.

"50 ft. front, 26 Wide, 2 stories high with a Cupola for a small bell the lower part to be for a dwelling wth Kitchen adjoining, and ye upper Story wch will be in one spacious room for the school."[9]

But misfortune plagued the best intentioned. Fire razed the New York Charity School, and some fifty pupils were forced to manage in quarters beneath Trinity Church steeple. A hurricane splintered Benjamin Dennis' combined dwelling and classroom in Goose Creek, South Carolina and it remained a wreck for want of workmen and money to repair it. Other S.P.G. pedagogues faced exceptional expenses. Andrew Wright at his own cost erected a schoolhouse in the North Division of Staten Island amid a poor neighborhood little likely to share expenses. Joseph Cleator used a small S.P.G. gratuity to purchase a little house for instructing his school children at Rye. And at Shrewsbury, New Jersey, Society schoolmaster Christopher Reynolds saw his £10 stipend quickly spent. There was in the Churchyard a schoolhouse started by inhabitants in years gone by, but never completed. Having purchased the high sheriff's £22 share in the superstructure, Reynolds set about finishing at his own expense what was to become "one of the largest School-Houses in the Province."[10] Hence, while Society pedagogues held no monopoly on working at uncomfortably close quarters with their

9. Thomas Morritt to the Secretary, "a Copy of a Letter to the Councill and the Honble. Assembly," [Charleston], October 1, 1723, *S.P.G. Letter Books,* Series A, Vol. XVII, p. 141; "Papers relating to Mr. Morritt and the School at Charleston, (Addressed to Assembly) S.C.," *ibid.,* Series A, Vol. XVII, p. 135; William Forster to the Secretary, Westchester, April 30, 1726, *ibid.,* Series A, Vol. XIX, p. 388; Joseph Browne to the Secretary, Stratford, March 28, 1734, *ibid.,* Series A, Vol. XXV, p. 142; Samuel Purdy to the Secretary, Rye, June 25, 1734, *ibid.,* Series A, Vol. XXV, p. 23; Ebenezer Punderson to the Secretary, North Groton, October 12, 1744, *S.P.G. Letters,* Series B, Vol. XIII, No. 120; Joseph Hildreth to the Secretary, New York, November 6, 1748, *S.P.G. Letters,* Series B, Vol. XVI, No. 54.

10. Joseph Hildreth to the Secretary, New York, April 6, 1750, *ibid.,* Series B, Vol. XVIII, No. 100; Benjamin Dennis to the Secretary, Boochaw near Goose Creek, South Carolina, February 9, 1713–14, *S.P.G. Letter Books,* Series A, Vol. IX, pp. 260–61; Andrew Wright to the Secretary, [Staten Island], n.d., *S.P.G. Letters,* Series B, Vol. XIII, No. 307; Joseph Cleator to the Secretary, Rye, April 29, 1718, *S.P.G. Letter Books,* Series A, Vol. XIII, p. 372; Church Wardens and Vestry Men to the Secretary, Shrewsbury, November 10, 1748, *S.P.G. Letters,* Series B, Vol. XVI, No. 84.

pupils, they shouldered a disproportionate amount of accommodation costs and fell subject as well to the vagaries of short-term leases and season-to-season changes of location.

There existed, to be sure, several reasons for the Society to refrain from buying a North American network of permanent school buildings. Some of their prospective teachers appeared only too anxious to strain S.P.G. charity to the limit. Furthermore, not only were local colonial educational needs at a given time exceptionally hard to predict, but also the question of how many pupils actually "attended" a given school caused no end of difficulty for London policymakers.

For a start, the pupil head-counting which justified a Society pedagogue's allowance assumed a variety of forms, one as complex as the other, although with progressively diminishing official community involvement. In centers like New York, almost any person of rank or importance might visit the S.P.G. school and attest to the number present. The Negro Catechetical School hosted as visitors not only Rector and Commissary Vesey of Trinity Church, but also such key figures as New York Mayor John Johnston, Governor Robert Hunter, prominent citizens like Lewis Morris, and City Recorder David Hamilton, together with an impressive list of justices of the peace and S.P.G. missionaries from the province's principal towns. Even then, reporting accurately appeared beyond the combined efforts of Elias Neau and his inspectors. "I must confess," he wrote, "that I have not been Careful Enough to Write all the Names. . . ." He might have appointed someone to determine the names of Negroes' and white apprentices' masters for proper recording, he explained,[11] but even then, approximation was the best he coud come up with.

Some adult pupils just passed through. White sailors, Negroes, and Indians arrived in port from Bermuda and elsewhere. They squeezed into Neau's upper apartment. "I am," confessed Neau,

11. "Certificate for Mr. Neau," [New York], n.d., *S.P.G. Letter Books,* Series A, Vol. XI, p. 357; "Certificate for Mr. Neau, Governour and Clergy of the Province of New York," New York, July 20, 1718, *ibid.,* Series A, Vol. XIII, p. 424; Elias Neau to the Secretary, New York, November 16, 1714, *ibid.,* Series A, Vol. X, pp. 162–64.

"busy to Catechise and after the Blessing the [sic] goe out Crowding one another I give them also Small Tracts of books & Catechism, that [they] may learn at Sea the Creed the Ten Command[ts] and the Lords Prayer." Other candidates became much more permanently involved, staying as much as a dozen years. In the long run, Neau reckoned as well as he could, collecting rough statistics whenever possible and periodically forwarding them to headquarters with the apparent blessing of his important visitors.[12]

Neu was not alone, either in the rank of his certifiers or the inexactitude of his attendance figures. John Beasley, who instructed Albany Negroes, supported an allowance claim for teaching a class of indeterminate size by securing the signatures of mayor, recorder, aldermen, and justices of that Dutch stronghold. The dynasty of William, Thomas, and Sarah Huddleston, New York Charity School teachers, merited the personal investigation for certifying purposes of a line of New York mayors extending from Caleb Heathcote, John Johnston, and Robert Walter, to Johannes Jansen, and Robert Lurting. City Mayor Holland gave similar attention to the same school under Joseph Hildreth in 1748.[13]

12. Elias Neau to the Secretary, New York, n.d., *ibid.*, Series A, Vol. X, pp. 195–96; Neau wrote
quand les Anfans Savent lire, on les met à apprehendre autre chose,—Mais Jay des Ecoliers qui viennent a mon Ecole depuis plus de douze anns; et se sont les plus vieux negres et negresses qui y viennent le plus constamment, il y 'en a plusieurs d' entreux qui ont apris a lire, par le [moien] des livres que Je leurs donne, et qui chantent les pseaumes á l'eglise comme les blans.
See Elias Neau to the Secretary, New York, May 2, 1718, *ibid.*, Series A, Vol. XIII, p. 397. Making due allowances for eighteenth-century French orthography, it is probable that Mr. Neau's letter suffered somewhat through transcription into the *Letter Book.* Neau estimated the number taught between 1704 and 1714 at 154, and added 58 more for the period 1714 to 1718. See "A List of Slaves taught by Mr. Neau Since 1704," New York, November 6, 1714, *ibid.*, Series A, Vol. X, pp. 220-23; "A list of Negroes instructed by Mr. Neau Since Nov. 1714," [New York], May 1, 1718, *ibid.*, Series A., Vol. XIII, p. 422.
13. John Beasley to the Secretary, Albany, June 15, 1734, *ibid.*, Series A, Vol. XXV, pp. 19, 20; *ibid.*, Series A, Vol. IX, pp. 179–80; Vol. XII, pp. 409–10; Vol. XIII, p. 485; Vol. XVI, p. 239; Vol. XVII, pp. 312–13; Vol. XVIII,

Somewhat earlier, however, the novelty of local governmental valuation of S.P.G. enterprises had begun to wear off. In 1732 Thomas Noxon wrote from New York that Mayor Lurting couldn't be bothered certifying the number of children taught on the S.P.G. bounty. Elsewhere, this form of schoolroom auditing generally fell to the Society missionary, backed up by various combinations of such churchwardens, vestrymen, or dependable inhabitants as could from time to time be persuaded for the purpose. The procedure was, nonetheless, still far from reliable. Daniel Denton reported thirty children busy at Oyster Bay in the winter of 1727. Some days previously, Hempstead missionary Robert Jenney wrote that whereas he found but twenty, he was assured there were usually thirty. Five years later, however, he had reason to doubt his previous endorsements. "I find from 3 Instances," he reported, "that Mr. Denton's Certificates of ye Number of his Scholars, have been Surreptitiously obtained." Evidently, neighbors signed on request any supporting statement at all out of pity for a poor teacher. Just the same, missionary certification of school attendance proved less cumbersome than documentation by public officials often unconnected with the S.P.G. excepting by Church membership. And when, in 1739, the Society formalized its system of accounting for its students by introducing the eight-question *Notitia Scholastica*, S.P.G. teachers may have counted with greater accuracy, and certainly counted more often.[14]

---

pp. 232–33; Vol. XIX, pp. 199, 206–7, 428–30; Vol. XX, p. 221; Vol. XXI, p. 358; Vol. XXII, p. 40; Vol. XXIII, pp. 343, 364; Vol. XXIV, pp. 29, 265; Joseph Hildreth to the Secretary, New York, March 26, 1748, *S.P.G. Letters,* Series B, Vol. XVI, No. 44.

14. Thomas Noxon to the Secretary, New York, February 24, 1733, *S.P.G. Letter Books,* Series A, Vol. XXIV, p. 463; Daniel Denton to the Secretary, Oysterbay, December 17, 1727, *ibid.,* Series A, Vol. XX, p. 205; Robert Jenney to the Secretary, Oysterbay, December 12, 1727, *ibid.,* Series A, Vol. XX, pp. 205–6; William Vesey and Robert Jenney to the Secretary, Hempstead, N.Y., June 12, 1732, *ibid.,* Series A, Vol. XXIV, pp. 207–10. *Notitia Scholastica* categories included daily attendance hours, numbers of students taught, number baptized into the Church of England, number of Negroes and Indians, number of children of dissenting parents, number of other schools in the vicinity, denominations of their schoolteachers, and other occupations of the school-

Precision notwithstanding, S.P.G. teachers served a body of colonial children and sometimes adults exceptionally sensitive in its attendance habits to a range of seasonal, occupational, and oppositional variables. At the commencement of the period, the Society expected and allowed for reasonable latitude regarding what constituted a schoolmaster's class. As the period wore on, though, apologies and explanations about how many boys and girls or grown men and women received instruction indicated both a growing sense of duty on the part of Society pedagogues to manage at least three dozen at a time and their corresponding expressions of failure when such numbers didn't materialize.[15]

Most obvious of all factors causing this fluctuation was the inhospitable winter chilling middle and northern colonies. In some instances, Negroes and day laborers lacking outdoor work during periodic cold snaps attended S.P.G. schoolmasters instead. Burlington's Rowland Ellis revealed in 1716 that twenty "Adult Persons, Prentices, etc." had come to his winter classes. William Forster of Westchester told of a similar-sized winter night school for young people, and his successor admitted twenty years later that a winter class of twenty-three, some grown men, made up his largest gathering for the year. But this occasional augmentation was more than counterpoised by the effect of gale, blizzard, or hard frost upon a child's ability or inclination to learn his alphabet in some drafty classroom. As George Taylor, S.P.G. schoolmaster at Providence explained things, his diminished class of eighteen pupils instructed during the sever winter of 1746–'47 was "small indeed, but owing to necessity—to wit,

---

master. For the Society, this administrative simplification greatly eased the problem of long-range planning. For the historian, the innovation has turned out to be frustrating. Before 1739, S.P.G. pedagogues wrote divergently and at length about their work and their private lives. After that date, a large proportion of their letters are terse, routine affairs, understandably numerical in their bias.

15. An examination of 172 "attendance" reports reveals a low of 3, a high of 74, and a mean of 37. As shown later, though, maximum numbers rarely attended all at the same time but received instruction sometime during the year.

the extravagant Price of Firewood (it being at 50 Shillings a Cord)."[16]

Nor was mere weather the only deterrent to prolonged, regular school attendance. For one thing, less affluent parents of either the frontier settlements or the wilderness towns saw little point in carrying instruction beyond the barest minimum. At Westchester, Society pedagogue William Forster claimed to have ruled over eighty-two pupils in a fifteen-month period. The greater part of these had, he maintained, learned all that their friends deemed necessary. As for the rest, the young men and women among them would come as they could spare the time. Such an arrangement affected Forster's statistics. "The Number of my Scholers [*sic*] at p^esent is 31," he informed London headquarters a decade later, "and the reason there are no more, is my teaching them Quick, and as they generally learn no further than the Double Rule of Three or Practice one Sett goes off, before another is grown up fit to come."[17]

For another thing, the seasonal demands of family agrarian labor added sporadic pupil attendance to an already foreshortened session of elementary formal education. In Rye, Joseph Cleator's students went farming in the summertime. In Westchester, William Forster's were "sometimes more and sometimes less as the people can spare their Children from their Country business. . . ." Rowland Ellis' Burlington children continued in number "very uncertain by reason their parents often want them for sundry occasions expecially about harvest time and seed time." Daniel Denton's Oyster Bay charges came and

16. Rowland Ellis to the Secretary, Burlington, April 19, 1716, *S.P.G. Letter Books*, Series A, Vol. XI, pp. 316–17; William Forster to the Secretary, Westchester, May 18, 1723, *ibid.*, Series A, Vol. XVII, pp. 228–29; Basil Bartow to the Secretary, Westchester, October 28, 1745, *S.P.G. Letters*, Series B, Vol. XIII, No. 337; George Taylor to the Secretary, Providence, R.I., June 2, 1747, *ibid.*, Series B, Vol. XIV, No. 65; *Notitia Scholastica*, June 3, 1747, *ibid.*, No. 66.
17. William Forster to the Secretary, West Chester, August 20, 1718, *S.P.G. Letter Books*, Series A, Vol. XIII, pp. 382–83; William Forster to the Secretary, Westchester, July 10, 1728, *ibid.*, Series A, Vol. XXI, p. 348.

went, for "the custom here is not to send them constant so that sometimes I have but few and in the last year for greatest part of the time, less than ever I had since I came to town and more unconstant for my scholars consist chiefly of the poorest peoples [*sic*] children." Joseph Browne said he taught forty-five Stratford children "when their parents Spare them from their Labour." At Providence, George Taylor "thought it not superfluous to add that as Soon as Children here are capable of Labour, they are immediately applied to it, either in Husbandry, or Some Trade." And Basil Bartow admitted that in the spring most of his older Westchester students closed their books and once more turned to the plough.[18]

Then, too, Society pedagogues found themselves by no means unique in their occupations. New York and Boston schools were plentiful. Joseph Hildreth of the former city's Charity School kept the S.P.G. apprised of the combination of city schools prevalent from 1745 to 1752. From one Latin, six English, two French, and three Dutch schools in action on the earlier date, Hildreth reported seven years later a shift to two Latin, ten English, one French, two Dutch, and one Hebrew establishments. As far as Hildreth was concerned there appeared sufficient teaching for all. Others in rural areas, though, saw the organized efforts of non-Anglican schoolteachers as a threat to their own welfare and that of the Society and of the Church as a whole. In Burlington, for instance, Rowland Ellis protested that Quaker schoolmasters prevented him from success in keeping with his own reputation as a man of learning. Less inclined still to mince words, Thomas Keeble of Oyster Bay notified the Society of six

18. Joseph Cleator to the Secretary, August 16, 1718, *ibid.*, Series A, Vol. XIII, p. 339; *ibid.*, Series A, Vol. XIV, p. 109; William Forster to the Secretary, Westchester, May 18, 1723, *ibid.*, Series A, Vol. XVII, pp. 228–29; Rowland Ellis to the Secretary, Burlington, July 12, 1726, *ibid.*, Series A, Vol. XIX, p. 397; Daniel Denton to the Secretary, Oysterbay, February 17, 1729, *ibid.*, Series A, pp. 384–86; Joseph Browne to the Secretary, Stratford, May 12, 1735, *ibid.*, Series A, Vol. XXV, p. 281; George Taylor to the Secretary, Providence, October 17, 1739, *S.P.G. Letters*, Series B, Vol. VII, No. 95; Basil Bartow to the Secretary, Westchester, October 28, 1745, *ibid.*, Series B, Vol. XIII, No. 337.

schools besides his own, one nearby, the rest at Norwich, Metinecock, Musketoe Cove, Cedar Swamp, and Jericho respectively. Those generally conducting classes were, as Keeble phrased it, necessitous traveling persons who rarely kept school above a quarter, or at most a half, year at one place. Meanwhile, in the South, Thomas Morritt complained that the slow start of his "regular school" was largely due to "a few pretending Pedagogues y^t are scattered abt the Country. . . ."[19]

What with the irregularities of pupil attendance, the fruitless appeals against supposedly unauthorized and certainly casual itinerant opposition, and the steady inroads the more reputable nonconformist teachers and schools made into their livelihoods, S.P.G. pedagogues were thus thrown upon their own devices. Survival in the widest sense was to depend on long hours, an open door, and a dependable method.

The leading category of *Notitia Scholastica* (daily attendance hours), though on first glance simple enough, elicited a variety of replies. Joseph Browne of Stratford responded with "Constant" or "Without Intermission." George Taylor in Providence merely echoed the question—daily attendance—whereas Thomas Keeble at Oyster Bay employed "every day except holidays." Some clues as to which holidays these were cropped up in Westchester. As was the case at "most places in the colony," William Forster was said to have allowed a fortnight at Christmas, a week at Easter, a week at Whitsuntide, and three days around Shrove Tuesday, as well as regular holidays. A decade afterward, Basil Bartow was following much the same routine, having forfeited the Shrove Tuesday break but indicat-

19. Joseph Hildreth to the Secretary, New York, November 21, 1745, *ibid.,* Series B, Vol. XIII, No. 221; Joseph Hildreth to the Secretary, New York, October 28, 1752, *ibid.,* Series B, Vol. XX, No. 59; Rowland Ellis to the Secretary, Burlington, April 12, 1717, *S.P.G. Letter Books,* Series A, Vol. XII, pp. 281–82; Thomas Keeble to the Secretary, Oysterbay, May 24, 1739, *S.P.G. Letters,* Series B, Vol. VII, No. 155; Thomas Morritt to the Secretary, [Charleston], December 11, 1723, *S.P.G. Letter Books,* Series A, Vol. XVII, pp. 115, 116.

ing a free Saturday afternoon for his two-dozen boys and girls.[20] For the most part, though, query number one, *Notitia Scholastica,* drew a more direct reply. A great number of Society schoolmasters expressed the day's labors in terms of regular time put in, the usual formula being five hours in winter, six in summer, and the most frequent guarantee "at least 6 hours." Some, on the other hand, claimed more than that. Christopher Reynolds' Shrewsbury pupils applied themselves, so their master said, from eight in the morning until five in the afternoon. And North Groton's demanding Samuel Hutchinson considered a winter's day from nine to four cause for apology, spring classes extending from eight to four quite normal, and an autumn session running from seven in the morning to five in the evening nothing extraordinary. As well as this, several S.P.G. schoolmen found it necessary to teach Negro and Indian slaves from sunset to nine during the winter,[21] a period of time varying from about a two and a quarter hour minimum to a four-and-one-half-hour maximum certain to tax Society men's energies.

Owing to the way *Notitia Scholastica* statistics were requested,

20. See Joseph Browne's letters, *S.P.G. Letters,* Series B, Vol. XI, No. 41; Vol. XV, No. 67; Vol. XVI, No. 20; Vol. XVII, No. 52; Vol. XVIII, No. 63; Vol. XIX, No. 49. See also George Taylor to the Secretary, Providence, May 1, 1741, *ibid.,* Series B, Vol. IX, No. 50; Providence, October 6, 1759, *ibid.,* Series C, Vol. IX, No. 39; Thomas Keeble to the Secretary, Oysterbay, March 26, 1742, *ibid.,* Series B, Vol. X, Nos. 105, 106; "A Deposition of Theodosius Bartow and John Bartow re. Mr. Wm. Forster," Westchester, January 30, 1735, *S.P.G. Letter Books,* Series A, Vol. XXVI, p. 58; Basil Bartow to the Secretary, Westchester, October 28, 1745, *S.P.G. Letters,* Series B, Vol. XIII, No. 337.

21. Typical of the described hourly routines are the reports of Basil Bartow, Flint Dwight, William Forster, and Samuel Purdy. See, for instance, *ibid.,* Series B, Vol. XIII, No. 337a; Vol. XVII, Nos. 109, 110; Vol. XVIII, No. 120; Vol. XX, Nos. 62, 63; Vol. VII, No. 151; Vol. VII (II), Nos. 157–59; Vol. VII, No. 149; Vol. IX, No. 76; Vol. XIII, No. 268; Vol. XIV, No. 115; Vol. XV, No. 116; Vol. XVI, No. 69 respectively. For other details, see Christopher Reynolds to the Secretary, Shrewsbury, October 15, 1748, *ibid.,* Series B, Vol. XVI, No. 84; Shrewsbury, October 8, 1750, *ibid.,* Series B, Vol. XX, No. 103; Samuel Hutchinson to the Secretary, North Groton, April 20, 1747, *ibid.,* Series B, Vol. XV, No. 49; [North Groton], April 1, 1758, *ibid.,* Series B, Vol. XXII, No. 166; Samuel Hutchinson to the Secretary, Groton, October 1, 1757, *ibid.,* Series B, Vol. XXII, No. 165; Groton, September 29, 1759, *ibid.,* Series B, Vol. XXII, No. 168; Edward Davies to the Secretary, Southton, N.Y., November 12, 1734, *S.P.G. Letter Books,* Series A, Vol. XXV, p. 41.

later reporters made few attempts to justify the long hours they said they spent in the classroom by explaining what they actually did to earn their S.P.G. allowances. But earlier pedagogues, as anxious to earn more as not to be called lazy, proved much more informative. Getting under way at eight, William Huddleston taught his New York charity scholars to spell, read, and write until eleven. Then, on the prompting of Trinity bell, he led his pupils to prayers "to the great growth and Encouragement of that Infant Church." At one o'clock in the afternoon through to five in the evening, he repeated his lessons in spelling, reading, and writing, and added exercises in cyphering. Then he read the psalm for the day, those who could follow making the responses, and all joining at length in "a Staff or two of the psalms we have read: And soe concludes the Day." In addition, Huddleston taught the Church catechism three times a week and on Sunday engaged in a strenuous program. This includes teaching graces and prayers by heart, attending prayers and hearing a Trinity sermon, returning to school to repeat texts and proofs, writing out as many portions of the sermon as could be recalled by those who knew how to write, answering from Lewis' *Explanation of the Catechism,* repeating the catechism, singing psalms, and offering prayers before final dismissal.[22]

While Huddleston and his pupils thus worked hard on the Hudson, Rowland Ellis and his charges did likewise on the Delaware. After prayers, each class read a chapter or two of the Old or New Testament, then turned to cyphering, writing, or reading. As at New York, Burlington's S.P.G. scholars hurried to church on the stroke of eleven, and their afternoons included reading and writing until four together with spelling and evening prayer during the last hour. On Tuesdays, Thursdays, and Saturdays, Ellis rehearsed his students in preparation for public catechizing at Sunday service in church.[23] Challenged by their

22. William Huddleston to the Secretary, New York, September 14, 1716, *ibid.,* Series A, Vol. XII, pp. 244–46.

23. Rowland Ellis to the Secretary, Burlington, October 8, 1715, *ibid.,* Series·A, Vol. XI, p. 262.

students' unpredictable attendance, Society pedagogues like Huddleston and Ellis worked them to capacity when they could.

Beyond their pursuit of thoroughly-employed, prolonged days of instruction, S.P.G. schoolmen also confronted the corresponding problem of whom to welcome to their classrooms in the first place. Society pedagogues often found themselves in an invidious position, particularly in the outlying districts. On the one hand, the S.P.G. expected them to teach at least three-dozen scholars. But on the other, they could achieve this figure only by persuading dissenters to send along son, daughter, slave, or servant. In view of S.P.G. charter provisions of a Society for Propagating the Gospel, such a necessity was normal. In actual fact, though, the more conservative S.P.G. teachers brought up on Keithian anti-Quaker invective never reconciled themselves with this otherwise logical facet of S.P.G. missionary commitment. A striking example was Rowland Ellis, who persisted throughout his reports in equating Anglicanism with Christianity while deploring the rise of New Jersey Quakerism, a term he linked with heathenism and paganism.[24]

Inevitably, the requirements of the situation dictated some form of compromise. Some Society pedagogues learned to accommodate non-Anglicans and, for the most part, upon non-Anglican conditions. In the minority were taskmasters such as Rowland Jones, who claimed to have easy liberty from Quaker parents to teach their children the Lord's Prayer, the Creed, and the Ten Commandments, and who indicated that by stopping short of the complete Church Catechism he won converts to the Anglican cause, children and parents alike. Relatively rare were men like George Taylor, who said he taught children

24. Characteristic of Ellis' view were such wordings as "Children of Christian Parents are abt 24 in Number, Quaker Six," or "Children of Christian Parents, 9, Quaker Children 15, Presbiterian [sic], 1," Rowland Ellis to the Secretary, Burlington, October 8, 1715, ibid., Series A, Vol. XI, p. 262; Burlington, April 13, 1719, ibid., Series A, Vol. XIII, p. 449.

of Providence dissenters all parts of the Church of England catechism.[25]

More often the S.P.G. pedagogue stood his ground on such decisions at the peril of a dwindling clientele. In South Carolina, to exemplify, Benjamin Dennis met the problem resolutely. Regardless of their wealth or status, he declared, Anabaptist and Presbyterian children under his care would submit to his rules of instruction, a sentiment endorsed by the Reverend Francis Le Jau, an S.P.G. missionary not given, as he put it, to observing any tenderness of conscience. But Dennis' efforts to dictate terms failed. In the meantime, others discovered the need for compromise. Certain Pennsylvania parents eager to have their children learn to read dispatched them to S.P.G. schools with the proviso that they refrain from learning the Church catechism and liturgy. In Westchester, William Forster took care to ask Quaker boys and girls "no questions that are improper for them to answer." Not so willing to bend, Samuel Purdy nearly three decades later explained diminishing classes by recounting "the attempts of some of our busy [Rye] dissenters, who don't like that their children should learn the Church Catechism." And at neighboring Westchester, Basil Bartow reported dissenter parental neglect of their children's Christian education and admitted his teaching "all parts of the Catechism excepting them [sic] relating to Baptism and the Lord's Supper."[26]

25. Rowland Jones to the Secretary, Chester [Pa.], June 17, 1730, ibid., Series A, Vol. XXIII, p. 159 ff; George Taylor to the Secretary, Providence, October 6, 1759, S.P.G. Letters, Series C, Vol. IX, No. 39.
26. Benjamin Dennis to the Secretary, Boochaw near Goose Creek, S.C., August 12, 1714, S.P.G. Letter Books, Series A, Vol. IX, p. 287; Francis Le Jau to the Secretary, S.C. Parish of St. James near Goose Creek, July 6, 1714, ibid., Series A, Vol. IX, p. 270; Richard Marsden to the Secretary, Chester, Pa., January 28, 1714/15, ibid., Series A, Vol. X, p. 143; William Forster to the Secretary, West Chester, November 3, 1717, ibid., Series A, Vol. XII, pp. 364–67; Samuel Purdy to the Secretary, Rye, December 6, 1744, S.P.G. Letters, Series B, Vol. XIII, No. 268; Cf. Basil Bartow to the Secretary, Westchester, September 29, 1746, ibid., Series B, Vol. XIV, No. 119, with Basil Bartow to the Secretary, Westchester, October 28, 1745, ibid., Series B, Vol. XIII, No. 337.

In fact, lines separating colonial conformity and nonconformity in the S.P.G. classroom were often flexible, as figures sampled from *Notitia Scholastica* show. Ultimately assured that their conscientious scruples about the Anglican order of service were not jeopardized, hundreds of dissenting parents took advantage of what S.P.G. schoolmasters otherwise had to offer. When, as was the case at Westchester between 1744 and 1752, the Society school held local monopoly on formal elementary education, children of several denominations arrived and many got free instruction. Of a total of 363 children which Basil Bartow reported over those eight years, he classified no fewer than 206 as non-Anglican. And even when they could choose, nonconformists sometimes preferred the advantages of an S.P.G. classroom. In Congregationalist Stratford between 1739 and 1751 Joseph Browne numbered some 174 non-Anglicans out of a total of 465 children, and with an Independent and a congregational school in session within a mile. Under similarly competitive conditions, Providence's George Taylor managed to attract 187 dissenters' children in a total of 387 reported between 1740 and 1761. Granted, Thomas Keeble, challenged at Oyster Bay by two to six other schools, recorded only thirteen Presbyterian pupils out of a 207 total from 1739-1744. But against this token performance, the sum of 952 dissenter pupils in a total of 2,269 reported by ten Society pedagogues between 1739 and 1761 testifies to the capacity of S.P.G. men to adapt to nonconformity, even though this signified for them an incomplete education.[27]

Yet, despite the long hours and the open doors characteristic

27. The above data are abstracted from 64 *Notitia Scholastica* received in London between 1739 and 1761 from ten schoolmasters located in Westchester, White Plains, New York City, Rye, Oysterbay, Hempstead, Stratford, North Groton, Shrewsbury, and Providence. Whereas it is not possible to determine the extent of overlap from one year's figures to the next, the relatively high fraction of non-Anglican pupils reported in the total bears out the inference of a very necessary latitude in a Society pedagogue's acceptance and instruction of children representing a variety of religious associations. The lowest proportion documented was zero dissenters in a class of 25; the highest, 35 dissenters in a class of 55.

of the S.P.G. classroom of mid-eighteenth-century continental America, a further effort—that of effective and rapid teaching— was required if young colonists of questionable attendance habits were to be fitted for trades,[28] as well as prepared for an active part in Church life and society. To this end, Society pedagogues counted on division of students into classes and logical presentation of material, coupled with heavy use of repetition and memorization.

In the first instance—division of classes—certain assumptions regarding those about to learn indicated particular groupings and procedures. For example, apart from their servile status, which tended in any case to band them together in evening classes, Negroes were variously described as incapable of pronouncing the English tongue, broken of speech, low of intellectual capacity, slow of apprehension, dull of understanding, and soon forgetting what they learned.[29] Accordingly, their instruction proceeded in the most familiar terms possible, and at a pace consistent with their sporadic attendance, their age, and the lateness of the hour at which they assembled.

But regardless of their views on race, age, or alleged lack of intelligence, S.P.G. pedagogues reasoned that to tackle one academic subject at a time was preferable to ranging over a variety of topics. Thus, in a simple school, like that of Joseph Cleator at Rye, some memorized their primers, some committed to heart the Church catechism, some read Psalter, Testament, and Bible, and some worked at arithmetic. As for writing, the Rye pedagogue acknowledged the bad example of his own script and

28. Several S.P.G. schoolmasters spoke regularly of apprentices coming for instruction at night. Most teachers, however, saw their task as that of teaching younger pupils to read prior to their being bound apprentices, and reported accordingly.

29. See Elias Neau to the Secretary, New York, October 8, 1719, *S.P.G. Letter Books*, Series A, Vol. XIII, p. 480; Edward Davies to the Secretary, Southton, N.Y., November 12, 1734, *ibid.*, Series A, Vol. XXV, p. 41; Richard Charlton to the Secretary, New York, December 15, 1739, *S.P.G. Letters*, Series B, Vol. VII(II), Nos. 103–107; William Sturgeon to the Secretary, Philadelphia, March, 26, 1752, *ibid.*, Series B, Vol. XX, No. 113; Joseph Ottolenghe to the Secretary, Georgia, September 9, 1751, *ibid.*, Series B, Vol. XIX, No. 149.

provided instead models of the best copperplate he could procure.[30]

Under more sophisticated conditions, such as those of William Forster at Westchester, the tasks appeared yet more varied and more difficult, but displayed much the same approach of facing one job at once. The parson's son, Forster revealed, was in grammar. Six others learned arithmetic, "whereof one in Practise three in Reduction one in Multiplication and the other seventeen learn to read and spell." Evidently Parson John Bartow's boy mastered his grammar, for, in six years time, when new country lads worked on "all the rules of Vulgar and Decimal Arithmetick," he was "about to learn Geometry Trigonometry Surveying and other branches of the Mathematicks."[31]

In the second instance—logical presentation—no system represented common practice better than that proposed by Rowland Jones, flamboyant teacher at Chester, Pennsylvania, and applicant (apparently unsuccessful) for the Society subsidy.[32] A wanderer, Jones had found plenty of opportunity to try out his technique. At Radnor, Pennsylvania, he had kept a classroom, but with poverty haunting some families, and with others pushing further and further into the frontier woods, he despaired of earning a decent living, and traveled to New England instead. There he soon lost interest, but upon returning to

30. Joseph Cleator to the Secretary, Rye, October 14, 1717, *S.P.G. Letter Books*, Series A, Vol. XII, p. 354. Cleator was certainly not unique in his embarrassment. From Rye, Samuel Purdy heartily wished himself better qualified in writing, but pointed out that "for those children that are anything advanced in writing, My Method is to procure copies writ by ye best Masters, & I find it answers ye end very well . . . ." See Samuel Purdy to the Secretary, Rye, August 29, 1733, *ibid.*, Series A, Vol. XXIV, p. 470. Thomas Gildersleve scrawled the information that he had forty scholars, "some readers sum Righters and sum Sy[p]herers." See Thomas Gildersleve to the Secretary, Hempstead, December 1, 1729, *S.P.G. Letters*, Series B, Vol. I, No. 47.

31. William Forster to the Secretary, West Chester, November 3, 1717, *S.P.G. Letter Books*, Series A, Vol. XII, p. 364; William Forster to the Secretary, Westchester, May 18, 1723, *ibid.*, Series A, Vol. XVII, p. 229.

32. It is interesting to note that in the general run of S.P.G. reporting, "method" was usually restricted to a list of subjects taught and hours kept. The answer to *how* teaching took place seemed crucial only at appointment time. Consequently, statements of method were mainly confined to letters of application. Doubtless applicants' "methodology" was sometimes more elegant in theory than in practice.

Pennsylvania was unable either at Chester or Newton, New Jersey, to make ends meet.

By contrast with his financial difficulties, Jones's method of instruction sounded well-articulated. "I endeavour (for beginners)," he wrote, "to get Primmers [sic] well furnished with Syllables vizt from One to 2.3.4.5.6.7. & 8. I take 'em several times over them," he went on, "till they are Perfect by way of repeating according as I find occasion, and then to some place forward according to their capacity, and I commonly every two or three leaves I [sic] make 'em repeat perhaps 2 or 3 times over, and when they get the Primer pretty well, I serve 'em so in the Psalter . . . ."

"We have," Jones continued, "some Psalters with the Proverbs in at the latter end, I give 'em that to learn, the which I take to be very agreeable, and still follows Repetition till I find they are Masters of such Places." Elaborating further, the Chester pedagogue declared "I [then] move 'em into such Places as I judge they are fit for either in the New or Old Testament, and as I find they Advance I move 'em not regarding the beginning nor Ending of the Bible, but moving of 'em where I think they may have Benefit by So making of 'em perfect in the Vowels Consonants and Dipthongs."

Jones further explained that

When they go on their Reading clean, without any Noising, Singing or Stumbling . . . then I set 'em to begin the Bible in order to go throughout. And when I begin Writers I follow 'em in the Letters till they come to cut pretty clean . . . and then to one Syllable and so to 2.3.4. and so to the longest words, and when they joyn handsomly, I give 'em some sweet pleasing Verses some perhaps on their Business some on Behaviour, some on their Duty to Parents . . . and when they come to manage double copies readily I give 'em some delightful sentences or Proverbs, or some places in the Psalms, or any part of the Bible, as they are of forwardness. . . .

Other subjects, too, came in for the same logical approach. "When I set 'em to Cyphering," Jones confided, "I keep 'em to my Old fancie of repeating and . . . go over every Rule till they are in a Case to move forward, and so on, and I find no way that goes beyond that way of Repeating both in Spelling, Reading, Writing and Cyphering . . . ." The results, claimed Jones, were highly gratifying. With a keen sense of rank, he flattered himself that "several Gentlemen Viz^t Ministers and Others has [*sic*] commended it and some Schoolmasters . . . ." To illustrate how good was his method, Jones added "one Girl exceeded all, she had great many parts in the Bible by heart and had the whole Book of St. John and hardly would miss a word . . . ."[33]

Eventually reconciled to long hours, open doors, and step-by-step instruction, S.P.G. pedagogues applied themselves to their assignments. Now and again, they sounded notes of optimism. But more often frustration furnished the principal theme of their letters.

Right from the start, Rowland Ellis, Burlington S.P.G. schoolmaster, labored under the fear of a Quaker plot. Upon arrival in 1714, Ellis had discovered another occupying his classroom. He proposed employing the alleged usurper as assistant. But he changed his mind when the latter "arrogantly withstood ye Societies Power and authority" by questioning the validity of the bishop's license, by maligning his rival, and by canvassing the neighborhood in order to find pupils for a school of his own.[34]

With fewer students than he thought he should have, Ellis drew to the secretary's attention the more serious dilemma of the Society pedagogue in the field. If, he argued, no bishop existed in the colonies to "suppress such irregularities," to whom should one turn? Certainly, Governor Robert Hunter was not likely to be much help, since he countenanced Quakerism as well as Christianity. Nor did it seem that the veteran S.P.G. minister, John Talbot, was in a position to forbid a Quaker

33. Rowland Jones to the Secretary, Chester, Pa., June 17, 1730, *ibid.*, Series A, Vol. XXIII, pp. 159–64.
34. Rowland Ellis to the Secretary, Burlington in West Jersey, May 20, 1714, *ibid.*, Series A, Vol. IX, pp. 155–58.

lacking the bishop of London's license to teach when and where he pleased. As for "obstinate" Quaker parents, Ellis considered them on the one hand as enemies to the Church, while on the other hand being obliged to receive their children and to instruct them not "as I wou'd but as near as I can without giving offence endeavouring to please everybody . . . ." Clearly, the Burlington teacher disliked his whole situation. "None knows who the shoe pinches but he that wears it—I have suffered enough already,"[35] he complained to headquarters.

Just the same, Ellis persevered. By spring of 1716, he had gathered twenty or so adult servants, apprentices, and Quakers' children "inclinable to Christianity" and had taught them the Church catechism with moderate success. But by summer his irritations regarding Quakers began to get him into serious political trouble. To the Society secretary he related his anger. West Jersey, he said, faced unparalleled calamities under the tyrannical administration of Colonel Robert Hunter. The Quaker schoolmaster took the very bread from the Society man's mouth. Men in high places preferred Quakerism to Christianity.[36]

Individually and collectively, Churchmen at first rallied to his aid. Missionary John Talbot informed the Society that Ellis was greatly discouraged by the Quaker being "set up in Opposition to his Lycence" and that subsequent complaints remained to no avail. The church wardens and vestry of Burlington's St. Mary's Church testified both to Ellis' diligence and to Quaker flouting of the bishop of London's license in a town with children sufficient for only one teacher. Their proposed solution seemed sensible enough. They requested that the Society beg George I to prevent through his instructions to the governor the corruption of youth by the allowance of Quaker schoolmasters, "espe-

35. *Ibid.*, p. 156; Rowland Ellis to the Secretary, Burlington, October 8, 1715, *ibid.*, Series A, Vol. XI, p. 264.
36. Rowland Ellis to the Secretary, Burlington, April 19, 1716, *ibid.*, Series A, Vol. XI, pp. 316–17; Rowland Ellis to the Secretary, Burlington, July 9, 1716, *ibid.*, Series A, Vol. XI, p. 323.

cially in Such Places where Persons sound in the faith and Qualified for that Employment are already Settled."[37]

Understandably reluctant to bother the king, the Society took quick action in addressing Governor Hunter, obviously anticipating that compliance exhibited by Governor Nicholson and other governors in earlier times. The Society had lately noted, said Secretary Humphreys, a letter from Mr. Ellis expressing "severall Difficulties and Obstructions" which he confronted as Society schoolmaster, "more particulary [sic] from a Quaker who teaches." The redress of Ellis' grievances, said the secretary, would be a great favor to the Society. But governors' compliance appeared no longer a matter of course. Ellis continued to speak against those he considered a threat. Quaker children, he charged, were tractable enough, but their conservative mothers and fathers "the most insensate and stupid of any." The Quaker schoolmaster continued to work to the S.P.G.'s detriment. As Society pedagogue, Ellis claimed to be met constantly with obstructions; stiff-necked nonconformists, he charged, thwarted both his welfare and that of the Church of England.[38]

Some time before, the secretary had routinely sent Ellis the usual sort of supplies—six Bibles, a dozen *Christian Monitors*, and a dozen each of Woodward's tracts on *Drunkenness, Swearing,* and *Lying*—with the Society's order to distribute them "with Great Caution" where they would do most good. But the more important problem—that of securing Hunter's intervention on behalf of Ellis' protection under his license, and preserving the S.P.G.'s good name—remained unsolved. Ellis continued to protest. The Quaker teacher, he said, continued in opposition.

37. John Talbot to the Secretary, Burlington, December 1, 1715, *ibid.*, Series A, Vol. XI, p. 329; The Church Wardens and Vestry of St. Marys [sic] Church at Burlingtoun [sic] to the Honble Society, n.d., *ibid.*, Series A, Vol. XI, pp. 336–37.
38. The Secretary to Gov. Hunter, [London], July 16, 1716, *ibid.*, Series A, Vol. XI, p. 339; Rowland Ellis to the Secretary, [Burlington], n.d., *ibid.*, Series A, Vol. XII, p. 262; Rowland Ellis to the Secretary, Burlington, April 12, 1717, *ibid.*, Series A, Vol. XII, pp. 281–82; Rowland Ellis to the Secretary, Burlington, August 29, 1717, *ibid.*, Series A, Vol. XXI, p. 379.

Attendance fell off. Under such untoward intrusion, raising a school was out of the question. England beckoned. Could not the Society find him a school in his native country near his parents and relations?[39]

The next year, however, perhaps through normal population increase in Burlington, or by dint of the instability of the teaching trade, Ellis announced a turning tide in his fortunes. Although but fifteen children attended his school, the Quaker had tired of his work, and for the moment prospects brightened. Indeed, over the years which followed, twenty-one, then twenty-five, and once even thirty-two pupils, sat at their benches under Ellis' eye, and this in face of a growing number of Quaker elementary schools, several conducted by women. Yet, rather than soften his disposition toward nonconformity, the trend in his favor only served to whet Ellis' appetite for renewed complaint. Burlington Quakers were, he alleged, of unsteady mind, and other inhabitants so poor they couldn't afford firewood for their schoolchildren in winter. Addressed to the S.P.G. secretary, such remarks would normally have reached a limited number of sympathetic ears. Unfortunately, Ellis' prior outcry that "in ye General education of his Charge [he] met with many hindrances from ye Quakers" had been printed in the S.P.G. *Abstract* appended to the bishop of Carlisle's 1719 *Annual Sermon,*[40] and widely circulated in the colonies. Burlington Quakers, among others, secured copies, and were distressed by what they read.

Naturally, Quakers who had received educational advantages from S.P.G. efforts abroad leveled their objections at the schoolmaster rather than at the Society that sent him. Far from hindering Ellis, the Society, or education, they maintained, their

39. The Secretary to Mr. Ellis, London, May 15, 1717, *ibid.*, Series A, Vol. XII, p. 425; Rowland Ellis to the Secretary, Burlington, N.J., July 10, 1718, *ibid.*, Series A, Vol. XIII, p. 378; Burlington, April 13, 1719, *ibid.*, Series A, Vol. XIII, p. 449.
40. Rowland Ellis to the Secretary, Burlington, June 23, 1720, *ibid.*, Series A, Vol. XIV, p. 118; Rowland Ellis to the Secretary, Burlington, December 1, 1721, *ibid.*, Series A, Vol. XV, p. 107; "Mr. Ellis's Certificate," Burlington, W. Jersey, October 21, 1722, *ibid.*, Series A, Vol. XVI, p. 242.

aim had been the promotion of piety and virtue in the world, their guiding principle Luke 2, verse 4—glad tidings of peace on earth and good will toward men. Ellis, on the contrary, had imposed upon the S.P.G. through his indifference to justice and his notorious falsehoods.[41]

Sensing that he was not carrying the town with him in his persistent castigation of Quakerism, the Burlington Society pedagogue attempted to smooth things over. Requested by his own Church to give an account, he proffered a formal statement. What he meant by the charge was, he said, that from the time he was sent by the Society as official schoolmaster, Quakers had been sending their children to Quaker teachers. Herein lay the hindrance. But, Ellis hastened to add, no physical interruption had taken place, apart from the request of a few Quakers who did avail themselves of his services that their youngsters might be excused from learning the Church catechism. The Burlington churchwardens, meantime, put the case more emphatically. The whole town knew, they assured the Society, that the offending paragraph in the 1719 *Abstract* was an error. "We have diligently enquired into the Same," they went on, "& find no ground for Mr. Ellis's writeing [*sic*] any thing of that nature nor do we tho' Concerned in the affairs of ye Church long before Mr. Ellis's arrival in the Country know of any hindrances the people called Quakers have given him . . . ." Missionary Talbot's signature was not on the document. For the time being, however, Ellis may have learned a little about the politics of education, for Talbot's next certificate referred to him as "circumspect";[42] and the schoolmaster's epistles thereafter became more informative regarding the classroom, less so touching the community.

Censure notwithstanding, and regardless of one Quaker

41. "Certificate of ye People Called Quakers in Burlington, N.J. dated Nov. 1, 1772," *ibid.*, Series A, Vol. XVI, pp. 244–46.
42. "Mr. Ellis's Certificate," Burlington, W. Jersey, October 21, 1722, *ibid.*, Series A, Vol. XVI, p. 242; Churchwardens to the Society, Burlington, November 1, 1722, *ibid.*, Series A, Vol. XVI, p. 211; "Certificate Pro. Ellis," Burlington, November 1, 1722, *ibid.*, Series A, Vol. XVI, p. 243; "John Talbot's Certificate Pro. Ellis," Burlington, September 14, 1723, *ibid.*, Series A, Vol. XVII, p. 236.

schoolmaster and several schoolmistresses teaching in Burlington, Rowland Ellis kept his school alive. Bearing in mind the practical bent of his neighborhood, he concentrated upon reading, writing, and arithmetic as subjects best suited to fit young boys for trades. For a time he enjoyed excellent health, and up to the end of the century's third decade reported upon his promotion of the business committed to his care, although not without remarking that the total number of children shared among five schools could handily be served by one—at most two—teachers.[43]

But a notable blank in the Society records after 1729 indicates that either an unusual quantity of Ellis' letters went suddenly astray, or (more likely) that he had good reason for his taciturnity. In any case, not until 1740 was a further communication from him received and filed by the S.P.G. Largely a "vindication of my conduct and behaviour," it abounded in pleas on behalf of a large family, denials of neglect, and charges of misrepresentation by Edward Vaughan, S.P.G. missionary in Elizabethtown, who had been requested to investigate but, according to Ellis, had rarely set foot in his school.[44]

This time the wardens and vestry of St. Ann's Church sided with the pedagogue, but to no avail. The Society hearkened to the Elizabethtown informer whose messages brimmed over with stories of scandal and of shameful neglect on Ellis' part. "I think Mr. Ellis has more Reason to blame himself than the Society," wrote the uncompromising missionary, "for the hard Fate he has mett with, as I lately wrote to him and begged of him seriously to consider whether he had not Deserved that Castigation . . . for his Notorious Neglect of Duty . . . ."[45]

43. Rowland Ellis to the Secretary, [Burlington], October 2, 1730, *ibid.*, Series A, Vol. XXIII, p. 82; Rowland Ellis to the Secretary, [Burlington], May 17, 1729, *S.P.G. Letters,* Series B, Vol. I, No. 63.
44. Rowland Ellis to the Secretary, Burlington, October 30, 1740, *ibid.*, Series B, (II), Nos. 223, 224.
45. "Petition of Wardens and Vestry of St. Ann's Church etc., freeholders & inhabitants," *ibid.*, Series B, (II), No. 221; Edward Vaughan to the Secretary, Elizabeth Town, N.J., May 29, 1739, *ibid.*, Series B, Vol. VII, No. 158.

Dismissal came, and the Burlington pedagogue faded into obscurity amid a flurry of protest about unjust accusations, enforced starvation, false statements, deprivations, wrongs, abuses, and unpaid retrospective allowances amounting to £95.[46] Even after a twenty-four-year probationary period, the S.P.G. would not offer continuing support to one deliberately stirring up animosity, whatever the legal niceties concerned. Indeed, with relationships between dissenter and conformist so numerically altered in the colonies in comparison with Britain, and with interconnections among governor, rector, schoolmaster, vestryman, town spokesman, and provincial assemblyman so unpredictable from the long range of metropolitan London, it was no easy task to discover where the path of legality lay. Under the circumstances, a cautious, if ruthless, plan of safety-first seemed the best S.P.G. policy.

The Reverend Thomas Morritt, S.P.G. schoolmaster at Charleston, South Carolina, once wrote that although poverty did not yet stand sentinel at his door, he predicted his becoming a financial prisoner sooner or later.[47] He always insisted that the influence for good of adequately supported S.P.G. pedagogues was limitless, and that without such backing, prospects for success were slight. As for the potential scope both of personal returns and institutional accomplishments, Morritt set his sights very high.

Like many of his countrymen come to propagate the gospel, the Reverend Morritt soon discovered a large discrepancy between his preconception of the places, people, and tasks ahead, and what he found upon arrival. Nothing, in fact, seemed right.

To start with, he had been obliged to lodge for seven weeks (at nine shillings per week) before the house he said was prom-

46. Rowland Ellis to the Secretary, Burlington, N.J., June 15, 1743, *ibid.*, Series B, Vol. XI, No. 173; Burlington, n.d., *ibid.*, Series B, Vol. XVI, No. 88.
47. "Thomas Morritt to the Secretary, containing a Copy of a Letter to the Councill and the Honble. Assembly," [Charleston], October 1, 1723, *S.P.G. Letter Books*, Series A, Vol. XVII, p. 114 ff.

ised was indeed provided, and to live in it an additional five weeks before it was properly fitted up. Carolina currency was depressed, too, and such commodities as schoolbooks so much dearer than in London that he was already heavily in debt. Moreover, "unauthorized" opposition sprang up on every side. One with "no Lycense either from my Lord of London or any Toleracon from his Ex^{cy} the Governor" kept as boarding pupils fifteen boys supposedly intended for the S.P.G. man. Others like him set up schools whenever they felt inclined, soon tired of their ventures, and moved on, to the detriment of progress. "These Intruders . . . ," objected Morritt, "baulk ye public School so much y^t I wish ye honble Society would be pleased to interest y^m selves & represent this grievance to ye Gov^{rs} from time to time."[48]

Morritt's resentment at such frustrations characterized his maiden year, 1723. What he confronted fell in his view so far short of expectations aroused by those "inviteing Termes in ye Lre for a Miss^y Schoolmaster," that remedy lay in being assigned a vacant parish to help support his family, or in securing leave to return to England.[49] There remained, however, a further alternative—the establishment of such a school as up to that time neither the Society nor any of its pedagogues had contemplated.

Morritt elucidated, drawing up estimates of his own requirements and the institution's needs and prospects, addressing himself simultaneously to the colonial assembly and the S.P.G., whose combined authority and resources seemed best suited to bringing about success. What Morritt had in mind was a classical Latin school, established under South Carolina's Free School Act, its main objective to produce scholars who themselves might serve eventually as schoolmasters.

48. Thomas Morritt to the Secretary, South Carolina, June 27, 1723, *ibid.*, Series A, Vol. XVII, pp. 90–92; Thomas Morritt to the Secretary, Charles City and Port, August 15, 1723, *ibid.*, Series A, Vol. XVII, pp. 104–5; Thomas Morritt to the Secretary, [Charleston], December 11, 1723, *ibid.*, Series A, Vol. XVII, p. 116.
49. Thomas Morritt to the Secretary, Charles City and Port, August 15, 1723, *ibid.*, Series A, Vol. XVII, pp. 105, 107.

In a proposal to Governor Nicholson, his council, and the assembly, Morritt outlined the methods and the subjects to be adopted. Teaching Latin was to be the central goal, and instruction would follow common practice in English grammar schools. This meant using Lilly first, then Corderius. Thereafter would follow Erasmus, Ovid, Virgil, Horace, Lucius, and Tacitus. Greek authors were to include Homer, Isocrates, Lucian, Hesiod, Euripides, and Dionysius. All the boys were to study basic chronology and geography, and works by Danet, Kennett, and Potter were to help provide acquaintance "with ye rights Customs & Ceremonies of ye Ancients." The latter pieces were to be read, along with the history of the heathen gods, "at Spare times or at home." Boarding students, meantime, would read translated ancient histories at least three evenings a week between eight and nine o'clock, and study as well the use of the globe.[50]

Here was an ambitious scheme, and the S.P.G. pedagogue, fully aware of the challenge at hand, looked for adequate pay. He stated such considerations as would satisfy both the requirements of his family and the dignity of his position. There would need to be a house, he explained, preferably in the country, so that the boys could be kept apart from city-given opportunities of absconding from school. A piece of land contingent to the house would be needed, too, in order to maintain a garden, a few cows, and some sheep and poultry. In turn, the proper care and increase of such amenities indicated slaves, whose purchase price would exceed initial profit. Morritt requisitioned three Negroes with the understanding that "provided they do not die within ye space of 3 years—I will engage to make that same good to ye province again should I either die or quit ye School." Separate from the dwelling house there would need to be a schoolhouse, fitted with forms and seats, and designed to over-

---

50. "Mr. Morits [*sic*] Proposal for keeping School in Charles Town, S.C., [Charleston], June 11, 1723, *ibid.*, Series A, Vol. XVII, p. 149.

come both breakage of personal property and overcrowding during hot summer months.[51]

To this proposal Morritt subjoined his salary expectations. He had come to South Carolina, he indicated, hoping for nothing less than the best of the ministers. But missionaries Thomas Hasel at St. Thomas, Benjamin Pownall at Christ-Church, William Guy at St. Andrews, Richard Ludlam at Goose Creek, Brian Hunt at St. John's, and Francis Varnod at St. George's each received £50 sterling and the schoolmaster but £30. Accordingly, Morritt hoped for the government's matching his Society stipend. On top of this, he felt a charge of £5.10s.0d., or £6 sterling per quarter per paying pupil, not unreasonable for instruction, accommodation, and diet, parents providing beds, linen, and "a Quarter advance that I may be enabled to go to market allway with ready money & provide myself with Necessaries Stores of Flour etc. when Ships arrive & not be obliged to run a Score." Finally, Morritt requested that such free pupils as may be accommodated under the fourteenth and fifteenth articles of the Free School Act might not be too numerous to begin with, and that as a final guarantee he be given leave to preach at appropriate times and places.[52]

To these far-reaching propositions, the South Carolina authorities reacted favorably; and although the Society granted no advance in salary, its silence regarding the dimensions of the plan likewise inferred permissiveness. In the interim, the assembly authorized a house, and with subsequent council endorsement set about procuring one. The Honorable Ralph Tyard, Chief Justice Bull, and Colonel Chicken held council with Commissary Garden, who agreed to relinquish the Charleston parsonage provided "Dr. Hutchinsons House on ye Green" could

51. "Papers Relating to Mr. Morritt and the School at Charlestown (Addressed to Assembly), S.C.," *ibid.*, Series A, Vol. XVII, pp. 133, 135.

52. *S.P.G. Abstract*, 1723, p. 58. Thirty pounds was the highest recorded S.P.G. schoolmaster's salary for the year. See also "Mr. Morits [*sic*] Proposal . . ., p. 150; "Papers . . .," pp. 131–32.

be hired at public expense as an alternative dwelling. This last arrangement was made at a fee of £100 per annum, but since Hutchinson could not move for three months Garden was allowed three month's lodging elsewhere, courtesy of the South Carolina government. The public treasury also produced £50 to put the house in order pending a more suitable meeting place, and notice was posted that a "Public School is to begin on midsummer day next" and that interested parents ought either to call on Morritt at the parsonage "near Charles City," or to refer to his proposal on record at the council office. The council, meanwhile, approved an advance of £50 for Morritt (£20 of which the governor immediately drew from his own account) and concurred with his request to act in his capacity as minister whenever the need arose. A further resolution called for commissioners named in the Free School Act to peruse that document to insure its harmony with laws since made, and recommended a salary of £100 proclamation money (about £30 sterling) for one year for the schoolmaster.[53]

After much letter-writing to headquarters during his first year, Morritt and those who knew him settled down to the more measured rhythm of semiannual reporting laid out in the S.P.G. regulations, although with a fullness typical of pedagogues' missives before the introduction of the statistically oriented *Notitia Scholastica*. Though he helped the Reverend William Guy with church duties on several occasions,[54] not all Morritt's hopes for remuneration were satisfied. But as far as the school was concerned, he rejoiced. It was, he assured the Society, in a flourishing condition. Very few, if any, exceeded it in all America. By the fall of 1724, twenty of a total of forty-five boys were in Latin. The next spring, these numbers had climbed to thirty-four

53. "House Committee Report," included in "Papers . . .," pp. 138, 139, dated May 18, 1723; "Council Reports," June 11, 1723, included in "Mr. Morits [*sic*] Proposal . . .," p. 151; Council Minute in "Papers . . ., p. 132; "Committee Resolution," *ibid.*, p. 136.
54. William Guy to the Secretary, St. Andrews, So. Carolina, January 7, 1723/4, *S.P.G. Letter Books*, Series A, Vol. XVII, pp. 118–19.

and fifty-four respectively, an assistant was fully occupied, and Morritt planned for a second one to look after mathematics, surveying, and arithmetic. The following October, Latin students were doing well. A credit to their mentor, some were reported capable of rendering a whole chapter of the English Testament into Latin in a single morning as well as translating Ovid or Erasmus into English on sight.

The name of the school meanwhile spread. Ten boys came from the surrounding country, one from Philadelphia, and one from the Bahamas. Ten others were charity boys recommended by the free school committee, and a twelve-year-old Indian boy was soon to take his place with the fifty-four other boys. To the sectaries the institution was an eyesore, Morritt declared. For the moment the only major obstacle appeared to be the discrepancy between the classical program the Society pedagogue had mapped out, and the scarcity of books to execute it. What a misfortune, wrote Morritt, that no library met the need. All he had were six "Classic Authors & those very Sorry editions."[55]

Innocent though the book shortage appeared, it nonetheless proved symptomatic of the fragility of the school raised so hopefully by the Carolina authorities on the one hand and the S.P.G. and its teacher on the other. Over the winter of 1725-26, Morritt had time to observe the effect of the project upon his domestic life, and in particular on his wife, who fed and quartered several dozen boys. A maid, brought from England, had married and departed. A Negro woman died, and six other slaves remaining had to be purchased with personal, not public, funds. Summer heat, foraging trips into town (on foot for want of a horse), and a late pregnancy sapped Mrs. Morritt's strength. Violent diarrhea wracked Morritt for weeks on end. Then, the following summer, a political debacle overwhelmed Morritt.

55. William Morritt to the Secretary, Charles Town, October 22, 1724, *ibid.*, Series A, Vol. XVIII, pp. 92–94; Charles Town, March 22, 1724/5, *ibid.*, Series A, Vol. XIX, pp. 61–62; Charles Town, October 27, 1725, *ibid.*, Series A, Vol. XIX, pp. 78–79.

Thereafter, the country life, riding, and a course of bitters were of no avail to health or status.[56]

Two major crises erupted. The first stemmed from the school's location. Ever anxious to secure a separate schoolhouse, Morritt had prevailed with the assembly to construct a building, and foundations were already built about a mile from Charleston center, just beyond the town boundary. But new city assembly-men soon called for a review of the question, arguing that to provide optimum service the school should be at the center rather than on the periphery of the South Carolina town. Two telling maneuvers lent cogency to their case. The first was the withdrawal of children, or their enrollment as day students on the pretext that the schoolmaster's house where they would otherwise sleep was unsafe. The second was the outright threat to vote for cessation of assembly subsidies in the event that Morritt's school continued to operate without the city limits.[57]

The second emergency much more closely concerned the Society itself because it involved the uncertain division of author-ity between the Carolina government and Commissary Garden, whose house Morritt had inherited but whose friendship he had not managed to cultivate. Their clash now had to do with Morritt's ministerial function in the province. According to previous arrangement with the government, Morritt had supplied Christ Church parish as Sunday minister. This had, he admitted, required his absence from Charleston now and then, but the river crossing was easy, and the extra salary a welcome relief. But Garden objected to the lost assistance at his own Charleston church that Mr. Morritt's Sabbath displacement occasioned. As he saw it, the pedagogue's gratuitous help at home held prece-dence over his paid labors on the opposite bank, and he backed up his opinions by confronting the assembly treasurer on the matter and successfully stopping payment of the government

56. William Morritt to the Secretary, Charles Town, April 6, 1726, *ibid.*, Series A, Vol. XIX, pp. 312–14; Charles Town, July 8, 1726, *ibid.*, Series A, Vol. XIX, p. 318; Charles Town, July 6, 1727, *ibid.*, Series A, Vol. XX, p. 93.
57. William Morritt to the Secretary, Charles Town, July 8, 1726, *ibid.*, Series A, Vol. XIX, pp. 319, 323.

allowance under the Free School Act, although not without inviting the assembly president's charge of meddling.[58]

The Charleston schoolmaster described in detail the demoralizing consequences of these and other contretemps. Every step he took, said Morritt, was watched and blocked. Such ill treatment caused "every impertinent Boy to think himself my Equal wch encourag'd my late Usher to fly in my Face for the People have no better notion of a Schoolm^{tr} than a Cobbler in this place . . . ." The commissary pressed him without respite to undertake the Charleston lectureship "wch in plain terms is to be his Curate, his Underlin [sic] and do on all occasions the Drudgery of the Parish y^t he may live at Ease." Children wearied of trying to learn under such circumstances, as did their parents of the expense. Debts amounting to over £1,000 Carolina currency remained his due. Mrs. Morritt's health declined. Despair stalked her spouse. Six weeks' recovery in the Bahamas were indicated, but penury kept Morritt confined, the financial prisoner he had once feared to become.

Discouraged, the S.P.G. pedagogue forgot his dream of a transplanted English grammar school and once more urged the Society either to recall him or assign him a Carolina parish. At the same time, he provided the school commissioners with early notice of his resignation so they might solicit the S.P.G. for a replacement. In 1728, after five eventful school years, Morritt achieved his quieter missionary post at Prince George's Wynaw (now Georgetown), not without immediately implying, however, that his Charleston school replacement, Mr. Lambert, was charging boarders more than was called for.[59]

Born in Connecticut in 1717, graduated Master of Arts from Yale College, and ordained Anglican minister at age thirty, ex-dissenter Jeremiah Leaming returned in 1748 via New York to

---

58. *Ibid.*, pp. 320–21.
59. *Ibid.*, pp. 322–24; William Morritt to the Secretary, Charles Town, April 6, 1726, *ibid.*, Series A, Vol. XXI, p. 314; William Morritt to the Secretary, South Carolina, April 8, 1728, *ibid.*, Series A, Vol. XXI, pp. 91–93.

take up his multiple post of assistant to Newport missionary James Honyman, catechist, and schoolmaster, under S.P.G. encouragement. Before Christmas that year, he was having second thoughts about what he had undertaken. "My duty here," he wrote, "is very hard, for I am obliged to preach two sermons a Week, for the Most Part of ye Time. And School to tend of Seventy and two, in Number, forty-four Latin, twenty-eight Readers, fifty and two of the Church, Nine Dissenters, Six Quakers, five Baptists, so you may see how much I have to do."[60]

For his part, the aging Honyman was relieved to get such a versatile helper, and a year before he died he informed the Society that Leaming was the very man he needed. But after his superior's death, the S.P.G. stopgap, Mr. Leaming, undertook the entire responsibility for all Church affairs in the Rhode Island community of over six thousand.[61]

Once more he begged the Society to consider his condition. It was bad enough, he argued, to preach two sermons every Sunday and an additional one for each fast and festival in the Church rubric, to read prayers constantly, to plan special services for the holy seasons, and to perform baptism. Worse, because his S.P.G. salary of £10 per annum for all Honyman's work as well as his own was insufficient, he faced a financial crisis, the solution to which disturbed him. "I am," as he put it, *"actually forced to keep school* [italics mine] for my daily Support," an obligation he hoped to renounce by suggesting he succeed the Reverend Honyman and be paid accordingly.[62]

---

60. Pascoe, *Two Hundred Years*, p. 853; James Honyman to the Secretary, Newport, R.I., October 19, 1748, *S.P.G. Letters*, Series B, Vol. XVI, No. 26; Jeremiah Leaming to the Secretary, [Newport], December 19, 1748, *ibid.*, Series B, Vol. XVI, No. 32.
61. James Honyman to the Secretary, Newport, R.I., October 13, 1749, *ibid.*, Series B, Vol. XVII, No. 70; Leaming gave 6,436 as Newport's 1748 population figure, see *ibid.*, No. 32.
62. Honyman had received £70 sterling, one of the S.P.G.'s highest stipends. See *S.P.G. Abstract*, 1748, p. 34. See, too, Jeremiah Leaming to the Secretary, Newport, R.I., December 26, 1749, *S.P.G. Letters*, Series B, Vol. XVII, No. 80; Jeremiah Leaming to the Secretary, Newport, R.I., July 26, 1750, *ibid.*, Series B, Vol. XVIII, No. 68.

For the time being, however, the Society's plan did not include a status change for Mr. Leaming. Honyman was succeeded in 1752 by the Reverend Mr. Beach, who gave way to the Reverend Mr. Pollen in 1755, both at the reduced salary of £50. Until the former date, though, the Society agreed to augment Mr. Leaming's salary as catechist by £10, an arrangement it did not rescind after the alternative appointments had been made. In the interim, some New Englanders supported Leaming. Boston's S.P.G. missionary, Henry Caner, pointed out that the Society catechist had not only kept Newport's pulpit alive after Mr. Honyman's passing, but had also assumed full ministerial functions when, during the last years of his life, a total paralysis gripped the elderly parson. Under the circumstances, thought Caner, Leaming deserved every consideration. The Newport vestryman and churchwardens wholeheartedly agreed.[63]

Unanimity regarding Mr. Leaming's hard lot was not universal, however. Since his designation as catechist did not require a schoolmaster's *Notitia Scholastica,* he occasionally acknowledged daily attendance or noted that school affairs were "in as Good Circumstances as can be expected," but generally was silent on the topic. On the contrary, the Reverend James MacSparran, Society missionary at Narragansett, proved more explicit. He set a much higher value on Leaming's annual income by detailing to the secretary the private venture the Yale pedagogue had associated himself with. Locally known as Mr. Kay's School, he explained, its sponsor, Mr. Kay, gave an annual donation, including a house, located in the schoolyard for the pedagogue's convenience, and worth £58 sterling. About fifty scholars paying £16 local currency (£1.13s.4d. sterling) per

63. *S.P.G. Abstract,* 1752, p. 31; The Secretary to Jeremiah Leaming, [London], October 22, 1750, *S.P.G. Letters,* Series B, Vol. XVIII, No. 213; *S.P.G. Abstract,* 1752, p. 31; 1753, p. 29; 1755, p. 36; 1756, p. 30; 1757, p. 36; 1758, p. 30; Henry Caner to the Secretary, Boston, July 12, 1750, *S.P.G. Letters,* Series B, Vol. XVIII, No. 12; Vestrymen and Church Wardens to the Secretary, Newport, R.I., November 6, 1752, *ibid.,* Series B, Vol. XX, No. 48.

year produced an estimated additional £55.13s.4d., an amount close to twice MacSparran's own allowance. Moreover, the latter added, Newport church had paid Leaming £4 local currency per week ever since Honyman's death.[64] In Mr. MacSparran's view, then, Leaming may well have been overpaid.

With his catechist's stipend pegged at £20 by an appreciative but firm Society, his school a going concern, and his Rhode Island ministerial duties finally taken up by others, the Newport pedagogue-parson pondered the relative satisfactions of teaching and preaching, the one task remunerative but hectic, the other modestly rewarded but relatively well-furnished with opportunity for study and contemplation. How Mr. Leaming arrived at his decision is not recorded, but by 1758 he had relinquished his catechetical-pedagogical status and fulfilled his previous missionary wish, not in Newport, but in the coast community of Norwalk, Connecticut, serving the S.P.G. there first for £30, then for £50 a year. Not till twenty years later did the Revolution dislodge him from his hard-won Norwalk retreat from the classroom.[65]

George Taylor, Providence schoolmaster from 1735 to Revolutionary times, stands unique in S.P.G. history for the length of his service and the brevity of his periodic reports. Very few of these preceded the *Notitia Scholastica,* which in any case discouraged discursive accounts, and from them the Society learned only that Taylor's classroom was in session with two dozen or so children. For the secretary's information, James MacSparran of Narragansett supplied additional details. Writing from Boston, he confirmed that of twenty-three scholars, the Providence

64. Mr. Leaming to the Secretary, Newport, R.I., February 3, 1752, *ibid.,* Series B, Vol. XX, No. 49; Mr. Leaming to the Secretary, Newport, R.I., March 27, 1751, *ibid.,* Series B, Vol. XIX, No. 56; James MacSparran to the Secretary, Narragansett, November 1, 1750, *ibid.,* Series B, Vol. XVIII, Nos. 65, 66.
65. *S.P.G. Abstracts,* 1759, p. 47; 1761, p. 31; Pascoe, *Two Hundred Years,* p. 853.

teacher instructed some gratis, others partly on the Society bounty, and the remainder at their parents' expense. Together, this constituted annual returns of about £24 sterling which, added to the £10 S.P.G. stipend, represented Taylor's means of looking after his wife and five children.[66] Upon the introduction of the *Notitia Scholastica* in 1739, however, Taylor complied with answers to each of the eight standard questions, adding in his covering letters such news as his economy of expression would permit.

Taken together, Taylor's *Notitia* related the development of a school that provided along with others a dependable community service, and of a pedagogue whose contentment with his calling kept him out of major political or personal trouble. Without specifying hours or their distribution, he informed the Society of daily attendance. Over at least a twenty-year period, he reported enrollments varying from two to three dozen, with the occasional reminder that not all his boys and girls appeared at the same time. Each year, anywhere from six to sixteen children of dissenting parents occupied classroom benches and half of these were put to learning the Church catechism alongside their Church of England schoolmates. Now and again one or two Negro children arrived, but their visits invariably proved short. Competition in the vicinity varied from one to three similar schools, staffed by Quaker, Baptist, or Independent schoolteachers, and upon occasion an Anglican pedagogue kept a private school, or one "lukewarm" toward the Church attended services the better to justify his free-lance teaching. In addition, women's schools, all of dissenter persuasion, became progressively more numerous within Providence boundaries. All this meant that Taylor found little time for idleness or recreation, and despite his steady but minimal S.P.G. stipend of £10 and

66. George Taylor to the Secretary, Providence, June 19, 1736, *S.P.G. Letter Books*, Series A, Vol. XXVI, p. 240; James MacSparran to the Secretary, Boston, September 21, 1738, *S.P.G. Letters*, Series B, Vol. VII, No. 33.

his other unstable revenues, he neither accepted nor contemplated any other employment.[67]

In comparison with many of his S.P.G. counterparts about the colonies, Taylor seemed to have recognized and accepted the gulf separating that logical theory underpinning all Society endeavors in America, and the multiplicity and confusion of demands which new world localities imposed on their S.P.G. schoolmasters. But this did not mean that Taylor remained silent when irritated.

Children in Rhode Island were taken out of school, readers or not, when they were big enough to go farming, he grumbled. Winters continued severe and firewood expensive. Dissenting neighbors, unpredictable as to where they sent their children to school, kept him guessing about the immediate future. On the one hand, he claimed instruction fees 20 percent lower than school charges elsewhere in the colony, with little discrimination between young Anglicans and young dissenters since the latter's parents owned the schoolhouse and could easily meet overcharges with dispossession. But on the other hand, he protested that his net business was "very disproportionate to the Demands of my numerous Family." In fact, he said, the times were hard for a man locally held to be a nonproducer. "Our Paper Currency," he continued, "daily depreciates, the Merchant raises the Price of his Commodities, and the Farmer follows his example in the Price of the Country's Produce: and between these another set of men who have nothing to sell, are ground and crushed to pieces . . . ."[68]

---

67. For Taylor's *Notitia Scholastica,* 1739–1751, and letters submitting equivalent data, see *S.P.G. Letters,* Series B, Vol. VII, No. 96; Vol. VII(II), No. 59; Vol. IX, Nos. 50, 51; Vol. X, No. 49; Vol. XI, No. 47; Vol. XIII, No. 147; Vol. XIV, No. 66; Vol. XV, No. 30; Vol. XVII, No. 71; Vol. XVIII, Nos. 24, 25; Vol. XX, Nos. 33, 34; Series C, Vol. IX, Nos. 39, 40, 41, 42, 43, 44, and 45.

68. George Taylor to the Secretary, Providence, October 17, 1739, *S.P.G. Letters,* Series B, Vol. VII, No. 95; George Taylor to the Secretary, Providence, May 1, 1741, *ibid.,* Series B, Vol. IX, No. 50; George Taylor to the Secretary, [Providence], May 13, 1751, *ibid.,* Series B, Vol. XX, No. 34. By 1743 Taylor had six children. See also George Taylor to the Secretary, Providence, October 6, 1747, *ibid.,* Series B, Vol. XV, No. 30.

In 1714 a half dozen S.P.G. schoolmasters reported from North America, four of them from the New York area, one from Pennsylvania, and one from South Carolina. During 1763 double that number wrote to advise the Society about their New World classrooms. In the intervening half century, as few as six to as many as seventeen dispatched in a given year news of their efforts and estimates of the results. Most wrote from the middle colonies, especially New York, where the S.P.G. concentrated its major pedagogical drive.[69] Before 1739 many fell into the expansive mood of the eighteenth-century correspondent completing page after page on the assumption that life was full and ships infrequent. After 1739 the necessary *Notitia Scholastica* furnished the secretary with hard figures, most useful to London policymakers, although they also enabled schoolmasters to remain silent on vital matters. But before or after *Notitia,* schoolmasters found it difficult to conceal very much from London. So vulnerable were they to public—especially dissentient—scrutiny, so important a component in the total Anglican missionary crusade, and of such special necessity to Society parsons, that whatever they neglected to mention would be filled in very rapidly by someone else. This was invariably the case whenever professional or personal shortcomings were involved, and they often were.

In far the majority of instances where parsons wrote beyond the mere signing of *Notitia Scholastica,* the message was one of dissatisfaction with pedagogues of their acquaintance. Christopher Bridge, missionary at Rye, constantly complained that veteran teacher Joseph Cleator was remiss in preparing the schoolchildren for public catechism, not only in his own erratic attendance in the classroom but likewise in the multitude of arguments he thought up for excusing his students from appearing at church—excuses, as Bridge termed them "that are Common among people of mean and low Circumstances." Gideon Johnston scored the "Incendiary and Firebrand" pedagogue

---

69. See Calam, "Parsons & Pedagogues," Appendixes C and D.

John Whitehead, who allegedly earned more money than his commissary for doing nothing at all. The South Carolina clergy jointly addressed the secretary with the information that William Morritt had finished with schoolteaching once and for all. An aspiring schoolmaster, Mr. Clowes, informed S.P.G. missionary Robert Jenny of the incapacity and negligence of Thomas Gildersleve, an S.P.G. pedagogue at Hempstead who by dint of winter inactivity had earned the local title of "ye Summer School Master." In turn, Jenney had notified the Society of schoolmaster Daniel Denton's neglect of the Oyster Bay classroom, for which truancy he still drew £10 sterling. The following year, Jenny joined Trinity Rector Vesey in a lengthy indictment of Denton, pointing out that his attendance figures were false, his certifying signatures surreptitiously obtained, and that he lived five miles from town, kept a tavern and brewery, set copy when he should be teaching, and was universally disliked, ill-mannered, and of a threatening disposition. Thomas Standard, sometime missionary at East Chester, censured Westchester's schoolman, William Forster, on two main counts. For one thing, his business abroad had kept him away from school for fourteen full months, although not from his £20 allowance. For another, he allegedly was "an Immorall man and an habitual Curser and Swearer, and frequently getts Drunk, and particularly last week was for days together guilty of Excessive drinking with one Underhill who openly Confessed it, he appears to be in the Interests of the Pretender." Edward Vaughan reported the shameful neglect of Rowland Ellis and welcomed his dismissal. Samuel Seabury supplied the news that £10 per annum S.P.G. pedagogue Thomas Temple of Hempstead had kept no school whatever for four years. And missionaries John Ross and William Smith independently declared unfit William Sturgeon, Philadelphia catechist drawing £50 from the Society but rendering no service in return.[70]

70. Christopher Bridge to the Secretary, Rye, November 14, 1717, *S.P.G. Letter Books,* Series A, Vol. XII, pp. 345–46. Joseph Cleator had often tried to explain that many poorer children owned no clothes suitable to wear at

Although reported pedagogical shortcomings such as these were more spectacular than average, and not a little colored by the inevitable jealousies common among men unused to the blurring of hierarchical boundaries, they nevertheless were representative of the serious problems facing the Society's attempt to establish the missionary pedagogue as the missionary parson's permanent right-hand man. Needless to say, everyone recognized the value of a well-qualified schoolmaster. Even George Berkeley found time among his papers in the Whitehall study to acquaint the S.P.G. of his high opinion of Thomas Scott, Newport grammarian, "a man of good Moralls, and a diligent Schoolmaster" who deserved Society encouragement. But as increasing demands were made upon limited Society resources,[71] S.P.G. men abroad both questioned the wisdom of subsidizing teachers and speculated upon the causes that produced less than satisfactory classroom results.

In the case of New England, the question of rival dissenter education was obvious enough. As early as 1727 Timothy Cutler described Boston's schools which were entirely at the disposal of the inhabitants who chose carefully and paid well the required schoolmasters. Shortly after Cutler's summary, Samuel Grainger, for a short time a Society teacher in Boston, sketched the school

---

regular Church services. Gideon Johnston to the Secretary, Charles Town, April 4, 1716, *ibid.*, Series A, Vol. XI, pp. 118–20. Whitehead shortly afterward witnessed Johnston's drowning and thereafter never recovered physical or mental health. He was dismissed from S.P.G. service only shortly before his death. Clergy of S.C. to the Secretary, [Charleston], January 2, 1727/8, *ibid.*, Series A, Vol XX, p. 106; Mr. Clowes to Mr. Jenney, Hempstead, March 30, 1728, *ibid.*, Series A, Vol. XXI, pp. 323–26; Robert Jenney to the Secretary, Hempstead, July 10, 1731, *ibid.*, Series A, Vol. XXIII, pp. 334–35; Mr. Vesey and Mr. Jenney to the Secretary, Hempstead, N.Y., June 12, 1732, *ibid.*, Series A, Vol. XXIV, pp. 207–10; Thomas Standard to the Secretary, East Chester, November 4, 1733, *ibid.*, Series A, Vol. XXIV, pp. 480–81; Edward Vaughan to the Secretary, Elizabeth Town, N.J., May 29, 1739, *S.P.G. Letters,* Series B, Vol. VII, No. 158; Samuel Seabury to the Secretary, Hempstead, October 13, 1752, *ibid.*, Series B, Vol. XX, No. 66; John Ross to the Secretary, Philadelphia, July 2, 1762, *ibid.*, Series B, Vol. XXI, No. 219; William Smith to the Secretary, Philadelphia, September 22, 1766, *ibid.*, Series B, Vol. XXI, No. 254.

71. Mr. Dean Berkeley to the Secretary [Newport], February 10, 1732, *S.P.G. Letter Books,* Series A, Vol. XXIV, p. 92; Pascoe, *Two Hundred Years,* p. 830.

picture. In the town of between 25 and 30 thousand inhabitants, there were two

Publick Grammar and 3 public Writing Schools, in which all per- swasions are priviledged with the benefit of Education of Inhabit- ants; and there are severall private Schools, but in none of them is the Church Catechism either taught or used, the Masters of them all being either of the Congregational or Baptist perswasion, and as to the other Towns in this Province wherever they consist of 100 Familey's [sic] every Town is Oblig'd by ye laws of the province to maintain an Orthodox Minister as the Law terms it and a School Master, both of which are without faile Congregationalists . . . .[72]

After Grainger's sudden death the following year, the minister, churchwardens, and vestrymen of King's Chapel, Boston, in- formed the S.P.G. of the accession of his son, Thomas, upon the approbation of the town selectmen, who were empowered by provincial laws "to grant Licence or Permission to school masters before they can open School." Thomas Grainger, then, found himself in the curious position of holding licenses both from the Anglican bishop of London and the dissenting select- men of Boston, in order to teach the Church catechism within hailing distance of Harvard College, and under the direct super- vision of a Society missionary lately resigned as rector of rigor- ously nonconformist Yale! Nearly a score of years later, Samuel Johnson said that Stratford pedagogue Joseph Browne's resig- nation from his S.P.G. classroom was not so tragic as all that since "our Schools are now better provided for by the Govern- ment than heretofore . . . ," an observation with which Browne entirely agreed.[73]

Elsewhere in the colonies a few others hazarded parallel opinions. Most articulate among them was the Reverend Samuel

72. Timothy Cutler to the Secretary, Boston, New E., October 10, 1727, S.P.G. Letters, Series B, Vol. I, No. 227; Samuel Grainger to the Secretary, Boston, November 25, 1732, S.P.G. Letter Books, Series A, Vol. XXIV, pp. 150–51.

73. Petition of the Ministers, Church Wardens & Vestrymen of King's Chapel, Boston, January 21, 1733, ibid., Series A, Vol. XXIV, p. 416; Samuel Johnson to the Secretary, Stratford, December 2, 1751, S.P.G. Letters, Series B, Vol. XIX, No. 49; Joseph Browne to the Secretary, Stratford, October 10, 1751, ibid., Series B, Vol. XIX, No. 50.

Cooke, who had succeeded William Thompson as missionary for Monmouth County, New Jersey, and who in 1760 considered seriously not just who should replace Christopher Reynolds, Shrewsbury's recently deceased S.P.G. schoolmaster, but also the wider question of whether he needed to be replaced at all. His letter contrasted sharply with others' reflecting the frustrations of Society clergymen who time after time complained of ineffective pedagogues.

"The Honble Society," wrote Cooke, "may perhaps expect a petition from the Congregation of Shrewsbury for the Continuance of their bounty towards the Support of another master —I have talk'd with my Vestry on that head: The Majority were for sending a petition, some were indifferent, & others against it. For my part," he went on, "I must own, I join the fewer Number & discourage the thing, as I, with Submission, think the Honble Society's Bounty can be better apply'd. School Masters may possibly be very useful Servants in some places —but I think it my Duty to Acquaint the Society, that, in Monmouth, it appears to me to be a needless Expence."

The missionary continued. "People here," he observed, "seem very willing & desirous to give their Children some Education —Even those who are indifferent and [care] less in Religion, and unwilling to Contribute anything towards the support of a Minister, are far from Backward to advance liberally to have their Children taught Reading, Writing and Arithmetic. As for the Poor," he urged, "whose Children I Judge are the design'd objects of this Charity of the Society's, there are none in this Country so poor but whose Pride is so great as to prevent their acknowledging it: And I have known Mr. Reynolds to have affronted & disoblig'd Several of the Congregation Offering to take their Children Gratis, when at the same time I have [thought] them proper objects of this Charity."

Cooke concluded that

There are others, it is true, whose minds being Narrower than their Circumstances, would gladly partake of this part of the Vanble

Society's Bounty had they it in their power—But if not—they would not in the least hesitate to pay their Childrens [*sic*] Schooling rather than they should be deprived of so great & so justly esteemed an Advantage. Tis with the greatest Humility and Deference to the Honble & Ven^ble Society and their Judgements, that I have here presum'd to offer my Opinion on this Subject—But I thought it a Duty incumbent on me to state the Case of this County, tho' in my Opinion and Sentiment I may possibly differ from some of my Brethren & Men of far superior Abilitys.[74]

That Cooke's remarks did not necessarily represent the picture in other parts of the colony may be deduced not only from the Society's continued subsidizing of individual schoolmasters elsewhere but also from the S.P.G.'s ongoing commitments in a diversity of institutions, including King's College, the College of Philadelphia, the Negro Catechetical School in New York, the Negro teacher-training school in Charleston, the Indian schools at Fort Hunter, the Mohawk Upper and Lower Towns, and the Charity School in New York. On the other hand, when read alongside the opinions of less analytical Society men, these later jottings by such sensitive observers of the colonial scene as Timothy Cutler, Samuel Johnson, and Samuel Cooke add up to the realization on the part of growing numbers of S.P.G. servants in the field that a Society pedagogue's role was so ill-defined, his tasks so numerous, his status so low, and his rewards so few that his relevance to propagating the gospel in foreign parts was questionable, particularly since school men of minimal capabilities brought ridicule to the Church, and since by the 1760s even poorer colonial parents were increasingly able to send their boys and girls to a greater variety of schools than ever before.

Whether a British expatriate or a native American colonist, the S.P.G. pedagogue accordingly had every reason to feel the tension between that ever-present realm of order expressed in Society propaganda, and a domain of modification to pressing

74. Samuel Cooke to the Secretary, Shrewsbury, Monmouth County, November 5, 1760, *ibid.*, Series B, Vol. XXIV, No. 101.

and often discouraging local circumstances obliging him to be something other than what he had anticipated or the Society had intended.

Much of this tension, it is true, sprang from the fact that the component parts of the religious hierarchy of king, archbishop, bishop, priest, and deacon, or the social/political hierarchy rising from beggardom to monarchy, were constantly subject to colonial redefinition or outright elimination. In the matter of licensing, for example, the S.P.G. pedagogue could never be certain whom he was dealing with or what prerogatives or protection a license really gave him. In theory, an S.P.G. appointment and the bishop of London's license guaranteed a dependable annual stipend and safeguard in face of unlicensed opposition. In practice, the license emerged as the merest formality. No colonial bishop existed to verify its correct use. Such bishop's delegates as Commissaries Johnston, Garden, or Vesey were preoccupied with their own parochial duties, and seemed only to catch up with those pedagogical irregularities that burgeoned into crises. Ministers saw in their schoolmasters subordinates who could conveniently relieve them from the tedium of preparing large groups of children for public catechizing in church and hence assessed a pedagogue's fulfillment of license-conditions largely in terms of his direct usefulness to Church liturgy.

As for security against rivals, an earlier shortage of qualified men, a growing appreciation of formal schooling in New England and elsewhere, and a general reluctance on the part of harassed governors to concern themselves with comparative trivia in face of war together erased the slightest trace of S.P.G. teaching monopolies in America. New York at first showed a high level lay-political involvement in the supervision of S.P.G. classrooms. But, as has been shown to be the case in Boston, other areas demanded of Society men licenses in addition to those issued at Lambeth Palace, London. Between these extremes lay the gamut of degree of complaint about how flimsy a warranty the license really was, once out of its London establishment context.

Throughout the period from 1714 to 1763, the Society pedagogue continued upon occasion to appeal for "official" help whenever his welfare or that of his pupils appeared threatened. More astonishing than what he overtly stated at these times, however, was the extent to which dilettante, opportunist, charletan, and devotée alike engaged in such improvisations as let the term "schoolmaster" mean whatever a given locale demanded of it.

The first major challenge to invention—that of identifying the real task at hand—showed men who in Britain might have successfully construed their jobs narrowly now straddling several roles at once. At the very least, the S.P.G. schoolmaster was *ex officio* catechist, whatever his capabilities or inclinations in the matter. In an emergency, too, he might be called upon to read prayers or sermons, although only the ordained could perform the sacraments. Then, as a result of the large-scale institution of slavery, of bonded servitude, and of apprenticeship, he often chose to become night schoolmaster as well.

The S.P.G. catechist, by dint of commanding a larger Society stipend, stood a cut above the pedagogue, but frequently, as with Neau and his Negroes, performed the pedagogue's job of teaching pupils to read. Sometimes an ordained minister in transit from college bachelor to schoolmaster to catechist to missionary, the catechist was called upon to substitute for his missionary colleague in the full range of Church ministerial responsibilities.

The ordained minister, in the meantime, combined the posts of parochial assistant and schoolmaster or, as with Jeremiah Leaming in Newport or Thomas Morritt in Charleston, acted in their simultaneous capacities of schoolmaster, catechist, *and* minister. As a result, classes under the tutelage of such a variety of mentors tackled work ranging all the way from the rudiments of repetition and memorization as practised in Elias Neau's second-story classroom to those academic sophistications attempted by Thomas Morritt and William Forster, although with most classrooms running heavily to the three R's.

The second distinct region of academic adaptation—that which followed when appeals to the Society proved barren—gave room for every imaginable association of S.P.G. colleagues with their surrounding communities and even with the local and provincial governmental bodies that demonstrated vested interests in their classroom performances.

Rare, indeed, was the man who actually subsisted on his S.P.G. allowance. Some begged their teaching positions as a charitable gesture from the Society, discovered they couldn't make ends meet, and branched out on their own, imaginatively —as clerks, scribes, farmers, physicians, traders, brewmasters, and sometimes even as retired men on pirated annuities. Some agreed to include in their already well-patronized classrooms a modicum of poor students in return for S.P.G. or provincial retainers. Some attracted private sponsorship, adding to their S.P.G. salaries a house, some land, and slaves to work it. Some, like Morritt, tapped the combined resources of Society, parents, private donors, and provincial government alike.

Thus, making a living where and how they could, S.P.G. pedagogues got by. But they scarcely made up as a whole that near "public school system" that William Webb Kemp identified them with in his very thorough New York study. Nor, for that matter, did mid-century America's S.P.G. Pedagogue quite fit Kemp's description of a "higher type of schoolmaster than most of the other colonial schools were able to secure—that is, one possessing college training." As the letters quite clearly reveal, many Society pedagogues held no such qualifications, and for those who did, the university degree guaranteed neither pedagogical prowess nor personal integrity. What it did ensure was that its bearer would not remain in the classroom very long. An S.P.G. missionary lived fairly well on his stipend and his perquisites, but an S.P.G. pedagogue faced at best a highly provisional series of occupations, and at worst a humiliating, marginal subsistence. Perhaps he read *The Husbandman's Manual* . . . with its alegorical references to bees "the meanest doing their Duty, with as much Chearfulness as the greatest."[75] In fact, though, North America was no apiary.

Collectively, then, S.P.G. pedagogues active between 1714 and 1763 were beset on the one hand by Society regulations while confronted on the other by an America that either prevented their obeying them or even tempted total disregard of them. After the French cession and a consequent feeling of security that made for keener colonial self-scrutiny, this tension would approach the breaking point.

75. William Webb Kemp, *The Support of Schools in Colonial New York by the Society for the Propagation of the Gospel in Foreign Parts* (New York: Teachers College, Columbia University, 1913), p. 277; *ibid.,* p. 56; Anon., *The Husbandman's Manual* . . . (London: F. C. and J. Rivington, 1811 edn.), p. 47, in S.P.C.K., *Religious Tracts Dispersed by the S.P.C.K.* (London: F. C. and J. Rivington, 1815), Vol. XI.

V

LEARNING AND LOYALTY

NO ASPECT of the American Revolution, wrote Carl Bridenbaugh, holds more fascination for the historian than the adjust-
ing, part conscious and part unconscious, of the colonists' view
of their past to meet the requirements of the changing social
and political conditions of the age. This "usable past" was, he
argued, constructed on the Puritan premise that arrival in the
New World constituted the preordained culmination of a historical process. Over the decades, such documents as Edward
Johnson's 1650 *Wonder Working Providence* . . . , William
Hubbard's 1682 manuscript drawing heavily on the Bradford
and Winthrop journals, Cotton Mather's *Magnalia* (1702),
Daniel Neal's 1720 *History of the Puritans,* and Thomas Prince's
Chronological History of New England (1736) further developed
and modified the theme. In addition, countless sermons, such as
Jonathan Mayhew's 1750 discourse *On Unlimited Submission,*
drove home the message of initial emigration for conscience sake
and re-establishment in a wilderness at length tamed to serve
God's glorious purpose.[1] As revolutionary hostilities approached,
such men as Jonathan Mayhew, Andrew Eliot, Charles Chauncy,

1. Bridenbaugh, *Mitre and Sceptre,* pp. 171, 172–78.

William Livingston, Ezra Stiles, Noah Welles, John Rodgers, Francis Alison, and others kept alive that sense of keen resentment at alleged intrusion into fundamental rights long ago established.

Ever since the 1702 exploratory journeys abroad of S.P.G. missionary George Keith, the Society had observed the sensitivity of colonials over encroachments on these established rights, and had grown accustomed to their protests over threats to colonial prerogative. During the last two decades of its American educational adventure, however, the S.P.G. had to contend not only with those creating a usable past but with equally articulate men mapping out a usable future, often radically different from the one the Society itself had envisaged for sixty years or more. Its chief polarities, as Curti has indicated,[2] were the ideals of nationalism and democracy.

Varied indeed appeared exponents of these extraordinary ideals. In his *Common Sense* (1776), Thomas Paine argued the absurdity of the monarchy. Charles Turner's 1783 *Discourse,* published in Boston, prophesied that even the masses could be brought to wisdom. Thomas Jefferson proposed in 1779 his educational plan which would guarantee basic instruction for all and advanced education for the gifted, to be repaid through public service. In 1783 Timothy Dwight accepted girls to be prepared in his school for college entrance, among other reasons so future mothers might teach their sons patriotism.

Nor were these mere gestures on the part of colonial malcontents. Up to and during the war with England, appeals for an American identity were realized in a variety of American institutions. Some appeared quite late in the Revolutionary War. But others developed well before hostilities. An American demand for reading material saw the establishment of at least seventy bookshops in Philadelphia and as many again elsewhere in the colonies before 1776. Serving those who could not afford

2. Merle Curti, *The Growth of American Thought* (New York: Harper and Row, third edition, 1964), pp. 147–48.

to purchase books were lending libraries in Charleston, New York, Boston, Philadelphia, and smaller centers—all going concerns prior to 1774. Between 1761 and 1766, over 4,000 titles emerged from American printing presses located in Philadelphia, Boston, New York, Newport, and Charleston. In roughly the same period, nineteen newspapers remained in business, printed on rag paper, and read not just by a few thousand subscribers but also by many others, particularly in coffee houses and taverns. In 1765, meantime, Ezra Stiles proposed a reconstituted American Academy of Science to "defeat episcopal intrigue" by honoring American literature and attracting all-American associates. Renamed the American Philosophical Association, this organization elected Benjamin Franklin as its first president in 1769.[3]

One must not presume that in reacting to a spirit of colonial independence the S.P.G. held the monopoly on conservative declarations. Americans who, like John Adams, viewed the American Revolution as a political, not a social, realignment of forces, continued to speak of two sorts of people—gentlemen qualified for high office, and simple men destined for toil. Similarly misleading, in view of one or two liberal S.P.G. anniversary sermons (not to mention Burke's conciliatory attitude toward America) would be the assumption that all appeals for colonial rights as Englishmen flowed from American pens as America and Britain drifted toward open war. On the whole, though,

3. Harvard Medical School started training American doctors in 1782. New American academies like those at Andover and Exeter, although characteristically classical, began to attract students from many parts rather than lose their best prospects through study abroad. Other schools, like Dickinson in Pennsylvania (1783), St. John's at Annapolis (1784), and Hampden-Sydney in Virginia (1782), typified the recognition of religious pluralism and the educational diversity stemming from it. Organizations such as the American Academy of Arts and Sciences, established in Boston, 1780, stimulated not just a knowledge of America's past but the planning of its future as well, in a wide field of enquiry, for the "interest, honor, dignity, and happiness of a free, independent and virtuous people." For a full treatment of the "revolutionary shift of emphasis" from an intellectually dependent to an intellectually independent American posture, see Curti, *ibid.*, pp. 123–48. For further details of America's cultural growth, see Carl Bridenbaugh, *Cities in Revolt* (New York: Capricorn Books, 1955), pp. 380–81, 382–83, 386, 388, 411, 412.

three striking peculiarities characterized the S.P.G.'s overseas educational effort as the colonies debated appropriate responses to preindependence provocation. One was a continued tendency to deal with abstracts rather than events or with the American protagonists involved in them. Another was a remarkable insensitivity to the serious intent and considerable accomplishments of such growing institutions as the colonial college. Yet another was a continuing investment in schools and schoolmasters under arrangements which, because of conflicting local circumstances, had proved detrimental to S.P.G. interests time and again for over half a century.

Peculiarities like these appear the more curious when it is realized that at the very heart of empire, in dockside taverns and coffee houses within sight and sound of S.P.G. headquarters, metropolitan Londoners conversed with American acquaintances about Quebec's restrictive boundary lines, the Currency, Sugar, and Stamp Acts, the Declaratory Act, Townshend's legislation, the Restrictive Tea Acts, and the Intolerable Acts paving the way to independence itself. Yet, in spite of such first hand contact, in spite of British military and naval involvement in North America up to the end of the French and Indian Wars, and in spite of the intermingling of Britishers and colonial Americans for reasons of travel or trade, the Society resolutely reached back to a Keithian perspective of North America to furnish the usable past it needed. In apparent disregard of compelling colonial actualities standing in the path of success, the Society determined throughout the crucial years from 1763 to 1783 to instruct recalcitrant colonials in the proper posture toward God and king.

During those years linking France's collapse in Canada and her return to North America as ally to a new American nation, men on either side of the Atlantic engaged in debate about freedom. How, it was asked, could colonies by definition ever achieve full stature within the British Empire?

In parliament, the "old Whig" faction opposed colonial taxation. For their stand on the subject, men like the Duke of Richmond, General Conway, the Marquis of Rockingham, Edmund Burke, Lord Camden, and Isaac Barré received American thanks by having American towns or counties named after them. Often cooperating with these men were William Pitt and his associates, including the Duke of Grafton and Lord Shelburne. William Pitt himself, as mover of the Stamp Act's 1766 repeal, was voted by the New York assembly as fit subject for a statue; Williamsburg, Virginia, and Dedham, Massachusetts, set up commemorative markers to "the Great Commoner."[4]

Both within parliament and beyond, however, less accommodating opinions regarding colonial duty could regularly be heard. And for persons able to join the congregations at London's St. Mary-le-Bow church, or to read printed versions of what was said on the occasion of the S.P.G. anniversary sermons delivered there, a vision of America progressively out of focus with America's prerevolutionary self-image was readily available. Never since the days of the itinerant Keith were words of such severity proffered as correct instruction in colonial subservience.

Granted, not all these later S.P.G. homilies attacked alleged colonial presumptuousness head on. Some earlier ones, like those preached by John Hume, bishop of Oxford, or Thomas Newton, bishop of Bristol, dwelt obliquely upon the inequalities of man. Others assessed the premises and conclusions of popular philosophy as insufficient to the solution of grave human problems. The pretended sufficiency of the law of nature, it was argued, could never guide one toward a good life, especially since no person could grasp all knowledge. Scepticism "which corrupted the Greeks" was now likely, said the bishop of Lincoln, to put authority and the Church of England to the most severe tests. A philosophic view of self-sufficiency, insisted the bishop of

4. Samuel Eliot Morison and Henry Steele Commager, *The Growth of the American Republic* (New York: Oxford University Press, 1962), Vol. I, pp. 150, 162.

Peterborough, is morally barren. Citing John Locke, he maintained that "natural religion was no where taken care of by the forces of natural reason," and that "it is too hard a thing for unassisted reason to establish morality . . . ." As for natural philosophy, the archbishop of York proffered warnings about the wanderings of curious and unsettled minds upon questions which it is God's providence to keep concealed.[5] Patently, here was no intellectual climate for Franklin or Jefferson.

Considerably more forthright, however, appeared those prelates who systematically applied themselves either to direct theorizing on colonial society or a deliberate downgrading of American life in terms scarcely calculated to win colonials to the Church cause overseas.

In the first case—that of social theorizing—hypothesizing upon colonial responsibilities usually took the form of connecting institutional religion and political fidelity, or, as in days long past, of linking Church missionary endeavors, military operations, and trade. For the bishop of Peterborough, "seeds of [established] Religion . . . will be the firmest bond, the most assured pledge of . . . fidelity." Largely in agreement were his colleagues, among whom a successor recommending prayer and a "proper sense of duty to the laws on one hand, and a just attention to the rights of our fellow subjects on the other," in order that "we and all the dependent members of the parent state, may happily and speedily be united again as one people." As for the connection between propagating the gospel and expansion overseas, the Indian again appeared pivotal. Armies, explained the bishop of Oxford, made him accessible to missionaries whose duty lay in teaching and enforcing the word of God. For, added his Peterborough counterpart, the deeper an

5. John Hume, *A Sermon* . . . (London: E. Owen and T. Harrison, 1762), p. 10; Thomas Newton, *A Sermon* . . . (London: E. Owen and T. Harrison, 1769), p. 9; Hume, *Sermon,* p. 7; John Green, *A Sermon* . . . (London: E. Owen and T. Harrison, 1768), p. 6; John Hinchcliffe, *A Sermon* . . . (London: T. Harrison and S. Brooke, 1776), pp. 4, 9; John Locke, *The Reasonableness of Christianity,* p. 532, folio edition, Vol. 2nd., cited in Hinchcliffe, *Sermon,* p. 10; William Markham, *A Sermon* . . . (London: T. Harrison and S. Brooke, 1777), p. viii.

Indian's religious conviction, the sounder subsequent transactions with him were likely to be. Encroachment on his territory, by Anglicans at least, was in no way lawless. On the other hand, alertness against the seductions of French Jesuits made it doubly important to win over interstitial tribes—particularly Mohawks —to ways of agriculture, episcopal Christianity, and military dependability. Charles Moss, bishop of St. David's, came more bluntly to the point. "In the late successes that attended . . . British arms," he showed, the Mohawks

had their full share of glory; they often stood foremost in the hour of danger, and shed their best blood in the common cause: and their friendship is the better worth securing, because the situation of their country, and their martial spirit and bravery are such, as to render them a natural barrier to some of the principal British settlements, against the invasion of enemies, as well European as American.[6]

In the second instance, that of portraying colonials in the worst possible light, S.P.G. anniversary sermonists spared no pains. If, during Queen Anne's reign, these lessons had been tentative or contradictory, or during mid-century condescendingly expressive of a class attitude that left little room for co-

6. Frank J. Klingberg has provided the best treatment of the S.P.G.'s operational triad of missionary, military, and trade activities. See his *Anglican Humanitarianism in Colonial New York* (Philadelphia: The Church Historical Society, 1940), *passim*. See also Richard Terrick, *A Sermon* . . . (London: E. Owen and T. Harrison, 1764), p. 28; John Hinchcliffe, *A Sermon* . . . (London: T. Harrison and S. Brooke, 1776), p. 16; John Hume, *Sermon*, p. 16; Terrick, *Sermon*, p. 25; Philip Younge, *A Sermon* . . . (London: E. Owen and T. Harrison, 1765), p. 22; Robert Lowth, *A Sermon* . . . (London: E. Owen and T. Harrison, 1771); Charles Moss, *A Sermon* . . . (London: T. Harrison and S. Brooke, 1772), p. xxiv. That these latter words bore direct relationship with what was actually going on in America is borne out in Frank J. Klingberg's excellent "Sir William Johnson and the Society for the Propagation of the Gospel (1749–1774)," *Historical Magazine of the Protestant Episcopal Church*, VIII (March, 1939), 4–37. Klingberg concluded that "the Society and its agent, Johnson, as has been seen throughout all the stages of European rivalry in seizing and settling these rich New York lands, tried to Christianize and protect the Indian, but also to use him as a 'Warlike Christian Man' in the battle lines of the day. Indeed, Johnson himself . . . , carried along by the conditions of his times, helped push the Indian boundary lines west and incidentally acquired large tracts of land for his own use," p. 36.

lonial initiative within an empire order, the Society offerings at St. Mary-le-Bow throughout the twilight era of the Atlantic coast colonies revealed every feature of an establishment rebuffed. Three themes recurred as the century advanced toward American dissociation—colonial greed, colonial luxury, colonial sectarianism.

The first line of argument held to the notion that the initial motivation for emigration to the colonies was material gain. But in the colonial setting, avarice was said to get the better of honest expectations, dishonesty to lead to jealousy, and jealousy to suspicion of all authority. Even the best intentioned emigrants, warned the bishop of Landaff, had quit their native soil only to turn brutal among the very infidels they ought to have brought over to Christianity. Some planters, he feared, too soon grew wealthy. Wealth gave way to irreligion, spelling the doom of social justice, truth, and fidelity. The bishop of Exeter concurred. Unlike earlier settlers, he maintained, newer colonists appeared far too deeply involved in their own welfare to bother with religion. Not only that, but relentless pursuit of wealth was responsible for political wrangling contrary to all just government.[7]

A second theme logically extended the first. Greed for gain as the colonists' fundamental social motivation was a bad enough prospect for a mother country anticipating dividends from its own colonial investments. But the realization of wealth, with all the attendant opportunities for misspent leisure time, seemed worse yet to contemplate. Furthermore, the outcome of colonial leisure most to be feared was freethinking, guaranteed to lure the unwary into a contempt for past traditions. At least the savage Indian, intoxicated with the returns of his trade, knew no better. But the "Philosophic Colonist"—the planter grown rich whether through hard work or good fortune—supposedly grew morally soft as the conveniencies of life multiplied. William

7. John Ewer, *A Sermon* . . . (London: E. Owen and T. Harrison, 1767), pp. 6, 12; Frederic Keppel, *A Sermon* . . . (London: E. Owen and T. Harrison, 1767), pp. 6, 12.

Warburton, bishop of Gloucester, voiced his disapproval in ringing tones. "The second venture of our Colonists," he regretted, "was for the *luxuries of life*: among which, the Commodity called FREETHINKING was carefully consigned to them, as that which would give a relish and a seasoning to all the rest." In complete agreement was the bishop of Lincoln, who spoke harshly of the "improved Colonist" who "as he advances in wealth and science may be for adopting those modish habits of thinking and living, which are too often the attendents of ease and affluence . . . ."[8]

A third theme, more vigorously developed as the colonies drifted toward empire separation, was the destructive effect of sectarianism. It appeared particularly galling to the Anglican prelates who addressed Bow church congregations (not to mention colonial readers of their printed words) to note that even the conquered French were allowed their Catholic bishops, and that all denominations abroad enjoyed full religious privileges, including disciplinary supervision, "except only the church here by law established." Under the circumstances, encouraging missionary teachers to serve in colonies now contemplating various modes of imperial defiance was an exceptionally delicate task. Striking a safe medium between a zealous fanaticism on the one hand, and an irresponsible nonchalance on the other, presented the utmost difficulty in home candidature for the important work, the anniversary preachers pointed out. But getting colonial candidates was just as hard. Not only did these need to qualify for holy orders by "crossing an immense ocean," but upon arrival they also had "the sad business to undergo, of presenting themselves unknown, to persons unknown, without any recommendation or introduction, except certain papers in their pocket."[9] But for sectarian advantages concerning ordination and a general sectarian suspicion of High Church Anglicanism, colonial-born

8. William Warburton, *A Sermon* . . . (London: E. Owen and T. Harrison, 1766), pp. 11–13; John Green, *A Sermon* . . . (London: E. Owen and T. Harrison, 1768), p. 11.

9. Ewer, *Sermon,* pp. 23, 21.

missionaries might have looked forward to S.P.G. service with confidence and faced the voyage to Britain with equanimity, transatlantic sailings being safer after the French wars. But as things stood, the very sectarianism that made missionary work necessary in the first place now prevented the Society from securing the missionary force needed to counterpoise it.

Amid the harsher tones employed to press home these messages of colonial shortcomings, more balanced sentiments, expressed with all the hope for better days ahead, occasionally reverberated at St. Mary-le-Bow. Prominent among these were the sermons of Jonathan Shipley, bishop of St. Asaph, and William Markham, archbishop of York. The first of these Shipley delivered in 1773, mere weeks after American Sons of Liberty heaved offending tea chests into Boston harbor. The other, Markham preached in 1777, when Washington's army had dwindled to just five-thousand regulars. Both, however, were deceivingly forgiving. Both appeared to leave open a way toward mending deteriorating relationships between England and America. But both looked to the same outcome—that of a chastened colonial child returning to the fold, although via different routes. Said Shipley, a colony treated with kindness will become good, hence obedient under the law. Said Markham, a colony made to submit to law will become good, hence an asset to a mother land.[10]

Installed with relative comfort in their British dioceses, the prominent Anglican prelates called upon to indicate the proper direction S.P.G. educators shold take in their efforts to save American colonies from moral and political ruin could offer their annual advice with a certain detachment. But growing

---

10. Jonathan Shipley, *A Sermon* . . . (London: T. Harrison and S. Brooke, 1773), p. xxii and *passim*. This sermon drew sharp criticism from colonial conservatives. "What a son of a b———h is the Bishop of St. Asaph!" wrote Myles Cooper to William Samuel Johnson. "They say at Philadelphia that the sermon was written by Dr. Franklin." This outburst is quoted in H. and C. Schneider (eds.), *Samuel Johnson, President of Kings College. His Career and Writings.* See also William Markham, *A Sermon* . . . (London: T. Harrison and S. Brooke, 1777), p. xxiv and *passim*.

American economic and political antagonism toward the old country after the Stamp Act crisis of 1765 presented Society parsons and pedagogues abroad with problems more urgent than ever before. A decade prior to independence, S.P.G. parsons throughout the Atlantic settlements began to sense a much more than ordinary reaction to their own pulpit or pamphlet observations as well as to those of their ecclesiastical superiors which they continued to distribute in printed form. Once hostilities commenced, an inept statement, a clumsy or inappropriate comparison, and Society parsons' lives and property were at stake. Under these conditions, Keithian diatribes were renounced by more careful S.P.G. colonials in favor of diplomatic equivocation.

The sort of caution forced upon Society men of divided loyalties may be examined in the writings of William Smith just prior to his serving the S.P.G. in Pennsylvania but before the 1775 shooting at Lexington. In a preface to university theses arguing close bonds with Britain, the renowned Pennsylvania provost carefully analyzed post-Stamp Act America. An act of the British parliament, he showed, had thrown union into jeopardy. Yet, it was Britain that had raised the college of Pennsylvania "from a helpless to a flourishing state," and thus England had every right to a return of gratitude, regardless of the political situation. Using such slogans as "tree of liberty" and "sons of liberty," so prevalent among later patriots, he nonetheless maintained that the full and free enjoyment of British liberty as well as protection from external attack could only be expected in return for colonial obedience under constitutional and legal restrictions and economic subordination. Given such obedience, Smith envisaged a state of colonial rapport which bent "our whole thoughts to a virtuous industry, beneficial to ourselves and Great Britain; acting as free, but not using our liberty as a cloak of maliciousness or licentiousness." Such cooperation would not, however, rule out the airing of views on such matters as empire propriety. On the contrary, in an oration delivered in 1773 to

The American Philosophical Society, Smith, by then S.P.G. missionary at Oxford, Pennsylvania, stressed that organizations such as he addressed should supplement schools by providing room for differences of opinion, freedom of discussion, and the general coordination of men of "different parties and persuasions in one grand pursuit" of peace and abundance.[11]

However, after April at Lexington and Concord, and June at Breed's Hill during the dark year 1775, and following such wartime disasters as the September fire which in 1776 wiped out nearly a quarter of New York's major buildings, the entire argument respecting British-colonial relations assumed a less academic aspect, and S.P.G. parsons were much pressed to favor one or the other cause. Even then, some of them vacillated.

Society missionaries in such scattered localities as Connecticut, Pennsylvania, and New York advanced Bishop Shipley's view that if only men would seek virtue, political differences would somehow work themselves out. In Wallingford, for example, Samuel Andrews, who later fled to New Brunswick, Canada, confessed that he was not so much afraid of the power of England as of the sins of America. Samuel Magaw, Dover missionary and later Vice-Provost of the University of Pennsylvania, stressed the urgency of public spirit, liberality, and disinterestedness. Leaning if anything toward the American cause, he predicted that from individual virtue would spring both political and spiritual salvation. John Sayre, soon to be imprisoned, then banished to New York, wrote and later published in the *New York Journal* a letter to the Fairfield Committeemen in which he simply interpreted the revolutionary struggle as God's judgment on England and America and hence felt obliged to "extend the kind offices of humanity" to those of either side who may require them.[12]

11. *Pennsylvania University—4 dissertations on the Reciprocal Advantages of a Perpetual Union* . . . (William and Thomas Bradford, MDCCLXVI), pp. i, ii, 5, 6, 7, 12; William Smith, *An Oration, Delivered January 22, 1773, Before the Patrons, Vice Presidents and Members of the American Philosophical Society* . . . (Philadelphia: John Dunlap, MDCCLXXIII), pp. 8, 15.
12. Samuel Andrews, *A Discourse, Showing the Necessity of Joining In-*

But other S.P.G. teachers devised infinitely more elaborate apologies in their desperation to satisfy the demands of Tory and patriot alike without compromising their own consciences. An especially fine example of such ambivalent exposition was provided in 1777 by Rye missionary Isaac Hunt, who quoted Montesquieu, Locke, and Bacon to embroider his basic endorsement of due colonial obedience. He added the counterbalancing argument, however, that strict adherence to the letter of the law often borders upon injustice. Parents (states), he added, ought not to provoke their children (colonies) to wrath. The state of minority, he went on, is temporary. When that state ceases, he concluded, the right of chastisement and absolute command ceases also.[13]

As hostilities wore on, these neutral appeals to both Britain and America to examine their hearts continued. In 1778 William Smith arrived at the accommodating thesis that divine authority could only stem from a free and common consent. That same year, Samuel Magaw unhesitatingly juxtaposed a notion of equality with one of subordination. Then, in 1780, the year General Lincoln surrendered Charleston to the British and Lord Cornwallis' cavalry leader, Patrick Ferguson, was wiped out by South Carolina backwoodsmen on Kings Mountain, S.P.G. parson Magaw dedicated to General Washington a Masonic sermon on America's British heritage. Not long thereafter, in a sermon which recommended the contradictory theories of local (as opposed to empire) obedience and the great chain of being,

---

ternal Repentence with External Profession of it . . . (Newhaven: Thomas and Samuel Green MDCCLXXV), p. 18; Samuel Magaw, *A Discourse* . . . (Philadelphia: Story and Humphreys, MDCCLXXV), p. 14; *New York Journal*, clipping, Evans No. 15078, n.d., pp. 3, 4.

13. Isaac Hunt, *The Political Family or a Discourse, pointing out the Reciprocal Advantages, which Flow from an uninterrupted Union between Great Britain and her American Colonies* (Philadelphia: n.p., 1775), pp. 6, 7, 11, 12, 29–30. Montesquieu argued that protection required dependence; that all inferior jurisdictions should flow from one superior fountain; that due subordination of lesser parts to greater is essential if both parts are to exist. Locke demonstrated that political society rests upon the consent of freemen capable of a majority. Bacon observed that colonies are children of the state and ought, therefore, after attaining youth or manhood, to evidence their gratitude "by pious love and filial obedience."

Magaw directed his dedication to the Chevalier de Luzerne, French Minister to the United States.[14]

Although 1775 was a year of uncertainty for some Society parsons, it was for others a time of decision. If available publications are any guide, relatively few S.P.G. parsons raised their voices in the American interest. Those who did often found themselves in circumstances where arguing otherwise would have proved embarrassing, if not dangerous. For instance, when required to preach at the request of colonial military men or before congress, William Smith justified colonial resistance to British oppression. Daniel Batwell, finding himself preaching before a congregation of colonial riflemen, insisted that the continental congress was motivated not at all by disloyalty, but by the quest to preserve long-established privileges. And David Griffiths, who resigned his S.P.G. position at Waterford, New Jersey, to become rector of Shelburne parish, Virginia, denied that colonial lives and property were at the absolute disposal of the king and his subjects in England.[15]

To be sure, cases of S.P.G. parsons bringing their missionary mandate in line with an emerging mood of American independ-

14. William Smith, *A Sermon* . . . (Philadelphia: John Dunlap, MDCCLXXIX), p. 20; Samuel Magaw, *A Sermon* . . . (Philadelphia: John Dunlap [1779]), p. 15 devoted in part to George Washington; Samuel Magaw, *A Sermon* . . . (Philadelphia: David C. Clatpoole, MDCCLXXXI), *passim;* Samuel Magaw, *A Sermon* . . . (Philadelphia: Hall and Sellars, MDCCLXXXIV), pp. 9, 20, preached in Philadelphia on December 27, 1783.

15. William Smith, *A Sermon on the Present Situation of American Affairs Preached* . . . *at the Request of the officers of the 3rd. Battalion of the City of Philadelphia* . . . (Philadelphia: James Humphreys, Jr., 1775), p. 21; *An Oration in Memory of General Montgomery* . . . *at the desire of the Honourable Continental Congress* (Philadelphia: John Dunlap, MDCCLXXVI), p. 25; Daniel Batwell, *A Sermon Preached at York-Town, Before Captain Morgan's and Captain Price's Companies of Riflemen* . . . (Philadelphia: John Dunlap, MDCCLXXV), p. 18. These command performances were in no way extraordinary. Robert Handy points out that to be an Anglican patriot was unexceptional, especially in the South, citing an estimate that two-thirds of the signers of the Declaration of Independence were nominally Anglican. See H. Shelton Smith, Robert T. Handy, and Lefferts A. Loetscher, *American Christianity: An Historical Interpretation with Representative Documents* (New York: Charles Scribner's Sons, 1960), Vol. I, p. 431; David Griffith, *Passive Obedience Considered* . . . (Williamsburg: Alexander Purdie, [1776]), pp. 12, 21.

ence were occasionally recorded in Society *Abstracts* printed during the war years. Collectively, however, by far the greater proportion of the Society's ministers abroad consistently and forcefully developed in sermons, pamphlets, and occasional pieces pro-British sentiments and Church establishment apologies inimical to the fathers of the American constitution whatever their religious affiliations.

In the days before the Stamp Act, for example, the S.P.G. had accomplished remarkable gains for the Church in the North, considering the firmness of Congregationalist opposition. When these gains were to be made in such localities as Cambridge, Massachusetts, however, it was to be expected that a fundamental aspect of Society work would be the educating of potential supporters in the legitimacy of the S.P.G. enterprise. Jonathan Mayhew's challenge of the Society's interpretation of its own charter typifies the sort of intellectual resistance the S.P.G. needed to overcome before it might expect major gains in such close proximity to Harvard. But Mayhew's queries took some answering. Had the Church of England correctly applied its royal charge by limiting its activities to converting heathens, Mayhew enquired, or had it not rather misplaced its warrant by maintaining episcopal churches in the towns and villages of North America?

East Apthorp, S.P.G. Cambridge missionary, reacted to Mayhew by alleging that the Society had considerable discretionary powers respecting its North American program. Conceding the point that certain inconsistencies occurred from one anniversary sermon to another with respect to what the S.P.G. was really about, he hailed Society rights as well as accomplishments. Religion, he observed with a characteristic thrust at New England congregationalism, "no longer wears among us that savage and gloomy appearance, with which superstition had terribly arrayed her—: its speculative doctrines were freed from those senseless horrors with which fanaticism had prevented [it]."[16]

In a 176-page rebuttal, Mayhew warned New England men of the dangers to their way of life of the S.P.G.'s presence among them. He catalogued ecclesiastical espionage, misuse of funds, erection of a "superb edifice" (Cambridge's 'Bishop's Palace'), and the possibility of mitered bishops rolling down Cambridge streets in gilded coaches bound for banquets[17] as prices the New World might have to pay for welcoming the Society.

Response to Mayhew varied from the caricature to the pedestrian. One sally, probably by Providence missionary Arthur Browne, showed New England puritans constantly opposing established religion "and yet . . . perpetually laying claim to an establishment!" Moreover, insisted Browne, puritanical remarks about ostentatious Church regalia being a deviation from apostolic plainness Biblically enjoined were wholly unfounded. Did Mayhew believe, he enquired sarcastically, that the fishermen of Galilee wore wigs and black coats and long sweeping cloaks, or that "a strip or two of lawn about the neck is more apostolical or fishermanlike, than the same stuff upon the arms?" A similar attack, attributed to Henry Caner of King's Chapel, Boston, rested its defense of S.P.G. activities on the authority of several earlier Society members and officers, including Governors Hunter and Dudley, Colonels Morris and Heathcote, Secretary David Humphreys, and even the Reverend George Keith. Similarly unrecent was his reference to a 1725 letter from the lords justices of England to Governor Dummer denying the existence of any church establishment in New England, information which

---

16. East Apthorp, *Considerations on the Institutions and Conduct of the S.P.G.* (Boston: Green and Russell, and Thomas and John Fleet, 1763), p. 7. Mayhew's reply entitled *Observations on the Charter and Conduct of the Society for the Propagation of the Gospel in Foreign Parts . . .* is carefully analyzed in Bridenbaugh, *Mitre and Sceptre*, pp. 224–29. See also Apthorp, *Considerations*, p. 14; *ibid.*, p. 17.

17. Cited in Bridenbaugh, *Mitre and Sceptre*, p. 226.

in Caner's opinion refuted Mayhew's right to question S.P.G. integrity.[18]

But many additional matters besides the propriety of S.P.G. New England work consumed the writing hours of Society parsons as America changed its posture toward empire authoritarianism. Society men sprang also to the defense of the Church of England as a whole. Some pointed to the actual lack of establishment threat in terms of minimal Church representation in certain colonial assemblies. They refuted, too, those cartoons of wine-bibbing, women-chasing Anglicans, too stupid for law or medicine, as drawn by Fairfield's Noah Hobart over a decade earlier. Some argued that the Church alone enjoyed a ministry vested with the proper authority from Christ, an advantage to which dissenters could lay no claim "unless every layman has authority to ordain; which appears so glaringly absurd . . . ." Others commended the Church liturgical ostentation so unacceptable to nonconformists—the "noble and majestic edifices," and the expensive adornments therein. Yet others recapitulated time-tried theories of episcopal divine right and objected to transmutation from establishment man to dissenter through the mere crossing of an ocean separating the old England from the new.[19]

In connection with this last point, S.P.G. parsons writing about the benefits of a colonial episcopate usually recognized, if they did not appreciate, their minority status to the North. But when it came to expressing opinions about the great ab-

18. [Arthur Browne], *Remarks on Dr. Mayhew's Incidental Reflections . . .* (Portsmouth: D. Fowle, 1763), p. 14, and *passim; ibid.,* p. 25; [Henry Caner], *A Candid Examination of Dr. Mayhew's Observations . . .* (Boston: Thomas and John Fleet, Green and Russell, Edes and Gill, 1763), pp. 5, 18.

19. John Beach, *A Friendly Expostulation . . .* (New York: John Holt, 1763), p. 33; *ibid.,* p. 5; Thomas Davies, *The Worship and Principle of the Church of England . . .* (n.p.: William Goddard, MDCCLXV), p. 11; Samuel Auchmuty, *A Sermon Preached at the Opening of St. Paul's Chapel in the City of New York . . .* (n.p.: H. Gaine, [1776]), p. 10; John Tyler, *The Sanctity of a Church Temple . . .* (Providence: John Carter, MDCCLXI), p. 13; Jeremiah Leaming, *Defence of the Episcopal Government . . .* (New York: John Holt, MDCCLXVI), pp. 4, 61, 62; *A Second Defence of the Episcopal Government . . .* (New York: John Holt, MDCCLXX), pp. 4, 5.

stracts—toleration, obedience, liberty—many loyal American parsons rose to the occasion with zeal unaccustomed since the days of George Keith. Thus, in their various colonial publications, East Apthorp, Samuel Andrews, Samuel Seabury, Charles Inglis, and other S.P.G. parsons tried to develop a viable theory of freedom. Their concept of civil liberty was of a service to God through conscientious subjection to law and government. Their appraisal of the colonial situation on the eve of revolution was that not only should America be grateful to Britain for past comforts, but that it also would be compelled to submit to Britain's might in the event of armed resistance.

Civil liberty, East Apthorp had said after the French conflict, had best not be confused with licentiousness. In occasional assessments of the proper limits of civil liberty, other colonial Society affiliates anticipated more serious discussion—by objecting, for instance, to the unpredictable loyalty of Benjamin Franklin, or by censuring "disloyal" articles (especially Dr. Mayhew's) in the *Independent Reflector,* the *Watch Tower,* the *American Whig,* and the *Philadelphia Centinel.*[20]

By the seventies, though, debate grew more violent. A sermon attributed to Samuel Andrews, who in 1786 left North Haven for New Brunswick, Canada, agreed that if liberty meant liberty of worship, all was well and good, but that if colonials "mean by their cry to hold the King's protection without yielding obedience to his authority, and the British Parliament," they ought to recall that they held their land titles by British law.[21] Dissenters, moreover, shoud bear in mind that in claiming liberties for themselves they might well avoid depriving others, and especially Church of England worshipers, of civil, natural, and religious liberties.

Samuel Seabury, driven by patriots from his Westchester mission in 1776, stated matters more forcefully still. Under cover

20. East Apthorp, *The Felicity of the Times* . . . (Boston: Green and Russell, MDCCLXIII), p. 25; [William Smith], *An Answer to Mr. Franklin's Remarks* . . . (Philadelphia: William Bradford, 1764), *passim;* [Charles Inglis], *A Vindication of the Bishop of Landaff's Sermon* . . . (New York: J. Holt, 1768), p. 8.
21. [Samuel Andrews], *A Sermon* . . . (New Haven: n.p.: 1770), p. 8.

of "lamentable cries about liberty," he charged, many colonists were merely degrading the authority of the British parliament over the British dominions. Four days later he began a close analysis of the nonimportation, nonexportation, and nonconsumption measures adopted by the Continental Congress, holding them to be a betrayal of colonial interest and predicting confusion, alienation, ineffectiveness, inflation, blockade, and colonial anarchy as a result.[22]

After the actual commencement of hostilities, such predictions intensified, particularly as voiced by Samuel Seabury and Charles Inglis. In his *Alarm to the Legislature* . . . , Samuel Seabury considered it bad enough to contend against the parent state, worse still to reject "moderate measures." What, he asked, was to become of colonies determined to affront the British ministry, parliament, nation, and king? How, he demanded, could colonies survive when they rejected peace offers as the machinations of slavery, confused freedom with sedition, and liberty with rebellion? How, he enquired, could New York's political contingent meeting at Philadelphia be considered representative of the people of the province when it had been "chosen in a tumultuous, illegal manner, entering into contracts, compacts, combinations, treaties of alliance with other colonies without any power from the legislature of the province?" How, he queried, dare these same delegates reject plans to accommodate the mother country, choosing instead to censure acts of the British parliament legitimately devised to prevent illegal trade and smuggling? In the interim, he complained, Rhode Islanders had dismantled harbor forts and taken cannon to deploy against His Majesty's forces. New Hampshire men had attacked and taken Portsmouth. Marylanders had assessed themselves £10,-000 in order to arm against the king. New Englanders, too, were arming, while New Yorkers had already selected a tax-gathering committee exclusive of regular legal government. Such a

---

22. A. W. Farmer [Samuel Seabury], *The Congress Canvassed* . . . (n.p.: John Rivington, 1774), p. 5; A. W. Farmer [Samuel Seabury], *Free Thoughts in the Proceedings of the Continental Congress* . . . (n.p.: 1774), *passim*.

ruinous state of affairs, Seabury warned, with its promise of
mob violence, its libel, its imposition upon New York province
of rule by a foreign power (not Britain but the delegates from
other colonies), and its threats of assassination at the hands of
Sons of Liberty, could only result in the most terrible consequences. Britain would not be intimidated. Parliament would
make a constitution detrimental to the colonies and thrust it
upon them. Republican courts would provide no appeal to higher
authorities. An American militia, unchecked by civil power,
would ravage the land. That Britain would prevail was a fore-
gone conclusion, as was the fact that thousands of occupation
troops would require quartering at colonial expense. Act now,
Seabury urged. Provide "deliverance from the tyranny of the
Congress and Committees."[23] Accommodation offered the only
escape from disaster.

More boldly stated still was *The True Interest of America . . .*
credited to Charles Inglis, the Dover S.P.G. missionary who left
the Society for the post of Rector of Trinity Church, New York,
became a refugee in England, and later assumed the first colonial
bishopric of Nova Scotia in 1787. To begin, Inglis charged
Thomas Paine with designing to tear the British Empire asunder.
Rejecting the premises of Paine and Hobbes that mankind is
naturally in a state of war, and government inevitably touched
by wickedness, he adopted instead Hooker's opinion that society
could not be without government nor government without law.
That government was agreeable to the will of God, and that the
first British emigrants were in a state of society before their
emigration, Inglis felt certain. He was equally sure of the fact
that absolute monarchy was the simplest form of government
and that, if Paine preferred simplicity, he could hardly choose
democracy. Granting that the expedition at Lexington was rash
and ill judged, he insisted that Great Britain's motives were ever
of affection and attachment as well as interest, and that the

---

23. Samuel Seabury, *An Alarm to the Legislature of the Province of New-
York Occasioned by The Present Political Disturbances in North America . . .*
(New York: James Rivington, MDCCLXXV), pp. 3, 5, 6, 7–12.

advantages to the colonies of a prompt reconciliation with the Old Country were numerous, including as they did the restoration of agriculture, commerce, industry, naval protection for trade, export bounties, and a guaranteed supply of European immigrants to fill up frontier settlement.[24]

On the other hand, Inglis presented disadvantages attending refusal to submit to the crown as overwhelming. There would be confusion of property ownership, he warned. Loyalists, considerable in number, would face dispossession. Easy avenues of peace with Britain would close off forever. Canada might be restored to France in the event of a successful American resistance, as might America itself be parcelled out to various European powers. Republican government, furthermore, could never succeed, for what were Americans but Britons, and Britons but monarchical subjects?[25]

But the Dover Society man abandoned any thought of American military successes in his final examination of what it would cost the colonies to prevail. Fifty-gun ships, he demonstrated, cost £14,355 sterling, and fifty-five such vessels, minimal for colonial defense, would accordingly drain from colonial coffers £789,525. Seventy-four gun ships at £27,200 each would bring a modicum of thirty to a sum of £716,000. Twelve frigates of thirty-two guns and another twelve of twenty guns would cost £89,760 and £52,440 respectively. With £542,-575 for cannon, the sum would approach £2,190,300, which annual incidental expenses would augment to £2,252,120. The addition of a thirty-regiment infantry and six regiments of cavalry would thus increase annual colonial expenses for defense alone to £2,821,532 sterling, a sum roughly equivalent to the thirteen colonies' total export value in the year 1769![26] Along

24. [Charles Inglis], *The True Interest of America Impartially Stated, in Certain Stictures* [*sic*] *On a Pamphlet intitled Common Sense, by an American* (Philadelphia: James Humphreys, MDCCLXXVI), pp. 10–17, 35, 40, 47, 48, 49.
25. *Ibid.*, pp. 50–52.
26. *Ibid.*, pp. 54, 60.

these classically-calculated, albeit theoretical, arithmetic progressions, Inglis predicted ruination for rebellious America.

Whatever lessons S.P.G. schoolmasters taught their school children in those American Society schools which operated until the war put them either out of operation or under new management, it is safe to guess that central to their teaching was that respect for British authority on any given plane so much a part of the S.P.G.'s total message; for such, at least, was the gist of S.P.G. anniversary sermons, S.P.G. colonial sermons, and the incidental pamphlets Society parsons found time to write and circulate. And doubtless Society pedagogues lost no opportunity to drive the message home to uncommitted boys and girls, servants, apprentices, Negro slaves, and Indians. But a less appropriate lesson for thirteen colonies struggling to unite against what they considered mounting contempt for their spirit of institutional and individual self-scrutiny could scarcely have been contemplated. Whether or not the Church's "usable past" upon which S.P.G. pedagogues presumably based their more specific classroom lessons found favor with colonial pupil, parent, or politician, is only sketchily recorded, for the years after 1763, and in particular the war years, saw many *Notitia Scholastica* lost or destroyed. A few clues exist, though, as to how the Society managed its school affairs in America as the Revolution approached, and, at length, played itself out.

Predictions of colonial doom notwithstanding, it at last became evident to Society pedagogues that the ruin of loyalist, not revolutionary, was in the offing. Admittedly, some S.P.G. schools evinced remarkable staying power during the mounting tension and eventual conflict, especially where British occupation and Society schools coincided geographically. The New York Charity School, which had risen from an initial S.P.G. grant to William Huddleston for £10 cash and £5 in tracts, burgeoned to a series of permanent buildings, housing in 1776 upwards of four score boys and girls. Under British occupation, Mr. Joseph

Hildreth, S.P.G. schoolmaster for over thirty years, died, and Charles Inglis, Trinity Church rector and author of *The True Interests of America,* assumed temporary charge. Under Amos Bull, the 1778 enrollment reached eighty-six, and in 1783, his successor, Ebenezer Street, drew a final £15 payment for services, the last the Society was to make to the benefit of the New York institution. Similarly, the New York Catechizing School, once the infant project of Mr. Elias Neau, managed under close cooperation with the Associates of Dr. Bray to sustain its efforts through to 1777, at which point Society support stopped. Thereafter, the project appears to have added impetus to the establishment of the New York African Free-School in 1787.[27]

As William Webb Kemp, J. W. Lydekker, and Frank J. Klingberg have shown, though, other S.P.G. educational institutions were quite incapable of accomplishing a smooth transition from colonial to republican America. Joseph Cleator's old school at Rye dwindled to nothing by 1776. Society schools on Staten Island did likewise. James Wetmore wrote in haste that

I continued my School at Musquito Cove on Long Island untill the 1st. of August last—to the Satisfaction of my Employers—but a number of my Neighbours being captivated by the Rebels and I very providentially escaping—and the Loyal Inhabitants being obliged to Lodge in the Fields for Safety—I have thought it Consistent with my Duty and prudence to quit the School, and am at present unsettled.

In the Mohawk Valley, too, military operations, loss of continued encouragement at the death of Sir William Johnson, and the eventual withdrawal for personal safety of all S.P.G. teachers in the vicinity forestalled any tangible Society progress. And, years before hostilities in North America, the Charleston Negro School likewise declined for want of suitably-trained Negro teachers.[28]

27. Kemp, *Support of Schools,* pp. 80, 101, 106, 115, 116, 121, 254, 260–61.
28. *Ibid.,* p. 145; November 1, 1779, *S.P.G. Letters,* Series B, Vol. III, No. 252, cited in Kemp, *Support of Schools,* pp. 187, 228; Frank J. Klingberg, *An Appraisal of the Negro in Colonial South Carolina* (Washington, D.C.: The Associated Publishers, 1941), p. 121.

The S.P.G. account of an accelerated harassment of Society pedagogues in the field is further revealed in the composite picture provided in the *Abstracts* through to 1783. Fewer and fewer English-born teachers ventured the dangerous Atlantic crossing to serve the Society abroad. Diminishing numbers of colonial-born pedagogues risked Society affiliation, no matter what their financial needs. *Abstract* listings of parsons and pedagogues in the various provinces grew shorter and shorter and, to an increasing extent, parson, catechist, and pedagogue became one and the same man holding on to a deteriorating local post.

Whereas the general mood of S.P.G. pedagogues' communications with Society headquarters during the last decades of the S.P.G. educational adventure in America is predominantly dark, few accounts of particular schools are complete enough to portray the decline and fall of particular institutions. One notable exception exists, however. A North Carolina school which ran full cycle from the time of the Stamp Act crisis to that of the Boston Tea Party so incensed its immediate community that a great deal of surviving correspondence was generated. Few accounts better exemplify the continuing inability of Society personnel at home and abroad to comprehend the innovative spirit of prerevolutionary colonial life and politics as it affected Society-sponsored schools.

News of the Newbern, N.C., project first came to S.P.G. attention in a 1764 letter from the Reverend James Reed, Society missionary at Craven Town and County for twenty years after 1755. Thomas Tomlinson, from Cumberland, England, had arrived in the parish, established a school, written home for an assistant, initiated a building subscription already totalling £200 colonial currency, and was teaching as many scholars as he could manage.[29]

29. James Reed to the Secretary, Newbern, June 21, 1764, *S.P.G. Letters,* Series B, Vol. V, No. 140.

Not only S.P.G. missionary James Reed but also the generality of the settlement had noticed the newcomer's initiative. The following year, inhabitants of Newbern and surrounding areas directed their memorial to William Tryon, Commander in Chief of the Province. They indicated that private subscriptions had already been absorbed in the purchase of building materials, and that local resources were unlikely to cover such additional expenses as salaries, schoolhouse construction, and costs of assistants. Informed of support in these matters through the S.P.G., the Newbern and district citizens accordingly requested Governor Tryon to apply on their behalf for a Society grant to enable Tomlinson to continue with his work. Similar appeals went to Lieutenant Governor Dobbs,[30] shortly after Tryon's death.

In anticipation of the petitioners' success, Tomlinson himself provided the S.P.G. with character references, and the Reverend Reed furnished progress reports. Some developments were less vigorous than might have been hoped. The schoolhouse rose slowly for want of money and materials. Subscriptions had been collected in the form of promissory notes, most long overdue. On the brighter side, though, Tomlinson continued without his assistant to instruct thirty scholars in return for £60 sterling per annum which enabled him to lodge at a public house for something like £25 per year. By 1766 the S.P.G. had granted its allowance and the Newbern teacher was reported to be getting along well. The schoolhouse, a "decent edifice for such a young country" was enclosed, 45 feet in length and 30 feet wide, and accounting to date for £300 Carolina currency—the entire local subscription—though still lacking floors and chimneys. The next step, reported the Reverend Reed, was that of advertising the undertaking from the pulpit at the next assembly session. For the time being, the Newbern vestry had agreed to pay the

30. *The Memorial of the Inhabitants of the Town of New-Bern* . . . , May 16, 1765, *ibid.,* Series B, Vol. V, No. 1; *ibid.,* Series B, Vol. V, No. 2.

schoolmaster £12 a year for attending the Newbern church in Reed's absence, a duty to be fulfilled with the aid of a copy of Tillotson's *Sermons*.[31]

Throughout the early days of his work as S.P.G. pedagogue, Tomlinson appears to have progressed satisfactorily. He promised in return for a slightly augmented stipend in 1767 to guarantee imprinting in the minds of his charges the doctrines of the established Church as well as to conform to whatever system of overseas exchange for salary purposes the Society deemed advisable. Next year he told about his newly appointed assistant and their joint efforts to teach nearly ninety pupils in a climate bound to sap the energy of the most resolute. Tomlinson paid the assistant, a candidate for holy orders, from his own pocket. By act of North Carolina's assembly a token duty upon imported rum was to provide enough money to discharge current debts, complete the schoolhouse, and furnish Mr. Tomlinson with about £20 per annum extra.[32]

As things turned out, the assistant's candidature for orders was well-timed with respect to his eventual career. No sooner had he presented himself for ordination in London than Tomlinson found it necessary to start cutting back on his initial plans for the Newbern school. For some time past, he wrote in 1770, the school had been on the decline, owing to high prices and scarce currency which prevented gentlemen from sending their children to board. Although the school trustees had lent every assistance, the building remained unfinished, the surrounding grounds lacked proper enclosure, and the property generally was sinking into disrepair as a result of recent hurricanes— facts that placed the future of free scholars in jeopardy. Faced

31. Mr. Tomlinson to the Secretary, Newbern, June 14, 1765, *ibid.*, Series B, Vol. V, No. 3; Mr. Reed to the Secretary, Newbern, July 10, 1765, *ibid.*, Series B, Vol. V, No. 142; Mr. Reed to the Secretary, Newbern, July 20, 1766, *ibid.*, Series B, Vol. V, No. 144.

32. Mr. Tomlinson to the Secretary, Newbern, January 26, 1767, *ibid.*, Series B, Vol. V, No. 4; Mr. Tomlinson to the Secretary, Newbern, January 26, 1767, *ibid.*, Series B, Vol. V, No. 5; Mr. Tomlinson to the Secretary, Newbern, January 20, 1768, *ibid.*, Series B, Vol. V, No. 6; Mr. Reed to the Secretary, Newbern, May 14, 1768, *ibid.*, Series B, Vol. V, No. 145.

with this financial crisis, trustees informed Tomlinson that non-paying pupils would have to be discharged in order that money raised through the tax on spirits might be used for repairing the school building. The extent of Mr. Tomlinson's own unreturned investment, amounting to over two hundred pounds, appeared in a statement of accounts dated December 25, 1771. Partial restitution had previously been ordered by the Society for Establishing a Public School in Newbern. But with it also came an unexpected announcement from that society. The same day, it notified Governor Josiah Martin that it had dismissed Mr. Tomlinson for negligence, and was recommending his second assistant, Mr. Joseph Parrot, be duly licensed to take up the vacant position.[33] What immediately followed was an intriguing discussion over the precise relationship between the S.P.G., the North Carolina assembly, the School Society, and the colonial governor.

Josiah Martin, governor of North Carolina, clearly was too busy to have the finer details of provincial educational matters at his fingertips. As a result, he took whatever legal counsel he could get. Attorney General Thomas McGuire responded succinctly. After carefully reading the act of the North Carolina assembly establishing the rights of Newbern school trustees, he concluded that whereas a schoolmaster could not be admitted without the governor's consent, the power of dismissal rested entirely in the hands of the trustee, whether or not the S.P.G. approved of him.[34]

The following winter, however, North Carolina lawyer Marmaduke Jones came up with a considerably more detailed

---

33. Mr. Tomlinson to the Secretary, Newbern, May 22, 1768, *ibid.*, Series B, Vol. V, No. 7; Mr. Tomlinson to the Secretary, Newbern, March 31, 1770, *ibid.*, Series B, Vol. V, No. 8; Samuel Cornell, James Davis, etc. to Thomas Tomlinson, Newbern, October 16, 1770, *ibid.*, Series B, Vol. No. 9; Account of Moneys due to Thomas Tomlinson . . . , *ibid.*, Series B, Vol. V, No. 13; Minutes of a meeting . . . , September 14, 1771, *ibid.*, Series B, Vol. V, No. 15; The Incorporated Society for Promoting and Establishing the Public School in Newbern to His Excellency Josiah Martin . . . , Newbern, September 14, 1771, *ibid.*, Series B, Vol. V, No. 17.

34. Thomas McGuire to the Governor of North Carolina, n.p., October 4, 1771, *ibid.*, Series B, Vol. V, No. 21.

opinion. From utmost attention to the letter of the law, he contended, it was necessary to be licensed, but not appointed, by the governor. The license, he continued, signified the governor's approbation of a particular person, without which he could not be admitted. Another requirement was the teacher's being of the Church of England. But with both these qualifications, he had not so much a right as a capacity of being admitted schoolmaster. The trustees still had the choice to make, and after making it reserved the right to dismiss and to recommend others. Put another way, the act empowered the governor to prevent the admission of any but such as he approved; but once admitted, the schoolmaster was subject to dismissal for cause by trustees. Nor was the precedent of an English schoolmaster licensed by the ordinary and, hence, not dismissed but by the ordinary's consent, exactly parallel. In Jones's opinion, indeed, even the English license was more of a diploma, "not to declare who shall, but who may be employed." This being the case, said Jones, Tomlinson's removal was quite regular.[35]

Precise as were the colonial legal standpoints regarding the Tomlinson case, those adopted by S.P.G. missionary Reed left a great deal more room for speculation. In a 1772 letter to the Society, Reed spoke of how difficult it was to determine the whole truth of the matter. Mr. Parrot, sometime assistant, Mr. Tomlinson himself, and a single dissenting trustee were the only available informants. When, Reed wrote, Tomlinson opened the school, he was warned of "the excessive indulgence of American parents, and the great difficulty of keeping up a proper discipline, more especially since his school consisted of members of both sexes." When pressed, though, he punished headstrong pupils and temporarily removed them, a policy which antagonized trustees whose children were affected. Also, Tomlinson had cause to be disappointed with unkept promises. When the act of assembly for establishing the school specified one penny a

---

35. Extract from a letter, Marmaduke Jones to the Governor of North Carolina, February 9, 1772, *ibid.*, Series B, Vol. V, No. 23.

gallon for a limited time to be laid on spirits imported into the Neuse River area, out of which Tomlinson was to have received £20 per annum for an assistant and to pay for poor children, the Newbern pedagogue brought Mr. Parrot over from London to help him look after a growing enrollment. But no sooner had he made this provision than the trustees required him to get rid of five poor students whom they claimed they could ill afford. The pretext was, said Reed, that the moneys thus saved might be applied to needed repairs; however, according to the one dissenting trustee, funds were adequate both for the poor children and for the reconstruction which in fact was never intended.

When Tomlinson found his school thus set upon, he was of course obliged, said Reed, to cancel the agreement with his assistant who, fortunately enough, was able to support himself by hack-writing and private tuition in mathematics. But this temporary expedient in no way reduced community antipathy toward a teacher temerous enough to expel the disobedient children of antagonistic trustees. The trustees, so went the story, urged assistant Parrot to open his own school and draw off Tomlinson's remaining source of revenue. Happily for Tomlinson, Parrot was a man of caution who for the time being waived what looked like an easy livelihood. Furthermore, Governor Tryon had taken an interest in the S.P.G. pedagogue and entertained no immediate notions of seeing him removed.

Tryon, however, was shortly thereafter transferred to New York. His successor sought the aforementioned legal advice so unfavorable, it transpired, to the teacher. This being the case, Martin had denied Tomlinson a public hearing. Meantime, the trustees worked quickly. If the Society missionary is to be accredited, they gave him no notice of meeting. Eight met. One dissented. Seven, therefore, dismissed the pedagogue, elected new trustees to fill two vacancies, and nine signed Mr. Parrot's nomination as teacher replacement.

But an impediment at length arose. Mr. Parrot, reported

Reed, declined the nomination, preferring to find less politically sensitive employment in the provincial secretary's office. Moreover, even after dismissal, Tomlinson stuck to his post. The School Society treasurer refused payment of money due. The pedagogue sued for above £200. This latest maneuver brought Reed to his next point. The majority of trustees, he indicated, were wealthy men, but for the most part lacking in schooling. In his opinion, they had little knowledge of any learned languages, of science, or of the difficulty of governing a school.

At length turning to the constitutional issues at stake, the Society missionary sincerely wished for the repeal of the act establishing the school. Such legislation, he urged, placed far too much power in the hands of uneducated trustees who should, he insisted, lay their accounts annually before the governor. Reed finally proposed that "if the Bishop of London would point out the Defects of the Present Act and get it repealed, I believe it would not be difficult to get a much better passed at the next session of the Assembly."[36] In this light Reed therefore saw the legitimacy as well as the necessity of S.P.G. intervention into North Carolina's local political affairs.

That the North Carolina governor was acutely embarrassed by his own invidious position in the affair is clear from his reluctant acceptance of the local legal advice he received. By the act of general assembly for establishing a public school in Newbern passed in 1766, he advised the bishop of London, the governor was invested with the power "perfectly nugatory" making his license necessary to the appointment of a teacher while the power of dismissal and removal was "reserved to the Trustees, and requires not his consent or participation." But Governor Martin's solution was not to step in with unilateral amendments, but rather to appeal to London ecclesiastical authorities for redress. The trustees, he complained, had acted capriciously in removing Tomlinson. Accordingly, he asked that

36. Mr. Reed to the Secretary, Newbern, February 15, 1772, *ibid.*, Series B, Vol. V, No. 147.

measures be taken to alter that part of the act making it possible for trustees to get rid of teachers without the governor's consent.[37]

Further letters to the bishop of London elaborated on the untenable position of a governor unable to make his voice heard in educational matters. Defending Tomlinson, Governor Martin sustained the cause of a master exercising a "just, moderate, and necessary exertion of authority of a pedagogue over contumaceous children." Once more repeating his complaint to the S.P.G., Governor Martin advised the bishop of London that the provincial law under which the school operated vested the trustees with power so absolute with respect to the dismissing of teachers that in the case of Tomlinson there was nothing he, the governor, could do except pray that the S.P.G. would continue to extend its subsidy, and lament over "ignorant and uneducated men . . . as little capable of judging the merits of a pedagogue as inclinable to justice."

To conclude, Martin appealed for official intervention from "home," writing

Matters of this nature falling particularly under your lordship's notice as patron of Religion and Letters, and coadjutor in the laudable and pious designs of the S.P.G. whose continuance and encouragement have been heretofore extended to this institution, I humbly beg leave to urge to your Lordship's consideration as a Member of His Majesty's most Honourable Privy Council the expediency of recommending the aforementioned Act of the General Assembly of the Province for His Majesty's Royal Disallowance as depriving the Governor of Power with which he ought to be invested to oppose the injurious and arbitrary proceedings of the Trustees, who left to the free exercise of their caprice must ruin an institution that might under proper regulations become of the utmost advantage to society by promoting useful knowledge.[38]

37. Extracts from two letters from his Excellency Joseph Martin, Esq., Gov. of N.C. to the Lord Bishop of London: the other to the S.P.G., dated June 20, 1772, *ibid.*, Series B, Vol. V, No. 26.

38. These last sentiments are set forth in Joseph Martin to the Bishop of London, Newbern, June 20, 1772, *ibid.*, Series B, Vol. V, No. 27; Josiah Martin to Thomas Burton [Bishop of London], n.p., June 20, 1772, *ibid.*, Series B, Vol. V, No. 28.

Thus, through such elevated channels would North Carolina's governor defend his authority against the Newbern trustees.

What is interesting about the Newbern episode is not that, like many S.P.G. schools, Tomlinson's institution was committed to oblivion by the ravages of military campaigns but that its Society parson and pedagogue both miscalculated on nearly every issue involving its establishment. They presumed that the pedagogue's initial investments were secure since less well-instructed colonists would welcome one qualified in teaching the humanities. They assumed that a growing popularity would necessitate the employment of an assistant and on speculation arranged for one to come. They believed that community appreciation for the Tomlinson régime would best be inculcated through an unbending discipline for pupils whose parents would thank the pedagogue for his objectivity. They trusted in the influence of the S.P.G. missionary superior—Mr. Reed—along with that of the provincial governor and lieutenant governor, for clearing the way toward operating as they saw fit. They failed to reckon with Carolina hurricanes or the debilitating effects of the Carolina climate. They understood that whatever matters could not be conveniently regularized by rector or governor could be brought to decisions through British parliamentary intervention. Lastly, they considered trustees and interested local supporters to be wealthy but ignorant men lacking in refinement, and they evidently failed to keep their opinions to themselves.

On these and other counts, Tomlinson and Reed were badly mistaken. Yet, misguided though they appear, they were in many senses typical of eighty years of S.P.G. parsons and pedagogues throughout the colonies, so optimistic in their hopes for good progress, so confident of the apparently self-evident worth of their American missions, so much out of contact with the realities of local power or the undercurrents of resentment constantly threatening their work. As an S.P.G. correspondent, Tomlinson soon vanished from the scene. In ten years time, revolutionary hostilities were at an end, thereby marking the settlement of the final salary remittance to the last S.P.G. preceptor within United States territory. There would be times when the new republic would again have to consider the benefits of subordination so eloquently extolled by the S.P.G. sermonists of old. But for the time being, Americans were to be getting their lessons in loyalty from other teachers or, in a few cases, from the same teachers with new outlooks on American politics.

At all events, as we have seen, the first phase of the S.P.G. educational thrust in the American colonies, brought to an end at Queen Anne's demise in 1714, was clearly characterized by a search for educational objectives among a mass of advice received from well-meaning friends of the Society. The second phase of the adventure, stretching from 1714 to 1763, was marked by the massing and implementation of propaganda deemed suitable to improving Church fortunes abroad, to inculcating colonial compliance, and to ensuring that these central contentions were not lost on young colonials, no matter how diverse their studies in S.P.G. schools. A period of retreat, phase three, which encompassed the two decades from 1763 to 1783, was punctuated by expressions of surprise and regret on the part of many Society teachers on both sides of the Atlantic, visibly perplexed to find their mother country imagery and attitude of unconscious superiority unacceptable as well as ineffectual in an alienated America. It now remains to speculate why four-score years of concerted educational effort should have produced educational results so different from those the S.P.G. had envisaged—results spelling colonial resentment toward the Society and what it stood for.

VI

PARSONS AND
PEDAGOGUES

THAT THE S.P.G. failed in its efforts to educate North America
to the sort of British Empire connection its High Church membership deemed proper is determined not so much by the fact
that life in wartime America proved untenable to S.P.G. servants as by the fact that their very presence was a contributing
factor to the Revolution.[1] Admittedly, propagating the gospel,
not educating in any narrow institutional sense of the word, was
what the Society set out to do. Early bylaws as well as subsequent policies governing appointment of parsons and pedagogues
indicated the S.P.G.'s understanding of the real breadth of its
missionary responsibilities. Extending Anglicanism according to
the charter was one thing, but beyond this overriding consideration the Society recognized its involvement in an American
colonial adventure in education, the specifics of which ranged

1. After massing substantial evidence to testify to this point, Carl
Bridenbaugh concluded that throughout the period here under examination,
"the minds and emotions of . . . generations of dissenting colonists were un-
consciously conditioned for revolt. There appears to be little doubt," he continued, "that if the American rebellion had been suppressed, not only the
dispatch of bishops but the establishment of the Church of England in the
colonies would have ensued," *Mitre and Sceptre*, pp. 335, 337.

from reading, writing, arithmetic, and catechism, through higher classical studies, to more abstracted concepts of empire loyalty couched in terms of social, political, and economic subservience. Unquestionably, the early members of the Venerable Society had every reason for optimism regarding this venture in provincial education. An Anglican organization already existed for the job. Administrative overlap appeared well-suited for maximum S.P.G. influence at home. This was especially true of bishops who not only knew the right people but also held seats in the House of Lords. Moreover, this phenomenon of multiple place-holding extended into the colonies, where governors in particular at first collaborated with Society missionaries and the Society secretary back in London in order to further Society interests. In short, from the standpoint of personnel the S.P.G. was a microcosm of the Church establishment itself.

Optimism notwithstanding, certain irreparable flaws in the S.P.G. edifice appeared quite early in the Society's experience as America's teacher. For one thing, it was never possible to match in North America the comparable components of England's established Church. First, the promotional pattern among Anglican diocesan seats linked rising responsibility and income with gravitation toward metropolitan London.[2] Candidates for American missionary or classroom assignments tended to include such men as were not only failing to fulfill their material expectations at the heart of empire but who were also facing severe financial difficulties unlikely to be rectified at the empire's periphery. Second, the most vigorous attempts on the part of the Society fell short of convincing Britain's government of the need to establish during any stage of the period here under scrutiny a resident colonial bishopric.

Left to shift for themselves, subordinate ranks of Society servants faced America with misgivings. Uncertain of their commissions, insecure respecting otherwise routine daily judgments,

---

2. For an excellent discussion of the topic, see Sykes, *Church and State*, Chapter IV, "The Ladder of Preferment."

they fed back to headquarters a picture of American life less deliberately distorted than inadvertantly colored by the frustrations of a nebulous charge. Missionary discipline had to be shared among such Church officials as senior rectors and colonial commissaries, or delegated to colonial governors. But these Church and governmental officers rarely found their ideal notions of colonial administration consistent with the exigencies of colonial life. To be sure, Churchmen like Rector Vesey of Trinity Church, New York, typified the man on the spot who simply assumed he had authority over subordinates like schoolmaster William Huddleston or catechist Elias Neau. But, for the most part, the commissary, that interstitial figure enjoying some of the bishop's responsibilities but few of his perquisites, fared badly. Holding power of recommendation but not of ordination, of censure but not of dismissal, men like Gideon Johnston and Alexander Garden of South Carolina soon discovered they occupied invidious positions exposing them to insults at the hands of their S.P.G. subordinates and submitting their written appeals for guidance to interminable ocean voyages and the chances of storm or naval combat.

Little better off were the colonial governors whose status steadily diminished as the century progressed. At the beginning of the Society's American adventure, Governor Cornbury was having difficulty enough regulating the licensing of teachers among Long Island Quakers, in checking the political outbursts of S.P.G. servants such as Thorougood Moore, and in defining with any precision his own duties concerning Society activities in early New York. Toward the end of the Society's régime abroad, governors like North Carolina's Joseph Martin discovered it impossible to decide and act on licensing questions which normally would have been handled by an English bishop or his immediate delegate. Under the circumstances, the only solution was to recruit into the mission field men of exceptional talent whose missionary zeal was least likely to conflict with their material ambition or to compromise their likelihood of staying out of trouble.

But judging from the ample documentation of financial disappointment and local rejection suffered by S.P.G. parsons and pedagogues who left Britain, the Society was far from successful in this last respect. The logical answer was to find volunteers in America, and this the Society did with a measure of advantage, numerically speaking. But the administrative vacuum created by the continuing absence of a colonial bishop, together with the ascending scale of Society stipends from token amounts for schoolmasters to substantial sums for missionaries, only served to compound an already unsatisfactory manpower situation. Resident colonials had to go to England for ordination and many were lost at sea as a result. Since there were no diocesan seats located provincially, the prospect of the miter formed no part of the colonial promotional scheme of things. As a general rule, though, schoolmasters aspired to catechists' roles, catechists to regional missionary assignments, and missionaries to rectorships of the leading city churches. Rare was the career S.P.G. pedagogue.

It is not surprising that throughout their active years of S.P.G. involvement Society men abroad wrote passionately and often to headquarters regarding the exceptional challenges of propagating the gospel in foreign parts. Had these periodic jottings been kept confidential, it is doubtful that nonconformists harassment of Society efforts would have achieved the persistence it did. But the S.P.G.'s propaganda program aimed at securing the subscriptions so vital to its operation depended for its verve upon wide circulation of missionary impressions. So these colonial *cris de cœur* as a matter of policy found their way into *Abstracts* and *Anniversary Sermons* and were redistributed in colonial America, bringing about an even more rigidly defensive posture on the part of an already beleaguered Society cadre facing irritated nonconformists who complained that the S.P.G. was habitually misinformed by its emissaries. The corresponding downward spiral in S.P.G. field morale, and its circuitous effect upon London-based concepts about the true nature of colonial life, could scarcely have been predicted by those responsible for developing the charter. Yet, one cannot deny that Society parsons and pedagogues engaged in an undertaking unique in its documentation of fresh impressions of colonial existence, impressive in its geographic scope, rich in the variety of its modes of teaching, diverse in its association with developing colonial institutions, and stubborn in the persistence of its messages for colonial consumption.

Eighteenth-century England suffered the human degradation of gin mills and poverty-motivated crime. The Society newcomer to eighteenth-century America likewise faced certain grim realities. An awesome solitude often pressed in upon the parson circuit rider. Stifling heat exhausted the conscientious pedagogue. Both shuddered at unaccustomed winter blasts; both languished with chronic disease; both advised headquarters of their predicaments.[3] Apart from this repetitive saga of sheer physical demands placed upon the Society servant abroad, however, S.P.G. impressions of America gleaned from the first startled confrontation with new ways of thinking and acting no doubt played an important part in determining the tone of subsequent educational efforts. In the beginning, stereotyping in the metaphorical mode made up a good part of eastbound communication. For George Keith, the Quaker was a snake in the grass. To John Urmston, "anythingarian" denoted the uncommitted

3. One may rightly enquire if at least *some* S.P.G. men did not report pleasure in their work and surroundings. Available evidence from thousands of Society letters indicates the negative. Vernon L. Parrington suggested that the eighteenth-century American conservative gentleman considered the frontier simply a "temptation to gross social laxity." More often, he argued, it was from the pens of such eighteenth-century democrats as Crèvecoeur that there emerged an America of "verdant fields, . . . fair navigable rivers, and . . . green mountains." See *Letters from an American Farmer . . .* (London: 1782), cited in Vernon L. Parrington, *Main Currents in American Thought: The Colonial Mind, 1620–1800* (New York: Harcourt, Brace and World, Inc., 1927, 1954), pp. 139–50.

parishioner. *Abstracts* told of lukewarm people, giddy-brained, raving enthusiastically, weeds and thorns to be rooted out from among the standing conformist crop. Far from mere irritability on the part of classically trained eccentrics endowed with poignant *tournure de phrase,* these figures of speech were symptomatic of a more deeply ingrained resentment of the unusual. Over the years stock phrases were replaced by more particular forms of complaint. But continued expressions of surprise at novelty tell of certain essential differences between eighteenth-century British and colonial life—differences significant to men occupied in the multifarious aspects of teaching.

Society pedagogues, for example, found much unusual about the American colonial schools. For one thing, the fact that these needed building at all, and with wide community involvement at that, was cause for comment, as was news of their achievement, often complete with dimensions and construction costs. Indeed, the mood of intense relief expressed by Englishmen Joseph Cleator at Rye, Thomas Morritt at Charleston, and Thomas Tomlinson at Newbern serves to underscore that fear of pedagogical itineracy experienced by men used to staying put. For another thing, the colonial pupil loomed as a threat to previously held notions of appropriate comportment for children. Morritt, for instance, found his boys to be exceedingly impertinent, while Tomlinson failed to survive continuing disciplinary difficulties which at length wrecked his plans for a North American school of the first rank. As for the colonial parent, his failure to pay overdue schooling bills and his tendency to regulate attendance of son or daughter to match the practical demands of the harvest or the extravagant claims of opposition schoolmasters at first caught the immigrant Society pedagogue off guard.

Recently-arrived parsons, with greater circles of responsibility than their pedagogue confrères, likewise were prone to react with wonder to new dimensions of the common round. Like their subordinates in the classroom, they yearned for a building in which to gather their congregations, and provided near stone-by-stone, board-by-board progress reports. Those newcomers obliged to travel in order to serve remote settlements explained to the S.P.G. the huge expenditures of energy required to oblige distant proselytes. Many, like John Urmston of North Carolina, found themselves embarrassed by less-rigid social lines than in the old land they could take for granted. Custom dictated their living with a degree of elegance; but minimal stipends precluded such appearances. Habit suggested they refrain from manual labor; but necessity, together with the normal colonial assumption that one man may range widely in his work, sometimes indicated physical involvement beyond mere genteel gardening. Tradition ordered their answering to one man in the ecclesiastical scheme of things; but New World Church organization made room for substantial powers of the vestry. Training demanded the careful preparation of sermons in the solitude of a well-furnished study; but practice necessitated getting by on a slender library and over-extended parochial duties. Previous associations ensured devotion to High Church doctrine and liturgy; but present contacts demanded confrontation with an often alarming latitudinarianism. Thus, some S.P.G. parsons—John Talbot, Gideon Johnston, and James Honyman, for example—found their tasks abroad sufficiently frustrating. Others, such as John Wesley, wrote off North America as a sort of purgatory.

Interestingly enough, colonial-raised S.P.G. servants, possibly by virtue of their continuing correspondence with metropolitan Society administrators in London, painted a picture of colonial life in many ways as critical as that of their British-born colleagues. Whatever exceptions to this general rule did occur tended to advise of superior provisions for education made in New England. For the rest, though, an ultra sensitivity to real or imaginary threats and a continuing appeal for the direction of authority indicated acute discomfort at a colonial society regrouping earlier patterns of prerogative. Indigent S.P.G. schoolmen like William Huddleston or Rowland Ellis regretted their

penurious circumstances, the drain upon their establishments
caused by opposition schoolmasters, the unsteady attendance,
their need for supplementary employment, the early placement
of promising children in a trade, the inroads of traveling teachers, the presumed dullness of Negro slaves, the fickleness of
Indians, the stupidity of mothers, the parsimony of fathers, the
fragmentation of effort among too many jobs, and the never-
ending struggle for accommodation. American-born Society parsons likewise expressed keen regret at the scarcity of books, the
duplicity of Indians, the machinations of congregationalism,
the stinginess of those occupying colonial pews, the rampant
colonial illiteracy, the insufficiency of American colleges, the
excesses of awakening enthusiasm, the chaos due to the lack of
a bishop abroad, the distance from British universities from
which numerous American Society men held honorary degrees,
and, toward the end of the period, the disloyalty of the republican patriot.

One cannot resist the conclusion, however, that native and
immigrant S.P.G. agent alike conjured up a depressing image of
America as a bench mark from which more safely to measure
progress. This, in fact, was the perspective about which W. R.
Cross once wrote of another age that "the missionary automati-
cally emphasized the situation of 'moral' waste before his arrival,
the obstructions thrown about him by his opponents, the erro-
neous and ineffective work of other churches, and his own
successful revivals."[4] It need hardly be said that in the Society's
case these impressions of the colonial scene bear at best partial
resemblance to the actualities of eighteenth-century American
life,[5] featuring measurable achievements in private and public

4. W. R. Cross, *The Burned Over District: The Social and Intellectual History of Enthusiastic Religion in Western New York, 1800–1850* (New York:
Harper and Row, 1950, 1965), p. 47.
5. Several interesting works verify various aspects of colonial culture.
Louis B. Wright, *The Cultural Life of the American Colonies* (New York:
Harper and Row, 1957) gives an excellent general treatment of books, archi-
tecture, science, and the press. Gordon C. Lee, *Crusade Against Ignorance*
(New York: Bureau of Publications, 1961) devotes its introductory essay to
the universality characterizing the range of Jefferson's intellectual achieve-

libraries, scientific, architectural, and literary arts, craftsmanship, and, above all, formal schooling.

In this last respect, a review of dominant types of colonial schools toward the later decades of the S.P.G. adventure in American education shows a burgeoning network of institutions reflecting religious diversity, trading class interests, and a growing aversion to such forms of central control as were implicit in the Society's own scheme. New England's educational tradition of local government initiative in school affairs stretched back to the very earliest seventeenth-century settlement. By the 1750s the northern provinces boasted dozens of town and district schools. Less amenable to public control by virtue of religious and national heterogeneity, the middle colonies leaned toward private control schools, many of which were referred to by Society missionaries stationed in various parts of New York and Pennsylvania. In the South, too, private incentive in school operation prevailed until the Revolution. The net result of these regional commitments, though, was a considerable array of common schools, Latin grammar schools, private English schools, academies, and colleges.[6]

Against this backdrop of American culture and education which S.P.G. men either failed to perceive or deliberately ignored, parsons and pedagogues strove to succeed. In S.P.G. history, however, "success" emerges as a highly relative term. To be sure, a certain statistical triumph—a function of headcounting—provides a fundamental theme. One senses, however,

ments. A similar essay introduces John Hardin Best's *Benjamin Franklin on Education* (New York: Bureau of Publications, 1962) and analyzes the colonial climate conducive to self-education. Frederick Rudolph's *The American College and University* (New York: Alfred Knopf, 1962) is less sanguine, but concedes the importance of the colonial college as educator of leaders. Daniel J. Boorstin, *The Americans: The Colonial Experience* (New York: Vintage Books, 1964) contends that before the Revolution America "had become one of the more 'civill' parts of the world."

6. The colleges included Harvard, 1636; William and Mary, 1693; Yale, 1701; Princeton, 1746; King's, 1754; Philadelphia, 1755; Brown, 1764; Rutgers, 1766; Dartmouth, 1769. For a good discussion of prevailing patterns of colonial education, see R. Freeman Butts and Lawrence A. Cremin, *A History of Education in American Culture* (New York: Holt, Rinehart and Winston, 1953), pp. 97–137.

the telling effect of America on Society parsons and pedagogues, as opposed to *their* influence on the colonies themselves.[7] Certainly, a review from the days of George Keith indicates a surprisingly high degree of inability to cope with the steady realignment of colonial social components and the threat posed by this process to a relatively inflexible Anglican transatlantic enterprise. The mortality roster, in fact, is startling.

George Keith himself, too zealous, perhaps, for the likings of S.P.G. liberals, returned to England for a life of rural obscurity. John Talbot was dismissed after nineteen years of service for tangling with the New Jersey provincial government. John Urmston retired under a cloud of disrepute. Elias Neau suffered summary removal (though he was at length reinstated) for failure to attune his Negro catechetical school to the requirements of New York slaveholders. Thorougood Moore was arrested on order of Governor Cornbury on charges of political meddling. Thomas Eager resigned his Braintree mission as a result of verbal as well as physical violence against townsmen. Francis Phillips was sent packing for maligning Governor Hunter. Thomas Poyer gave up following twenty-one years of service after being cautioned against too forceful dispute of parsonage ownership. Richard Marsden had his missionary appointment cancelled for misconduct even before it took effect. James Giguillet quit his South Carolina post, allegedly to live off the savings of his elderly bride. Jacob Henderson resigned his S.P.G. Newcastle mission after accusing Lewis Morris of misusing a missionary's talents. Robert Sinclair resigned after two years. Dismissal came to Burlington's pedagogue, Rowland Ellis, for neglect. Resignation in favor of a parish charge was Thomas Morritt's choice. Rejection for inability to reconcile the

7. Various renderings of the "cutural shock" theses are to be found in such works as Oscar Handlin, *The Uprooted* (New York: Grosset and Dunlap, 1951); Howard Mumford Jones, *O Strange New World* (New York: Viking Press, 1952, 1964); Bernard Bailyn, *Education in the Forming of American Society* (New York: Vintage Books, 1960); Oscar Handlin, *The Americans* (Boston: Little, Brown and Co., 1963); Louis Hartz, *The Founding of New Societies* (New York: Harcourt, Brace and World, 1964).

conflicting demands of local agencies was the reward of Newbern's schoolmaster Thomas Tomlinson. Less spectacular than
these open breaches, yet apparent as common expressions of
ressentiment on the part of eighteenth-century S.P.G. correspondents, are endless confessions of frustration, disillusion-
ment, antagonism, fear, envy, suspicion, and confusion, as well
as despair at ever achieving minimal personal ambition, let
alone fulfilling the major provisions of the 1701 S.P.G. charter.

In spite of inability to comprehend, hence to adapt, personally, to a less-rigidly defined social order lacking the automatic
safeguards of Britain's Anglican establishment, S.P.G. parsons
and pedagogues were nonetheless engaged in an educational
undertaking the scope of which was without precedent in English missionary history up to the time. Indeed, the seriousness
of the Society's intentions from 1701 to the severence of North
American connections in 1783 may be graphically demonstrated
by the simple exercise of matching marking pins with centers
of S.P.G. educational activity as plotted on suitably mounted
maps. The resulting chart fairly bristles with signals.

To the north, a pin at Brunswick, Maine, denotes the spot
from which in 1779 Jacob Bailey fled revolutionaries and
headed for Nova Scotia. To the south, a similar sign at St.
George's, Georgia, indicates the mission from which John
Holmes was removed for unsatisfactory conduct in 1777 after
four years of Society affiliation. Between the two, a band of pins
hugging the southeastern coastline, but thickening inland from
the New Jersey shore and northward, replicates the very wide
distribution of ministers, catechists, and schoolmasters engaged
in Society work. Major colonial centers such as Boston, New
York, Philadelphia, and Charleston sprout rich clusters of these
labels. Thriving towns like Portsmouth, Providence, New London, New Haven, and New Brunswick feature less dense but
still noticeable concentrations. Relatively isolated markers show

how at one time or another S.P.G. men pushed upstream along
America's waterways—up the Piscataqua to Dover; the Housa-
tonic to Great Barrington; the Hudson and Mohawk to New-
burgh, Poughkeepsie, Albany, Schenectady, Fort Hunter, and
Johnstown; the Delaware to Phillipsburg; the Susquehanna to
Pequea; Albermarle Sound and the Chowan to Edenton; the
Pamlico to Bath; the Neuse to New Bern; the Cape Fear to
St. Pauls; the Santee to St. Paul; the Savannah to Augusta; and
the St. Mary's to St. George's, the most southerly S.P.G. post,
southeast of the great Okefenokee Swamp.

Numerical rather than visual representation of the total Society educational effort abroad is every bit as impressive. Altogether, some three hundred and forty missionaries at some two
hundred central stations strove to improve the minds and
morals of their colonial congregations. While they were thus
occupied, at least one hundred and twenty of their catechist
and schoolmaster colleagues busied themselves teaching a variety
of subjects ranging from catechism and the singing of psalms
to Latin and mathematics. Despite chronic complaints that
S.P.G. stipends fell short of a colonial subsistence level com-
mensurate with the proper social standing of an officer of the
Anglican establishment, the Society laid out not inconsiderable
sums of money in aid of its American program. Annual expenditures varied from a minimum of £452 sterling in the 1701
inaugural year to a maximum of £8,860 in 1771, and reached
a cumulative total for the eighty-two years here in question of
£357,528. Illusory though such particulars tend to be when
one takes no account of the chronological overlap of educational service or of the passage of time, the Society's American
representation in given years along the way is still striking. By
1714, for example, six schoolmasters and twenty-six missionaries occupied themselves at teaching tasks. At mid century,
seventeen pedagogues and fifty-eight parsons were at work.
Granted, many careers in S.P.G. service were short. On the

other hand, some stretched twenty, thirty, even forty years, now and again continuing in insular or continental British North America following the Revolution.

In addition to this creditable educational coverage of colonial America, the S.P.G. drew on a remarkably wide range of instructional modes. Central to their work, of course, were church pulpit and classroom dais, and from these vantage points Society parsons and pedagogues taught generations of colonists, slaves, and Indians the fundamentals of literacy and of Anglican Christianity as well as the benefits and responsibilities of close association with empire-building Britain. But schools and churches by no means exhausted S.P.G. educational resources.

To start with, the Anglican propensity for punctilious sermon-preparation not only provided steady work for printers like London's Downing or Philadelphia's Dunlap, but likewise assured a continuous supply of inexpensive reading material available, as many a preface immodestly maintained, "upon unanimous request of the congregation," and dealing not just with Old and New Testament apologies for routine missionary practices, but providing as well a good deal of currently significant civic and political opinion. From London anniversary sermons bound together with S.P.G. abstracts not only radiated to the provincial towns of eighteenth-century Britain but also furnished a chance for Society servants abroad and the better instructed of their parishioners to read about colonial life among distant compatriots as perceived by headquarters officials. From colonial presses the printed sermons and occasional essays of missionaries in the field also found eager readers, not a few of whom responded in kind. Moreover, scores of thousands of Bibles, Common Prayer Books, Church Catechisms, and pamphlets of every description were annually packaged and dispatched to America for distribution among Church vestryman and proselyte alike. As incentive, each missionary and many schoolmasters received a box of appropriate titles or an allowance which might be spent according to individual requisition.

Further to these lesser provisions, valuable bequests enlarged already distinguished colonial collections. As C. F. Pascoe has pointed out,[8] the Reverend Dr. Millington of Kensington bequeathed in 1728 some 1,600 volumes, the possession of the New York clergy until largely decimated by British troops and used as legal tender in Long Island taverns. In 1758 nearly 1,500 books, mostly the donation of the Reverend Dr. Bristowe of London, were assigned to King's College and arrived intact five years later, many to suffer the same fate as the Millington gift.[9] Christ Church, Boston, benefited from a substantial donation in 1746, and Harvard College was twice the recipient of Society philanthropy, once at the bequest of George Berkeley in 1748 and later, after the 1764 fire, through the forethought of East Apthorp, sometime missionary at Cambridge. Added to this bibliophilistic missionary tradition springing from the earlier work of Thomas Bray and his associates was the Society's persistent effort to provide translated reading material for Indians as well as for European immigrants.

When it came to making best possible use of their resources, S.P.G. parsons and pedagogues were forced to find such opportunities as arose. Especially during the first decade of its North American adventure, the Society expected its representatives to take their cues from George Keith, and travel far and wide to gather the uncommitted to the Church fold. Men like Gideon Johnston, John Urmston, and John Wesley in the South, or John Talbot in New Jersey, and numerous of their colleagues in New England's outlying districts or the well-spaced Hudson and Mohawk villages, rapidly learned about the hazards of overland circuits or the perils of waterway travel in aid of spreading the gospel among frontiersmen. In the fullness of time, colonial centers boasted structurally aesthetic places of Anglican worship furnished within according to the highest standards of Old Country taste. But along the fringes of settlement, S.P.G. parsons

8. Pascoe, *Two Hundred Years*, p. 798.
9. Austin Baxter Keep, "The Library of King's College," *Columbia University Quarterly*, XIII (June, 1911), 275–84.

continued to pursue waterways and trails, holding communion wherever and whenever they could, leaving catechist or schoolmaster to tend the central church while they themselves comforted the sick, buried the dead, and gave out their supplies of books and tracts for study pending their return.

Society pedagogues also utilized an astonishing variety of means to accommodate their pupils and fulfill S.P.G. obligations. Actual physical arrangements included private dwellings, rented premises of every description, church buildings, log cabins, fieldstone meeting houses, and upstairs apartments. Various combinations of boys and girls, young men and women, white, Indian, and Negro, free, indentured, and slave, Church and dissenter, made up classes learning the gamut of subjects from catechism to classics.

Because slaves and bonded servants could not attend day school, many S.P.G. teachers opened their schools at night and often instructed older people at that time regardless of their state of freedom. In some areas, pupils preoccupied with spring planting or fall harvest could take advantage of summer classes and achieve rudimentary literacy in the shortest possible number of hours. Even sailors with a day or two shore leave might drift into such harbor towns as New York and pick up a tract and a word of encouragement before re-embarking.

One might have imagined that a teaching mission so widely applicable and apparently flexible could have survived the most radical colonial innovations. As it transpired, the Society's intervention in rapidly changing American institutions and its struggle to ensure empire compliance failed to sustain initial impetus, and eventually came to a halt.

To the charter members of Britain's Venerable Society, there was not much doubt as to the sort of schoolteacher fitted for the onerous task of taking in hand errant colonial children and patiently leading them to the knowledge of letters, hence, of

God. Lest there should have been any hesitation concerning a pedagogue's qualifications, S.P.G. administrators laid out detailed instructions which were aimed at preserving the Society's good name while simultaneously ameliorating the ignorant condition of American pupils. Commentators since the days of David Humphreys have rightly indicated the humanitarian thinking which, in a brutal age, could allow for kind and gentle methods of instruction as well as the mere mechanics of reporting on educational progress. The fact remains, however, that lacking a complete colonial episcopal superstructure, the Society's educational program abroad was obliged to rely on a highly fragmented series of connections with the communities in which its schoolmasters operated. As a result, there seemed little hope of ensuring that anyone other than the pedagogue himself and his students actually knew what took place in the classroom during the normal course of events. Much, there is no doubt, was kindly. Some, presumably, was also efficient. But a good deal, it seems probable, fell far short of S.P.G. expectations.

To Society members at home, the initial notion of dispatching schoolmasters from England itself constituted the best means of ensuring execution of the proper sort of instruction. A case in point was Joseph Cleator, who had left his West Cumberland residence, accepted a £20 annual S.P.G. stipend, secured the personal backing of the influential Colonel Heathcote, and managed, with prompting from his missionary superiors, to satisfy the humanitarian intentions of the Society as well as the instructional requirements of the boys and girls of colonial Rye. The very limitations placed upon such an ambitious American educational program by the volunteer nature of S.P.G. financing rendered the wholesale employment of men like Cleator exceptional, not regular. Indeed, even Cleator relied to some extent on Caleb Heathcote's patronage, on local Church perquisites, and on community donations in order more or less effectively to ply his trade. In most cases, essential to Society educational progress was some already ongoing educational enterprise which the S.P.G. might subsidize, but not wholly underwrite.

Among the many alternative means of accomplishing the latter end, one in particular—granting an allowance to a pedagogue already established on his own—served as the basis for all subsequent administrative elaboration. But the ensuing network of community involvement contrasted with the apparent simplicity of the pedagogue's task as the Society conceived of it. To start with, regardless of their Church membership, those holding municipal office often had to be judges of which poor children deserved a free education in an S.P.G.-subsidized school. Once such decisions were made, inspection of school premises and effectiveness of instruction fell to a variety of civil officers, often including governor, mayor, alderman, or magistrate, as well as to prominent Society members abroad. In addition, provincial governors, whatever their religious affiliation, initially stood in the place of London's bishop whenever the urgency of licensing could not wait for the slow business of transatlantic communication. Thus, from the earliest days of the S.P.G. colonial adventure in education, boundaries of Society control in school affairs overlapped those of local civil interests in educational matters.

In one sense this blurring of the understood limits of school control was not unlike the situation among English charity schools,[10] hospitals, workhouses, and insane asylums of the same period, featuring certain taken-for-granted coordination between church and state along a broad spectrum of philanthropic undertakings, among which the S.P.G. with its royal charter and parliamentary connections was but one example. But, in other senses the Society found itself increasingly incapable of containing the role of schoolmaster within the frame of reference provided either by the charter or by custom in Britain, and

10. See especially M. G. Jones, *The Charity School Movement,* (Cambridge, England: 1938).

progressively unable to rely on the supposition that civil authorities which concerned themselves with what S.P.G. schools were about would necessarily approve of them.

The first of these two difficulties—that of realizing some more-or-less common expectation of a pedagogue's job—was compounded by the previously indicated fact that subsistance on a Society stipend was not possible. Additional employment proved customary, despite a missionary convention that labor other than that strictly connected with Church affairs was beneath the dignity of a Church parson. When this auxiliary occupation took the form of minor church or civic office, nothing was subtracted from pedagogical effort but time. When, however, Society schoolteachers went farming, practiced the rudiments of medicine, undertook copying and hack writing, kept shops, or worked as hired help in a multitude of community occupations, something of the mystery, the authority, hence the dignity of the title "schoolmaster" seems to have suffered.

The same phenomenon of apparent pedagogical insufficiency loomed large whenever shortcuts to full S.P.G. teaching qualifications were dictated by local circumstances. In Charleston, for instance, the training and use as teachers of minimally literate Negro boys failed as a result of their inability to be at once slave and master. Among the Mohawk encampments west of Albany, Indian schoolmasters were either lured by their fellows to abandon for hunting their occupation with children in the classroom, or held in open contempt for being mere cripples. In similar fashion, Dutch interpreters[11] serving to help non-Indian-speaking Society teachers could rarely be relied upon to transmit to Indian children a notion of the importance of a Society pedagogue unable to communicate with them.

The second problem—relying on the support of community authorities other than S.P.G. delegates—became extremely complex as Society teachers accepted payment from quarters other

11. For a stimulating discussion of the theology of mission-as-translation, see Bengt Sundkler, *The World of Mission* (Grand Rapids: Wm. B. Eerdmans Publishing Company, 1963, 1965), trans. Eric J. Sharpe.

than the S.P.G. itself, or relied on different agencies for liberty to operate. Even when such income or permission was forthcoming from a Church vestry, matters could be complicated enough. Rowland Ellis, for instance, discovered to his downfall that his Burlington churchwardens were far more tolerant of their Quaker associates than he was. When, as in the case of Thomas Grainger, a license to teach had to be secured from Boston's dissenting selectmen as well as from the bishop of London, the scope of S.P.G. educational influence was doubly restricted by the recognized nonconformist intervention into Society educational affairs as well as by the admitted excellence of Boston's own schools. By far the most troublesome of all, though, was the sort of school operation which left the Society pedagogue responsible to an S.P.G. notion of missionary education on the one hand and a developing concept, particularly in the South, of a "free" or "public" school established and, to some degree at least, funded through provincial legislation. Just how delicate was the Society pedagogue's task under this two-fold, and sometimes conflicting, responsibility may best be judged by recalling the similar experiences of Thomas Morritt and Thomas Tomlinson, both of whom proved incapable of reconciling their personal ambitions either with the Society's regulations governing schoolmasters or with the stipulations of colonial acts of assembly.

In Morritt's case, initial government support under South Carolina's Free School Act had secured him a house, a promise of a school building, an advance on salary, and authorization to act as minister whenever appropriate occasion arose. The Society, moreover, had assured him of a salary of £30, a reasonably high figure for those times. Unfortunately, a shift in the composition of the colonial assembly brought about a corresponding shift of opinion regarding the school's location as well as a three-way disagreement among Morritt, Commissary Garden, and some of the more experienced provincial government officials concerning the legitimacy of the schoolmaster's parallel duties as parson and pedagogue. Even if Morritt had been obliged to contend with only one of the two above adversaries, the lack of their support would have spelled disaster for an already extended personal investment in colonial education. Morritt faced both reprimand from the S.P.G. via the Church commissary and the sudden termination of provincial funds; his school could not possibly have escaped closure.

Some fifty years later, Thomas Tomlinson found himself in even more direct conflict with civil authorities, although now with the S.P.G. missionary Mr. Reed on his side of the argument. Whereas Morritt at least had not needed to confront a board (in South Carolina, commissioners had been requested simply to study the correctness of operating the Charleston "free" school under the act), Tomlinson was directly answerable not just to the Society but likewise to the trustees of a fully established organization bearing like the Society itself an impressive title— The Incorporated Society for Promoting and Establishing the Public School in Newbern. Partially funded by a duty on imported liquor, the latter group conceded the governor's licensing prerogative for their teachers but concluded that theirs was the exclusive right to dismiss, a privilege they unhesitatingly exercised in Tomlinson's case, in spite of the governor's uncertainty about the propriety of the matter and of the S.P.G. parson's vehement protest.

There is admittedly much evidence testifying that the Society wished by means of its missionary parsons and pedagogues to establish churches and schools with as little local friction as possible and to withdraw their support once such institutions had arrived at a durable self-sufficiency. The churches' relatively easy transition to post-revolutionary American episcopacy suggests that their vestry democracy successfully combined Church form of worship with a new republican spirit.

Schools, on the contrary, were infinitely more sensitive to problems of ultimate control. In fact, the apparent flexibility of the S.P.G. schoolman's relationships with the community at

large indicated not so much his virtuosity in manipulating contradictory interests as the fact that, with growing confidence,
the community could get along without him. From the first days
of William Huddleston's New York experience through to
Thomas Tomlinson's failure in Newbern, the inroads of opposition schools occupied substantial portions of schoolmasters' reports to S.P.G. headquarters. Acts of assembly in the South,
municipal involvement in the middle colonies, and combinations
of town and provincial enactments in New England added a wide
variety of alternatives for the consideration of colonial parents
seeking proper instruction for their children. As early as the
1720s, Society pedagogues like Samuel Grainger were describ-
ing in detail the Massachusetts laws providing "public" grammar
and writing schools and the obligation of provincial citizens to
maintain them. By 1751 schoolmaster Joseph Browne and his
illustrious Stratford missionary superior, Samuel Johnson, were
to agree that the former's resignation was nothing to regret, in
view of the provincial government's backing of good schools.
Less than a decade later, Samuel Cooke explained to the S.P.G.
secretary that Monmouth County, New Jersey, parents—even
those lacking religious feelings—were anxious to provide fundamental education for their children, willing to make considerable
personal sacrifice to achieve this goal, and at times upset by
charity implications when offered free classroom services. Much
more upsetting, though, for large bodies of Americans were the
infinite variations upon a theme of Empire subordination con-
stituting one of the Society's foremost educational preoccupa-
tions in North America.

Upon consideration of the annual traffic across the Atlantic
throughout the 1700s, the hopes of wealth overseas, the naval
engagements, the Indian wars, the brave explorations, the lure
of the slave trade, the riches to be had in land, furs, timber,
and fish, the letters to relatives and acquaintances abroad, and
the conversations all these things must surely have engendered,

one could reasonably assume that by mid century the S.P.G.
might have arrived at a fairly detailed picture of the political
complexity and social variety of colonial America.

That later Society officials like Samuel Seabury of New York
should refer to neighboring American provinces as foreign powers provides an extreme case of latter-day provincialism doubtless provoked by the political exigencies of the 1770s. Under
quieter domestic circumstances obtaining during the Society's
first dozen years or so of operation, however, the S.P.G. was
inclined to lump American colonies together as one undifferentiated national asset—the romantically vague "Plantacons, Colonies, and Factories beyond the Seas" of charter fame.

Along with this fabulous, albeit durable, concept of North
America, so prevalent in the range of media from letters to
anniversary sermons, several important assumptions about
American inhabitants held currency. Most persistent of these
was the near-axiomatic allegation of the inferiority of all colonists who, had their antecedents been made of sterner stuff,
would not have needed to exchange their native shore for a
wilderness. Thus, with only rare exceptions, the primary recipients of Society education were portrayed as objects of pity who,
despite their rights as Englishmen, might be expected to aspire
but to a modified empire citizenship.

A second, not unrelated, social notion held that Christianity
was compatible with slavery on a large scale and that, accordingly, Negro bondsmen could benefit from Christian teaching
and kindly treatment while their owners profits through increased output. Here was no questioning the institution of Negro
slavery itself. In fact, such a challenge would have proven particularly embarrassing to a Society whose missionaries were
themselves slaveowners and whose income was annually bolstered both by means of private donations from slaveholder
members and from earnings of the large scale slave-operated
Codrington plantation in Barbadoes. What was involved, rather,
was the endorsement of a production system whereby the exer-

tion of human muscle-power was delegated to a caste, designated as inferior, but entitled to humane treatment.

A third belief about American society, commonly elaborated in earlier S.P.G. pronouncements but seriously reviewed after bloody wars, concerned American Indians. These peoples, at first considered as autonomous nations subject to regular diplomatic overtures, certainly appeared as hopeful converts to an agricultural way of life, and, eventually, to Christian faith and Anglican liturgy, sufficiently simplified to match their naive dignity.

Hence, in the Society's first years its nebulous, sometimes distorted understanding of the geographic, spiritual, and political composition of colonial America, coupled with a rudimentary view of a monolithic American society, subordinated by definition to Britain, but stratified within itself above a Negro slave base, permeated its entire educational undertaking.

With the growing S.P.G. dependence upon American-born parsons and pedagogues the way lay open for on-the-spot reporting of American colonial life. Understandably, indigent colonists pressed into Society service, and required to submit relatively restricted data of their progress according to pre-arranged questions, rarely provided in their routine letters especially sweeping analyses of the proper posture for America to adopt in Britain's shadow. For those who, on either side of the Atlantic, developed theories of empire relationships carefully enough to commit them to print, however, the events of the five middle decades of the eighteenth century furnished the challenge to work out much more sophisticated ideas of colonial/mother country rapport suitable to the work of the Anglican missionary arm.

At the foundation of most of the arguments lay a most confident statement of colonial economic dependency. Anniversary sermonists unhesitatingly represented personal as well as national dividends as the just returns of investment abroad of money and energy. *Abstract* compilers urged that enterprising

merchants reaping monetary harvests through American speculation were indebted to the Society and should recognize the
fact tangibly. Historians listed potential or actual colonial resources—stands of oak and pine, acres of tobacco, herds of
livestock, superabundent fish, and endless territories in which
to dispose of criminals otherwise menacing London's crowded
lanes. Clerical, military, and political observers, meantime,
rarely lost the opportunity of reminding their audiences of the
hinterland beyond colonial settlement and its usefulness to
Britain, assuming proper Indian relations.

Upon this foundation the S.P.G. tried to raise an educational
structure designed to support its constantly recurring theme of
colonial obedience. Such of their books as found a way into
personal and institutional libraries of Society parsons and pedagogues relentlessly applied figurative or logical arguments to the
question of man's station in life. Their authors belabored the
concept of duty, metaphorically through astronomical or natural
references, systematically via endorsements of sumptuary laws,
parliamentary prerogatives, royal authority, the power of the
magistrates, and the ever-present threat of chaos that would
result should overly ambitious men attempt to advance beyond
their right place in society. Pamphlets, supplied in very large
quantities, stressed the tight interconnection between family and
church as a means of ensuring effective transmission of acceptable ideas about social and political hierarchies. Their composite
message was that man should keep his place and be thankful for
it. And parsons and pedagogues, themselves intellectually drilled
in such notions of obedience as the S.P.G.-sponsored books and
pamphlets underscored, doubtless worked the latter values into
their daily lessons.

What marks the declining decades of the S.P.G. colonial
educational adventure is not the refinement or modification of
fundamental views about a closed society drafted under Queen
Anne and developed with greater precision up to the French
capitulation in Canada. It is rather the stiffening of these views

and their resulting brittlenesss before jolting contrary opinion nurtured by the spirit of colonial self-scrutiny made possible by the diminished French threat of encirclement, broadcast through the very same media that traditionally carried S.P.G. propaganda, and expressed by parsons and pedagogues of different religious and political persuasions.

Some Society men either through a true liberal spirit, or because of impending personal danger, modified their objections to colonial defiance. The bulk of S.P.G. parsons and pedagogues, however, declared for the British cause, leaving with their Low Church American compatriots the problem of how to reconcile Anglicanism with republicanism. Needless to say, with the commencement of hostilities, and throughout the war, those S.P.G. servants who continued to engage in the rhetoric of colonial obedience did so at their peril.

Quite unwilling to support representatives subscribing to the tenets of colonial independence, and at last convinced of the hopelessness of its educational cause in America, the S.P.G. withdrew from the American scene in 1783. Some of its envoys left their churches and classrooms and returned to Britain, one or two of them at last finding in the war adequate motivation for fulfilling the retirement yearnings of men who spoke of their careers in terms of foreign service. Others, with financial and emotional investments in what they considered their colonial homes, abruptly uprooted their families and joined the loyalist processions to Upper Canada, Lower Canada, the Maritimes, or the West Indies, there to teach other generations about the hazards of republicanism. Many, too, quietly relinquished Society stipends, stayed put, and became part of a disestablished American Episcopal Church. On its part, the Society turned toward Canada, the Indies, and Africa to continue its work so sharply interrupted in the new American republic.

Customarily, institutional histories end with a list of successes. Society historians from Humphreys to Klingberg have certainly

managed to look on the bright side of S.P.G. history in this
respect, despite the admitted harassment of their dramatis per-
sonæ at various stages of their Society careers and the personal
disaster many suffered after the Revolutionary War.
Generous is the catalogue and varied the categories of these
traditionally expressed S.P.G. accomplishments. Some tributes,
moreover, are irrefutable. It is, for instance, a fact that hundreds
of parsons and pedagogues contributed to the Society's American
work. It is a fact that thousands of pieces of printed material
saw distribution abroad at S.P.G. hands. It is a fact that in
scores of S.P.G.-subsidized schools scores of pupils of all ages
learned to read. It is a fact that in dozens of churches generations of Anglican congregations enjoyed sermons delivered by
Society parsons. It is a fact that hundreds of Negro slaves memorized their prayers under S.P.G. tutelage. And it is also a fact
that scores of Indians got a taste of white man's culture and a
smattering of letters thanks to S.P.G. patience.

Other accolades cannot be denied. The mood of the Society's
American enterprise, for all its imperial implications, was unquestionably humanitarian. In theory at least, parsons and pedagogues were warned against peremptory dealings with their
charges, and many instances of their self-sacrifice are documented in the S.P.G. archives. If the Society condoned slavery,
it was to be at least a more kindly bondage than that obtaining
prior to S.P.G. advent. If it abetted traders bent on profit, the
chances of Indian exploitation were reduced. If it helped hold
frontier savages at the beck and call of military commanders,
it was in the knowledge of Christianity that these forest dwellers
would face mortal dangers.

Continued sifting of the rich S.P.G. archival material is, I
believe, unlikely to refute either statistical or philanthropic
measures of Society accomplishments in colonial America. Certainly, there is no quarrel with such assessments here. But when
it comes to certain other yardsticks of attainment, one must
measure with great care. If, for instance, one argues that the

historical treasure trove of the Society archives themselves constitutes a measure of S.P.G. success, one may well be confusing the mere accumulation of paper with the fulfillment of designs formulated in 1701 and dignified by charter. Similarly, if one maintains that there existed in the early years of the United States a graceful good will between the Church of England and the American Episcopal Church, and attributes this circumstance to the successful work of a Society so recently dismissed, one may also be overlooking a much more fundamental question, namely, had the S.P.G. enterprise abroad proved successful, would there have been an American Episcopal Church at all, or, for that matter, a United States of America? In assessing the admissibility of this last query, one is obliged to turn again to the charter itself and to the consensus of Society opinion over eighty years of its American work to determine what it was the S.P.G. actually tried to teach colonists as a whole and how well it did so.

As far as the charter was concerned, what was needed was maintenance for an orthodox clergy to live among loving subjects and instruct them in the principles of true religion. This, S.P.G. parsons, British and American born, attempted, but found opposition, not so much from atheists, infidels, or "divers Romish Priests and Jesuits" but from dynamic Christian nonconformity, not a little assisted by Low Church latitudinarianism. Just how ultimately ineffectual proved S.P.G. teaching in face of such adversaries can be deduced from the abrupt 1786 Anglican disestablishment in Virginia, seat of Anglicanism in America, hence, model for emulation by other states. As for any sustained influence, the Anglican churches which in 1700 stood second in number by a narrow margin to those of Congregational denomination, in 1780 were fourth behind Congregational, Baptist, and Presbyterian churches, and, by 1820, transmuted to American Episcopal churches, were numerically outdistanced by Baptist, Congregational, Lutheran, Methodist, and Presbyterian churches alike, numbering but six-hundred out of a total of over ten-thousand American church buildings.[12] At least on a numerical basis, the showing is far from encouraging. Only by a most generous interpretation of the term could it indicate success.

The other question—the extent to which the S.P.G. achieved its broad teaching objectives as articulated over four-score years of trial—may likewise be answered with reference to other streams of contemporary American thought. Not that authoritarianism went completely by the board in the new republic. On the contrary, patriot aristocrats continued to poke fun at an unseemingly democracy whereby

> Down at night a bricklayer or carpenter lies,
> Next sun a Lycurgus, a Solon doth rise.[13]

Just the same, long before the Revolution it was clear from the statements and writings of such diverse men as Jonathan Mayhew and Tom Paine, William Livingston and Ezra Stiles, that there was nothing inconsistent about being simultaneously a dissenter and a good citizen. Yet, this was a conclusion the S.P.G. seemed incapable of drawing. With all the power at its disposal, it delivered a monotonous, unchanging message of unquestioning colonial subservience, never quite grasping the infinite variety of American religious, political, or social life. As Carl Bridenbaugh concluded, it is not beyond the data to propose that the Society inadvertently shared responsibility for eventual colonial dissociation.[14] Again, here was no crowning success.

Yet, neither the S.P.G. of Jefferson's era, nor of ours, nor all the men and women who travel abroad in our times to propagate their own special gospel in the foreign parts of a progressively closer-knit world, know from day to day whether or not they are on the right track. Historians to come will doubtless

12. See Edwin Scott Gaustad, *Historical Atlas of Religion in America* (New York: Harper and Row, 1962), p. 3, fig. 4; p. 4, fig. 6; p. 43, fig. 31.
13. Cited in Merle Curti, *The Growth of American Thought* (New York: Harper and Row, 1964, third edition), p. 134.
14. Bridenbaugh, *Mitre and Sceptre*, p. 338.

scrutinize our twentieth-century foreign aid programs and cultural missions, our student exchanges and peace corps, our traveling lectureships, our joint publishing enterprises, our overseas industrial empires, our olympic competitions, our diplomatic establishments, our world-wide radio and television transmissions, and, perhaps, our military expeditionary forces. When they do, they may well find themselves more tenderly disposed toward the parsons and pedagogues of this brief study, and their adventure in American education.

BIBLIOGRAPHICAL NOTE

FEW AUTHORS of texts in the history of American education have omitted to mention the S.P.G. Most, however, treat the subject lightly, leaving the impression that the S.P.G. was specifically founded for educating colonial American children, and that modest Society beginnings at length grew into America's public school system.

An early proponent of this view is Richard G. Boone, whose *Education in the United States: Its History from the Earliest Settlements* (1890) devoted a dozen lines or so to the Society's association with certain colonial Latin schools, with New York's Trinity School, and with King's College. A little later, Edwin Grant Dexter declares in *A History of Education in the United States* (1904) that the S.P.G. was active in promoting education, the proof being that its missionaries taught school.

By the end of World War I, Ellwood P. Cubberley's *Public Education in the United States* (1919) was available to add its authority to the S.P.G. myth. Stating flatly that the Society was chartered "to train children . . . through the direct agency of the schools," (for which statement one searches the 1701 charter in vain), it goes on to identify the S.P.G. charity schools as approaching a free school *system*. Thereafter, the attraction of his school-centered history seemed irresistable. In *Education in the United States* (1929), for example, Edgar W. Knight notes that the S.P.G. maintained schools, thereby promoting education. Then, citing both Knight and Cubberley, Stuart G. Noble in *A History of American Education* (1938) hazards the extraordinary observation that the Society confined its activities mainly to the field of elementary education. Although it goes into some detail regarding missionaries and libraries, Paul Monroe's long delayed *Founding of the American Public School* (1940) stresses schools, routines, curricula, texts, and methods. Moreover, his insistence that "the schools of the Society did constitute a *system* [italics mine]" continues in the Cubberley tradition of institutional educational history.

Perhaps through renewed interest in European roots, there followed during and after World War II a more thorough coverage in American educational history books of S.P.G. work. Howard K. Beale's *A History of Freedom of Teaching in American Schools* (1941) notes governors' instructions to license orthodox teachers, speaks of the S.P.G.'s humanitarian approach to child care, and indicates certain social obstructions blocking Negro instruction. In *The School in the American Social Order* (1947), Newton Edwards and Herman G. Richey employ the term "colonial evangelization" to suggest a somewhat broader field of educational action. But, with Cubberley and Monroe, they maintain that the "Society furnished the nearest approach to a *public school* [italics mine] founded in the South before the Revolution."

Among the dunes of the public school theme, shifting and reforming between Cubberley and Edwards and Richey, R. Freeman Butts's and Lawrence A. Cremin's *A History of Education in American Culture* (1953) is something of an oasis. Here, the emphasis is on change—changing attitudes toward child nature as illustrated in S.P.G. instructions to teachers, changing cultural composition of colonial America, changing concepts of the importance of books as outlined in Bray's *An Essay Towards Promoting All Necessary and Useful Knowledge,* and changing interpretations of the expression "free school." Beyond the oasis, however, lie the familiar sand hills. William E. Drake's *The American School in Transition* (1955) produces the old misstatement that the S.P.G. was founded "to train children . . . through the direct agency of the schools." H. G. Good deals briefly and conservatively with S.P.G. schools and colonial legislation supporting them in *A History of American Education* (1956), while R. E. Callahan, in his *An Introduction to Education in American Society* (1956), merely lists S.P.G. teacher qualifications as enumerated in E. W. Knight and C. L. Hall, *Readings in American Educational History* (1951). Adolphe E. Meyer's *An Educational History of the American People* (1957) does manage to break from this casual pattern of S.P.G. treatment by assessing S.P.G. schools as "less than fair" and proposing that "under the sugar of . . . charity was the pill of Anglicanism." Unfortunately, though, Meyer's references to "the band of evangelical pedagogues" and to "the Gospel Propagators" for all their freshness tend to caricature the Society man and his colonial work in education.

MANUSCRIPT SOURCES

Although one does not expect histories of American education for undergraduate study or graduate survey to deal at length with the S.P.G., one is nonetheless struck by the distance separating many such works from the richness and current availability of the primary sources, especially when these are consulted with a broad definition of education in mind. Granted, original documents are of uneven readability. Certain items, moreover, have disappeared "during the perigrinations of the Office," as S.P.G. Archivist Belle Pridmore puts it. Not unexpectedly, the best research to date has been based on the most legible items, and since these tend to cluster either at the beginning of the Society's history or according to colonial regions, the whole problem of historical sampling remains acute and will so continue until patience or science helps decipher illegible papers, or historian-sleuths locate missing pieces. Exceptions to the problem are the *S.P.G. Journals,* which run continuously from 1701 to the present day and are of good physical quality.

The investigator wishing to probe more deeply into S.P.G. history, however, will find the archives conveniently arranged. The *S.P.G. Letter Books,* Series A, 1702–1737, consist of manuscript letter books kept by the first three secretaries of the Society. Since most of the originals (of which the letters are copies) have disappeared, the *Letter Books* are vulnerable to external criticism. It is highly likely, however, that apart from small transcription errors, these materials are reliable. As Miss Pridmore indicates, Volumes I–VI contain in-letters and Volumes VII–XXVI both in and out-letters from S.P.G. missionaries, governors, private citizens, church wardens, English subscribers, and continental church officials. The letters are arranged chronologically but there is some overlap in dates, as inland letters were transcribed before those of the same date from overseas. The volumes as rendered on microfilm by Micro Methods Limited have their own contemporary index.

The *S.P.G. Letters,* Series B, 1701–1786, preserve original in-letters from America and drafts or copies of out-letters. Volumes VII–XX contain general correspondence, beginning in 1738 after the A Series ends and continuing to 1753, and all volumes have contemporary indexes. The microfilmed B Series does not always show letters in chronological sequence. As is explained in the micro-filmed introduction, some volumes are regionally arranged, thus: Volume I, New York and New England, mostly 1712–14 and 1725–33; Volumes II and III, New York, 1755–82; Volumes IV and V, North and South Carolina, 1715–91; Volume VI, Bahamas, Barbadoes; Volume XXI, Pennsylvania, 1700–82, and a few letters from New York during the Revolution; Volume XXII, Massachusetts; Volume XXIII, Connecticut, 1754–82; Volume XXIV, New Jersey, 1754–82; Volume XXV, Nova Scotia, 1760–86.

The *S.P.G. Letters,* Series C, is a collection of original missives from colonial America, arranged chronologically by colonies (including 80 letters from Georgia, 1758–1782) together with 65 out-letters (mostly routine) from Society Secretary David Humphreys, written between 1731 and 1733. With the excellent *S.P.G. Index to Letters, Series A, B, and C,* cross-catalogued under "letters from" and "persons mentioned," and the *S.P.G. Journals* complete from the June 27, 1701 inaugural meeting, these items make up a primary manuscript resource of matchless importance. Students of education, philanthropy, economics, political and church history, anthropology, and sociology will be delving into it for decades to come.

S.P.G. ANNIVERSARY SERMONS AND ABSTRACTS

Thanks to the use of exceptionally durable rag paper, and to wide distribution throughout the American colonies, S.P.G. *Anniversary Sermons* and *Abstracts* may be found in a number of North American repositories. Those employed in this study are part of a nearly complete collection shelved in the Missionary Library of New York's Union Theological Seminary. The *Abstracts* are of special value in locating names and stations of S.P.G. personnel. Both the *Anniversary Sermons* and the *Abstracts* show by their high standard of authorship and editorship, clarity of print, and beauty of adornment, the talent the Society was able to bring to bear on its propaganda campaigns.

SERMONS AND OCCASIONAL PIECES BY S.P.G. SERVANTS IN AMERICA

The sermons, essays, and "letters" written by S.P.G. men resident in the colonies, and cited in Chapters III and V of this study, are too numerous to mention here. All of them, however, are listed in Charles Evans' *American Bibliography,* Volumes I to VI of the Peter Smith edition (New York: 1941). The numbers they are assigned in this prodigious index may be used to locate them in the excellent Micro-Card rendering of *Early American Imprints* (first series). They reveal the reactions of establishment men confronted with disestablishment ideas.

STANDARD HISTORIES DRAWING ON S.P.G. PRIMARY SOURCES

As indicated in the Preface, the S.P.G. has not lacked historians. The first of these was S.P.G. Secretary the Reverend David Humphreys, D.D., whose *An Historical Account of the Incorporated Society for the Propagation of the Gospel in Foreign Parts Containing Their Foundations, Proceedings, and the Success of their Missionaries in the British Colonies to the year 1728* (1730) is every bit as thorough as its title. Its central idea is that the Society brought a measure of culture to otherwise crude American colonies. Society Secretary Ernest Hawkins' *Historical Notices* (1845), a didactic history supplying "lessons both of warning and instruction," perpetuates his precursor's view of the S.P.G. as an instrument for colonizing and civilizing the world's less enlightened populace.

Two important later works, by an S.P.G. Keeper of the Records and an S.P.G. Editorial Secretary respectively, bring to the forefront of S.P.G. historiography a marked sense of the enormous S.P.G. manuscript resources and of the alluring yet frustrating impression their brimming volume makes on even the most patient scholar. The first such tome is C. F. Pascoe's *Classified Digest of the Records of the Society for the Propagation of the Gospel in Foreign Parts, 1701–1892* (1893), which reappeared in expanded form as *Two Hundred Years of the S.P.G.: An Historical Account of the Society for the Propagation of the Gospel in Foreign Parts, 1701–1900* (1901). In scope alone, these editions are exceptionally ambitious, as more than half a century of scholars' footnotes have since testified. Nor is Pascoe merely a compiler. Although he gives little or no attention to internal criticism of his data, his narrative is very readable. The second book, H. P. Thompson's *Into All Lands: The History of the Society for the Propagation of the Gospel in Foreign Parts* (1951) brings the account of Society work up to mid-twentieth century. But in its section on colonial America, it follows Pascoe's pattern of taking at face value missionary reports of colossal colonial ignorance.

MONOGRAPHS ON SELECTED S.P.G. TOPICS

In addition to standard histories, many very useful, if less comprehensive, books address themselves to various aspects of S.P.G.

largely uncriticised but nonetheless absorbing. The third, by a Klingberg student, is indispensable to an understanding of the tension between S.P.G. humanitarian efforts and S.P.G. slave-ownership.

In a class by itself, Carl Bridenbaugh's *Mitre and Sceptre* (1962) presents by far the best-balanced attempt in terms of documentation. Arguing the Society's inadvertent contribution in provoking the American Revolution, Bridenbaugh draws his battle lines rather finely, and, to borrow Richard Hofstadter's wording, even regards "conspiracy as *the motive force* in historical events." But in relating the transatlantic ebb and flow of ideas and interests surrounding the Anglican quest in colonial North America, he presents a highly provocative allegation of an Anglican lust for power which subsequent writers on the topic need to reckon with.

COLLECTED PAPERS, BIOGRAPHIES, DIARIES, AND JOURNALS

On account of the relative ease with which researchers may now work through the S.P.G. archives having the papers of a certain individual in mind, biographies have come forth in quantity. Edgar Legare Pennington initiated this trend and sustained it almost single handedly to World War II. His short biographical sketches, such as *The Reverend John Checkley* (1935), *The Reverend George Ross* (1937), *The Church of England in Early Colonial New Hampshire and the Reverend Arthur Browne* (1937–1938), *Apostle of New Jersey John Talbot 1645–1727* (1938), and *John Wesley's Georgia Ministry* (1939), lack any interpretive rigor but provide well-documented narratives and the sense of challenge experienced by S.P.G. envoys in America. His *Nathaniel Evans, a Poet of Colonial America* (1935) falls into the same category, as does the more recent *Thomas Bray* (1954) by H. P. Thompson.

Much more sophisticated are two works done in the forties. Ethyn Williams Kirby's *George Keith: 1638–1716* (1942) is a scholarly, highly readable account of the controversial first S.P.G. missionary whose name became a household word in subsequent S.P.G. history. The work is particularly well balanced with respect to Keith's personal struggles to arrive at a viable religious faith and to resist or persuade those set against him. Frank J. Klingberg's edition, *Carolina Chronicle: The Papers of Commissary Gideon Johnston, 1707–1716* (1946), furnishes transcripts of Johnston's long letters from Charleston. The introductory essay is the best in

XII (1815). This collection, though generally of editions postdating the 1783 limit of this study, features several works mentioned in the S.P.G. archival documents, probably little changed from earlier printings, and available at New York's Union Theological Seminary Library. Included are the anonymous *The Husbandman's Manual* (1811 ed.), White Kennett's *The Christian Scholar* (1811 ed.), and five of Josiah Woodward's pamphlets—*A Disswasive from Gaming* (1811 ed.); *A Disswasive from the sin of Drunkenness* (1812 ed.); *A Kind Caution to Prophane Swearers* (1812 ed.); *The Seaman's Monitor* (1812 ed.); and *The Soldier's Monitor* (1810 ed.).

Much earlier printings of titles recommended for colonial use are William Stanley's *The Faith and Practice of a Church of England Man* (1688), available in the Auburn Collection, Union Theological Seminary, together with Richard Allestree's *The Works of the Learned Author of the Whole Duty of Man* (1723) and a later volume, *The New and Complete Whole Duty of Man* [1744]. William Beveridge's *The Church Catechism Explained* appears in *The Theological Works of Wm. Beveridge, D.D.* (1844). A principal thrust of all these works is the advice to readers to be content with their station in life.

ARTICLE, PAPERS, AND THESES ON THE S.P.G.

The S.P.G. archival materials have given rise to many shorter themes. For a splendid account of the scholar's elation at rediscovery of S.P.G. documents in a flooded London basement, Miss G. E. Edwards, "Life in Old S.P.G. Documents," *S.P.G. Archives Lectures 1936–7* (1937), pp. 13–22, is hard to match. More elegant is Frank J. Klingberg's response to the transit of culture idea in "Contributions of the S.P.G. to the American Way of Life," *Historical Magazine of the Protestant Episcopal Church,* XII (September, 1943), 215 ff. Another of Dr. Klingberg's essays admirably portrays the missionary as agent of empire—"Sir William Johnson and the Society for the Propagation of the Gospel (1749–1774)," *Historical Magazine of the Prostestant Episcopal Church,* VIII (March, 1939), 4–37. Although not so analytical, Ruth M. Winton's "Governor Francis Nicholson's Relations with the Society for the Propagation of the Gospel in Foreign Parts, 1701–1727," *Historical Magazine of the Protestant Episcopal Church,* XVII (September, 1948), 274–86, gives a good impression of a colonial governor's military, trade, and missionary responsibilities. Charles W. Parker's

"Lewis Morris, First Colonial Governor of New Jersey," *Proceedings of the New Jersey Historical Society*, XIII (July, 1928), 273–82, ignores Morris' S.P.G. affiliations but provides useful background to an antecedent of Gouverneur Morris, Minister to France and U. S. Senator.

On the broader topic of total Anglican aspirations in early North America, Evarts B. Greene's "The Anglican Outlook on the American Colonies in the Early Eighteenth Century," *The American Historical Review*, XX (October, 1914–July, 1915), 64–85, contrasts Church strength in Britain with its "humiliating weakness" overseas. Two other useful articles dealing with the breadth of accomplishment of an S.P.G. pioneer are John Wolfe Lydekker, "Thomas Bray (1658–1730) Founder of Missionary Enterprise," *Historical Magazine of the Protestant Episcopal Church*, XII (1943), 186–224, and Joseph Towne Wheeler, "Thomas Bray and the Maryland Parochial Libraries," *The Maryland Historical Magazine*, XXXIV (September, 1939), 246–65, both generously documented. Another work of wide interest is Edgar Legare Pennington's "The S.P.G. Anniversary Sermons 1702–1783," *Historical Magazine of the Protestant Episcopal Church*, XX (March, 1951), 10–43, which contains an excellent appendix of anniversary preachers and the ecclesiastical posts they held up to the date of their performance at St. Mary-le-Bow.

Among many papers showing Anglican-Congregational friction, Louis Leonard Tucker's "The Church of England and Religious Liberty at Pre-Revolutionary Yale," *William and Mary Quarterly*, XVII (July, 1960), 314–28, and Glenn Weaver's "Anglican-Congregationalist Tensions in Pre-Revolutionary Connecticut," *Historical Magazine of the Protestant Episcopal Church*, XXVI (1957), 269–85, both examine the notion that some colonial Anglicans with S.P.G. mandates worked for religious freedom by pressing for Congregationalist disestablishment of one sort or another rather than for Anglican establishment.

Typical of several doctoral dissertations on various facets of the S.P.G.'s North American work are Charles Bronislaw Hirsch's "The Experience of the S.P.G. in 18th century North Carolina," (Indiana, 1954), plus two earlier pieces, W. A. Bultmann's "The Society for the Propagation of the Gospel in Foreign Parts and the Foreign Settlers in the American Colonies," (California, 1952), and F. D. Gifford's "The Church of England in Colonial Westchester; a Study of the Work of the S.P.G. Missionaries in the

Parishes of West Chester, Rye and New Rochelle," (New York University, 1942). A more recent study, John Kendall Nelson's "Anglican Missions in America 1701–1725: A Study of the Society for the Propagation of the Gospel in Foreign Parts," (Northwestern, 1962) provides the most comprehensive coverage of the topic, and serves as a most reliable reference. Characteristically, these works are regional and descriptive, but make fine use of the primary materials. For a graphic representation of missionary stations and missionary career lines, see my own "Parsons and Pedagogues," (Columbia University, 1969), Appendixes A–F.

BOOKS ON EUROPEAN BACKGROUND TO THE S.P.G.

Edward Eggleston's classic, *The Transit of Civilization* (1900) and Louis Hartz, *The Founding of New Societies* (1964) provide fundamental background reading for a study having to do with transatlantic modification of ideas. Although one deals with an image of "mental furniture" and the other with a notion of "fragmentation" in a culture developing uniquely in isolation, both are helpful as heuristic devices for internal criticism of the S.P.G. primary sources.

Several works on general aspects of eighteenth-century English life contain good contextual data. Dorothy George's *London Life in the 18th Century* (1965) brings alive the crowded chaos of the empire metropolis. Basil Williams' *The Whig Supremacy, 1714–1760* (1939) has many excellent chapters on English culture. M. G. Jones's *The Charity School Movement* (1938) deal with the British institutions upon which the S.P.G. attempted to model some of its colonial American educational enterprises. Alan Fager Herr, *The Elizabethan Sermon: A Survey and a Bibliography* (1940) shows with brilliance and succinctness the educational centrality of pulpit oratory and its careful commitment to shorthand or print for further study. John Beresford (ed.), *The Diary of a Country Parson: The Reverend James Woodforde, 1758–1781* (1926) presents the daily social and political round of a minor Church figure. Invaluable for its content, style, and documentation is Norman Sykes, *Church and State in England in the XVIIIth Century* (1934). A stimulating companion piece, G. V. Bennett and J. D. Walsh (eds.), *Essays in Modern English Church History in Memory of Norman Sykes* (1966) contains splendid contributions on episcopacy, the evangelical revival, and the nonconformist conscience. The Central Council for the Care of Churches' *The Parochial*

Libraries of the Church of England (1959) has many first-rate photographs of chained volumes and portable libraries such as were once dispatched to S.P.G. missionaries in colonial America.

More specialized are such books as Dudley W. R. Bahlman's *The Moral Revolution of 1688* (1957) which distinguishes between reform and religious societies and shows Bray's involvement with both. Christopher Hill's *Puritanism and Revolution* (1958) reviews recent interpretations of the English Civil War and examines men and movements coming after it. His *The Century of Revolution 1603–1714* (1961) maintains that the struggle for freedom in England at the end of Queen Anne's reign was far from complete. How religious societies approached the problem of propaganda in such an age as Hill and Bahlman describe is treated in a highly readable book, *Henry Newman: An American in London 1708–43* (1956) by Leonard W. Cowie.

Other volumes which treat with great force the English roots of Puritanism include Gerald Cragg's *From Puritanism to the Age of Reason* (1950), *Puritanism in the Period of the Great Persecution, 1660–1688* (1957), and *Reason and Authority in the Eighteenth Century* (1964). Two books examining the nature of English Church establishment and of nonconformist attitudes toward it arrive at opposing conclusions. Charles H. George and Katherine George, *The Protestant Mind of the English Reformation 1570–1640* (1961) stresses the "variety in unity" theme of Protestantism to conclude that Anglican and Puritan shared much common ground. John F. H. New, *Anglican and Puritan: The Basis of Their Opposition, 1558–1640* (1964) speaks of alien "universes of discourse" from which grave conflicts emerged. For an understanding of nonconformist parliamentary lobbying which doubtless had a bearing on the failure of establishing an Anglican bishopric in colonial America, N. C. Hunt's *Two Early Political Associations: The Quakers and the Dissenting Deputies in the Age of Sir Robert Walpole* (1961), and Bernard Lord Manning, *The Protestant Dissenting Deputies*, O. Greenwood (ed.) (1952) are excellent. First-class references for setting seventeenth- and eighteenth-century England into a wider European intellectual context are the classic *The European Mind 1680–1715* (1935), by Paul Hazard, and his *European Thought in the Eighteenth Century From Montesquieu to Lessing* (1946), both translated with great sensitivity by J. Lewis May.

BOOKS ON AMERICAN BACKGROUND TO THE S.P.G.

A most stimulating slim volume to which in part this study owes its motivation is Bernard Bailyn's *Education in the Forming of American Society* (1960), which urges a very broad concept of education and thereby justifies further S.P.G. exploratory studies. Vernon L. Parrington's *Main Currents in American Thought, Volume I: 1620–1800: The Colonial Mind* (1927), Merle Curti's *The Growth of American Thought* (1964, third edition), and Perry Miller's *The New England Mind From Colony to Province* (1953) are indispensable for keeping track of the many beliefs making up the American composite and explaining some of the frustration suffered by S.P.G. men in face of them. An interesting work which produces with great literary skill a vision of the vastness of American space, Howard Mumford Jones's *O Strange New World* (1952) is much in sympathy with many S.P.G. missives from abroad.

Absolutely essential to counterbalancing the Keithian invective concerning the morals and abilities of colonists is a series of works with general cultural approaches. Among these, Daniel J. Boorstin's provocative *The Americans: The Colonial Experience* (1958) argues the case of the undifferentiated American whose range of abilities must have greatly surprised the S.P.G. man abroad. Other exceptional accounts of the growth and scope of colonial culture are Carl Bridenbaugh's *Cities in the Wilderness: Urban Life in America 1625–1742* (1938), *Cities in Revolt: Urban Life in America 1743–1776* (1955), *Rebels and Gentlemen: Philadelphia in the Age of Franklin* (1942 with Jessica Bridenbaugh), and *The Colonial Craftsman* (1950). Likewise helpful in this regard are Louis B. Wright's *The First Gentlemen of Virginia: Intellectual Qualities of the Early Colonial Ruling Class* (1940), and his *The Cultural Life of the American Colonies: 1607–1763* (1957). Also very useful as resource material for debates over American religious enthusiasm is Alan Heimert and Perry Miller (eds.), *The Great Awakening: Documents Illustrating the Crisis and its Consequences* (1967).

An excellent standby for crosschecking the primary sources is Everts Boutell Greene, *The Provincial Governor in The English Colonies of North America* (1898), which lists numerous governors' instructions between 1610 and 1771. Privately printed, *The Patriot Preachers of the American Revolution with Biographical Sketches, 1766–1783* (1931) is useful in demonstrating that S.P.G. ideas about class structure were by no means unique. Marcus W. Jernegan,

Laboring and Dependent Classes in Colonial America, 1607–1783 (1931), and Richard B. Morris' *Government and Labor in Early America* (1946) also shed much light on Society envoys' epistolary remarks about cost of living, purchasing power, and the teaching of adults. Alden T. Vaughan's *New England Frontiers: Puritans and Indians, 1620–1675* (1965) provides an antidote for the contention that all white-Indian relationships in North America were exploitative. Splendid for graphic representation of the balance of religious denominations at various points of colonial American history is Edwin Scott Gaustad's *Historical Atlas of Religion in America* (1962).

GENERAL CHURCH HISTORY AND REFERENCES

The most useful guide for both English and American backgrounds, and point of entry for S.P.G. studies, is Nelson R. Burr, in collaboration with J. W. Smith and A. L. Jamieson (eds.), *A Critical Bibliography of Religion in America,* Volume IV, Parts 1–5, *Religion in American Life* (1961). The introduction to William Wilson Manross, *The Fulham Papers in the Lambeth Palace Library* (1965) not only maps out a great collection of papers pertinent to the period but also gives an excellent treatment of the relevance in America of English canon law, a question constantly troubling the S.P.G.'s emissaries. For background material on numerous prominent S.P.G. members, a reliable and rich source is Sir Leslie Stephen and Sir Sidney Lee (eds.), *The Dictionary of National Biography* (1959–1960). The most rewarding general reference with respect to bibliography, introductory essays, and original documents is H. Shelton Smith, Robert T. Handy, and Lefferts A. Loetscher, *American Christianity: A Historical Interpretation with Representative Documents, Volume I, 1607–1820* (1960). Among a vast number of titles on missionary work in general, the Eric J. Sharpe translation of Bengt Sundkler, *The World of Mission* (1963) is suggestive with respect to "the environment in which the [mission] church exists, and with which it interacts." More specific to the S.P.G. American adventure are two doctoral theses, "The Anglican Middle Way in Early Eighteenth-Century America: Anglican Religious Thought in the American Colonies, 1702–1750," (Wisconsin, 1965), by Gerald Joseph Goodwin, and Borden W. Painter, Jr., "The Anglican Vestry in Colonial America," (Yale, 1965). A collection of exceptional quality is Brian Holmes (ed.), *Educational Policy and the Mission Schools: Case Studies from the British Empire* (1967), which prefaces a most useful introductory essay with the caution that although related to stated intentions, results of missionary achievement were "never exactly those aimed at." Winthrop S. Hudson, *Religion in America* (1965), Parts I and II, provides a clear overview of the colonial and early national American religious climate.

INDEX

Abstracts, 43, 191, 193; as propaganda and promotional literature, 55, 68, 73; colonial objection to, 57; compiled from *Journals,* 73; complementary to *Anniversary Sermons,* 73; Ellis' anti-Quaker charges, 129; Ellis' statements in error, 130; Great Awakening assessed, 75-76; late accounts of harassment, 178; preferential treatment for Anglicans, 73; printed during war years, 169; re. economic dependency, 210; thanks for gubernatorial help, 74

Account of the State of Religion in the English Plantations in North America (Dudley), 13-14

Adams, John, 13, 157

Admission to S.P.G. schools, 120-22

Advantages of Unity, The (Browne), 81

African Free School, 177

Alarm to the Legislature (Seabury), 173

Albany, 45, 47, 48, 104; Beasley at, 112, 199

Alison, Francis, 156

Allestree, *The Whole Duty of Man,* 97-98

Alliance between Church and State (Warburton), 66

America Dissected (MacSparran), 87-90

American Episcopal Church, 212, 214

American Philosophical Society, 157, 166

American Revolution, 155, 157, 176, 215

American Whig, 172

Anabaptists, 121

Andrews, Samuel, 166; at North Haven, 172; views of liberty, 172

Andrews, William: arrival at Fort Hunter, 48; discouragement, 49; *Horn Book, Primer, and Prayers* (with Barclay), translated for Mohawks, 92; lack of language skill, 47; life at Mohawk castle near Albany, 42; salary, 48

Anglican apologies, 43

Anglicanism: Ellis's concept of, 120; High Church, 163, 188; Low Church, 212, 214; New World style, 65; special benefits, 95

Anglicans: as New England dissenters, 56; children, 97; preferential treatment, 73

Anhalts, University of, 6

Anniversary Sermons, 157, 191, 200; Christianization as means of productivity, 71; colonial class distinction, 70; colonial objections, 57; composite picture of colonies, 33-35; economic dependency, 210; imagery, 72; location and attendance, 32; missionary priorities, 72; Negro education, 54; personal and national benefits of empire economics, 69; political views, 70; propaganda, 55, 68; publication, 32-33; purpose, 32; social rank, 72

Annual Report, French version, 91

Apprentices, 95, 101

Apthorp, East: concept of civil liberty, 172; gift of books to Harvard, 201; good account of colonies, 82-83; S.P.G. missionary at Cambridge, Mass., 36-37; *The Felicity of the Times,* 81

Archbishop of Canterbury, *ex officio* S.P.G. president, 5

Archbishop of York, 160

Aristotle, 77